WAKE UP AMERICA!

The Ongoing War on Christian America

By Kip Caudill
President and Founder, Caudill Foundation

Preface by Rev. Don Swarthout
President, Christians Reviving America's Values

Published By
Christians Reviving America's Values
Rev. Don Swarthout, President
P.O. Box 96493, Washington, D.C. 20090-6493

ISBN 0-9715291-0-8

This book is dedicated to:

To the memory of Mom, my best girl, and Dad, who possessed the greatest integrity I have ever witnessed; and to to all the people who came my way and those who helped me that I called friend;

Thank you, may God bless you
and may God bless America.

PREFACE

The United States of America is a Christian nation. The Founding Fathers were men of God, and they expressed their belief in a Divine Creator in virtually every major document of that era. From the Declaration of Independence's "endowed by their Creator" language to the reference in the Articles of Confederation to the "Great Governor of the World" to the First Amendment's freedom of religion clause, it was perfectly clear that God and religion was part and parcel of the American way of life.

What was so evident then has become a major issue of contention now. A small group of anti-religious radicals have thwarted the will of the Founding Fathers and driven God and religion out of American culture whenever and wherever they could. *From removing crosses on state seals to keeping Christmas manger scenes off of public property to, worst of all, keeping children from praying in school, our Christian society has suffered from assault after assault from these radicals.*

It is time for America to wake up to this threat! Kip Caudill has written a book that tells us exactly what the threat is, and what we must do to combat it. It is up to us and our elected officials to stop these assaults and restore God and religion to America as it was meant to be! We need to join together and with our Congressmen and make sure – once and for all – that the anti-prayer radicals never again take religion away from us. Only with voluntary prayer in schools, the Ten Commandments on public display, and religious freedom restored, can we once again truly call ourselves "One nation, under God, with liberty and justice for all". Amen.

Pastor Don Swarthout, President
Christians Reviving America's Values

TABLE OF CONTENTS

I. INTRODUCTION—WAKE UP AMERICA!

There is a war going on, a war against Christian America. It is a war being fought both from without and within. This book will discuss America's founding as a religious nation, and how in the last 40 years the opponents of God and faith have fought a war to make the United States secular. If Americans of faith don't wake up to the threat, the United States will be stripped of its greatest legacy – the legacy of Christian morality in government.

> **Genesis 12:2**
> And I will make of thee a great nation, and I will bless thee, and make thy name great; and thou shalt be a biessing.

America is a Christian nation. It was founded by Christian men, using Christian principles. It credits the source of the rights guaranteed by the Constitution and the Declaration of Independence to a Supreme Being. And as a reward for our Christian foundation, God has made America by far the most blessed nation in the history of the world.

American citizens have unprecedented freedom and the opportunity to undertake nearly every endeavor of life for which they are inclined. America's God-given freedom and prosperity are a shining beacon of hope to people around the world. However, our freedom and prosperity – and our Christian heritage itself – are also the source of great hatred by radicals around the globe, and in America itself.

As I write this, mere days have passed since the despicable terrorist attack on the World Trade Center in New York and the Pentagon near our nation's capital. President George W. Bush has named Muslim terrorists led by Osama bin Ladan as the guilty party. And America is going to battle against these Muslim terrorists who have waged war on Christian America.

But the war on Christian America is not just being fought by militant Muslims around the world. It's also being fought by an equally sinister, and possibly even more deadly, force – one within the United States itself. That force is the group of liberal elites in America, who despise our Christian heritage and promote their own Godless version of secular humanism.

In 1962 the liberal Supreme Court took the Bible and prayer out of America's school system. This was the first shot fired in a 40 year long war over our religious freedom. A small group of liberal elite secular humanists – people who don't believe in God and who arrogantly place man over God as the prime mover of events in the universe – is trying to remake the United States in its own image. They do not like the Christian America the Founding Fathers bequeathed to us, and so they are using every weapon in their arsenal to beat religion down so hard that Americans of faith dare not leave their churches.

The America our Founding Fathers bequeathed to us no longer exists. Over the years, elected and appointed officials of this land have slowly but surely chiseled away our rights. Taxes have become oppressively high – as bad as some socialist nations in Europe. Bureaucrats rule our lives. The United Nations has been allowed to dictate our foreign policy. Government agents kill American citizens with barely a peep of protest from the media. And most insidious of all, God and religion is being systematically struck from all aspects of public life. Soon I fear that even the tax exempt status for churches that teach the Bible and fight for your right to freely worship God will be curtailed.

These people who are fighting this war against Christian America, those who have foisted their secular doctrines on America, are simply put, criminals. They have assaulted our Constitution and our Bill of Rights – and they have nearly destroyed them. If Americans like you and I don't do something, and soon, to stop these secularists from destroying Christian America, we will surely witness the destruction of the United States.

We have two enemies in this war – secular humanism and ignorance. The secular humanists are leading the charge to stamp religion out of public life. The ignorant are the people in America who refuse to believe or refuse to care that Christian America is at war with the liberal secular humanists. We must fight back against the first group in this war. And we must educate the second group to the dangers, and bring them onto God's side.

Simply stated, God will not bless a secular nation. We have already seen that in the terrorist attacks on our nation. And we all need to realize that the future will be even more grim unless we return to our Christian heritage. When a nation loses more people in one morning from terrorist attacks than in any day during the Second World War, something is terribly wrong in America. There is only one solution now and forever – return to God's grace by returning to our Christian heritage.

America is a christian nation! And everything we hold dear as a christian nation is under attack!

It's time to wake up america, and fight this war for our country's heritage!

II. AMERICA'S RELIGIOUS HERITAGE

The United States of America is a Christian nation. The Declaration of Independence and Constitution are based on the Judeo-Christian ethic. The Holy Bible is the basis for our founding documents, and our system of laws. And America's leaders, from the Founding Fathers to politicians of today have made the point that "America is a Christian nation". Now, this does not mean that all the people were or are Christian. But what it does mean is that Christian tenets were the basis for all of our founding documents, laws, moral codes and institutions.

Psalms 33:12
Blessed is the nation whose God is Lord; and the people whom he hath chosen for his own inheritance.

Now, there are many today who would argue that America is not a Christian nation. But an examination of just a few parts of American history bears the fact that America is a Christian nation out quite clearly. Here are just a few examples:

A portion of the Charter for the Virginia Colony said: "To the glory of His divine Majesty, in propagating of the Christian religion to such people as yet live in ignorance of the true knowledge and worship of God."

When the Pilgrims signed the Mayflower Compact, they agreed: "For the glory of God and advancement of ye Christian faith ... doe by these presents solemnly & mutually in ye presence of God and one of another, covenant & combine our selves together into a civil body politick."

Nearly all of the men who wrote the U.S. Constitution were professing Christians. (M.E. Bradford, A Worthy Company, Plymouth Rock Foundation., 1982).

When Alexis de Tocqueville wrote his famous book on the great experiment in Democracy by the United States, called Democracy in America, he said: "In the United States of America the sovereign authority is religious ... there is no other country in the world in which the Christian religion retains a greater influence over the souls of men than in America."

Abraham Lincoln, the man who kept our nation together, said: "In regard to this Great Book, I have but to say, it is the best gift God has given to man. All the good the Savior gave to the world was communicated through this book. But for it, we would not know right from wrong. All things most desirable for man's welfare, here and hereafter, are to be found portrayed in it." (George L. Hunt, Calvinism and the Political Order, Westminster Press, 1965, p.33)

And even the United States Supreme Court has stated that America is a Christian nation: "Our laws and our institutions must necessarily be based upon and embody the teachings of the Redeemer of mankind. It is impossible that it should be otherwise; and in this sense and to this extent our civilization and our institutions are emphatically Christian ... this is a religious people. This is historically true. From the discovery of this continent to the present hour, there is a single voice making this affirmation ... we find everywhere a clear definition of the same truth ... this is a Christian nation." (Church of the Holy Trinity vs. United States, 143 US 457, 36 L ed 226, Justice Brewer)

THE FOUNDING FATHERS AND NATURE'S GOD

When in the course of human events it becomes necessary for one people to dissolve the political bands which have connected them with another and to assume among the powers of the earth the separate and equal station to which the laws of nature and of nature's God entitles them, a decent respect to the opinions of mankind requires that they should declare the causes which impel them to the separation.

Those are the words written by Thomas Jefferson in the Declaration of Independence. And the most important of these words to the Founding Fathers were those that declared the rights endowed to all mankind by "nature's God".

From the foundation of our country, America has relied on God and the rights bequeathed to us by Him. Thomas Jefferson made that crystal clear when he cited "nature's God" in the Declaration of Independence. And the other Founding Fathers made it equally clear in the Constitution of the United States when they guaranteed religious freedom in the First Amendment. But what is "nature's God", and what rights are granted by Him? The Founding Fathers clearly believed that nature was created by God, and that the Holy Scriptures contained the laws of the God and the rights given to man by God.

From the time this country was founded, it was understood by our leaders that God had granted us certain rights that no government should curtail. It was also understood that, in order to continue to be a good and just nation in the eyes of the Lord, America must maintain that Christian heritage and give thanks to God for granting it to us. One of the first official acts of that Congress was to open in prayer. Virtually every President, upon taking the oath of office, invoked God in one way or another and asked Him to guide our nation. Congress also established a national day of Thanksgiving, praising God for granting our young nation its freedom.

But today, opponents of faith and prayer outrageously assert that the Founding Founders actually meant to strike God from the public domain when they approved the First Amendment to the Constitution. Such an assertion is blatantly false. The Founding Fathers explained that the First Amendment was merely to prevent a single denomination from being federally established. The Founders wanted to avoid in America what had occurred in Great Britain; all becoming- by government decree- Anglicans, Catholics, or any other denomination. Even the most superficial examination makes it clear that the Founding Fathers were devoutly religious men, and wanted their nation to be devoutly religious as well.

When America was founded, it was founded by Christians. In fact, 52 of the original 56 who signed the Declaration of Independence were avowed Christians. There were no Buddhists, Mormons, Muslims present at that time. Those are simply the facts.

And these men were devoutly religious Christians, as well. It is as interesting as it is informative to look at some of the quotes from our Founding Fathers. These quotes indicate the founders' strong sense of Christian values and their perceived importance in the foundations of our nation:

George Washington: "It is impossible to rightly govern without God and the Bible."

John Adams: "The general principles upon which our founders achieved independence... were the principles of Christianity.

Andrew Jackson: "The Bible is the rock upon which our republic rests."

James Madison: "Religion is the basis and foundation of government."

John Adams: "Religion and virtue are the only foundations of free government."

Patrick Henry: "It cannot be emphasized too strongly or too often that this great nation was founded … by Christians; not on religions, but on the Gospel of Jesus Christ. The Bible is worth all other books that have ever been printed."

Abraham Lincoln: "The Bible is the best gift God ever gave to man."

John Quincy Adams: "From the day of the Declaration...(the American people) were bound by the laws of God, which they all acknowledge as the rules of their conduct."

James Madison: "A nation that will not be ruled by the Ten Commandments, shall be ruled by tyrants."

James Monroe: "The liberty, prosperity and happiness of our country will always be the object of my most fervent prayers to the Supreme Author of All Good."

William Penn: "Let men be good and government cannot be bad."

James Madison: "The future of America rests not in the laws of this Constitution, but in the laws of God."

GOD AND THE PRESIDENTS

Clearly our Founding Fathers were deeply religious men, who took their faith seriously and who used Christian principles to build a nation. But it wasn't just our Founding Fathers who've demonstrated their strong Christian faith. From George Washington to George W. Bush, our U.S. Presidents have nearly unanimously invoked God when embarking upon their presidencies. The appendix at the end of this book lists every reference to God that every president has made during an inaugural address.

Now, some of these invocations are far more sincere than others, to be sure. When Calvin Coolidge said "America seeks no earthly empire built on blood and force ... The legions which we send forth are armed, not with the sword, but with the cross ... all mankind [is] of divine origin. She cherishes no purpose save to merit the favor of Almighty God," he was sincere in his faith. When Herbert Hoover asked "the help of Almighty God," he was genuine. Dwight Eisenhower honestly and openly prayed to "Almighty God". And when Ronald Reagan claimed that "with God's help, we can and will resolve" our problems, he felt it to be true from the bottom of his heart.

Now, when Bill Clinton came out and invoked God in his inaugural address, his subsequent actions proved he didn't feel it in his heart. But the point is that even fallen presidents like Bill Clinton felt the American people would expect him to invoke God in his inauguration, even if he never planned on following His divine plan.

So, there is no doubt that our national leaders, from our Founding Fathers right up to President George W. Bush, have felt the need to invoke God's help for their stewardship over our nation. And there is no doubt that the reason they invoked God's help is that America is a Christian nation. But what is in doubt is whether or not the secular humanists who are fighting to strike God from our public lives will eventually even provide a future U.S. president with a court order preventing him from even mentioning God in his inauguration address.

III. THE WAR ON RELIGIOUS FREEDOM

The Constitution of the United States is pretty clear about our religious rights. The First Amendment to the Constitution states clearly that:

"Congress shall make no law respecting an establishment of religion, or prohibiting the free exercise thereof".

Ephesians 6:12
For we wrestle not against flesh and blood, but against... spiritual wickedness in high places.

Despite the relentless efforts of the secular humanists who attack our religious freedoms, this clause of the First Amendment to the Constitution is unequivocal. It states that the United States government can never sponsor or establish any particular religion, to be sure. The First Amendment also established the right of every citizen to freely practice his or her religion in America.

But the true intent of the First Amendment, and the right to freely practice one's religion, has been under assault for the past forty years. And these attacks have ranged from banning children from praying in school to curbing the religious rights of all Americans.

SCHOOL PRAYER

School prayer has been effectively banned since the Supreme Court – for all intents and purposes – struck prayer from our public schools in 1962.

From the foundation of our nation in 1776 to that disastrous 1962 Supreme Court decision, the United States was a Christian nation. Church attendance was high. Education in America was very often religious. Students prayed and read the Bible daily, even in public schools. And the establishment clause of the First Amendment was never interpreted as prohibiting religion in any state-run institution.

But in the early 1960's, a secular movement began in America to stamp out religion in every corner of the public square. In 1962 the Supreme Court began what was to become a series of disastrous decisions that would obliterate prayer in schools. In the *Engel v. Vitale* case, the Supreme Court ruled that the formation of an official prayer by the state of New York was unconstitutional. It also ruled that aid to all religions was as equally impermissible as aid to any one religion. Most incomprehensible of all, the Court said that even voluntary prayers by students violated the First Amendment.

Buoyed by their 1962 victory, the opponents of school prayer won another victory in 1963. In *the Abington School District v. Schempp*, the Supreme Court prohibited the then common practice of opening the school day with a prayer or Bible reading. The reasoning behind this decision was that the primary effect of opening the school day with a prayer was the advancement of religion, which according *to Engel v. Vitale* was now unconstitutional. Never mind that opening the school day with a prayer or a reading of the Bible also advanced the secular goals of promoting morals and good values, the Court said. It advanced religion, and that the Supreme Court would not allow.

Since these disastrous rulings in the early 1960's, the Supreme Court has stood steadfastly by its decision to ban prayer and Bible readings in public schools. The Court even banned a copy of the Ten Commandments in a Kentucky public school, despite its historical, secular importance.

However, the American people have not stood idly by while a few misguided men and women on the Supreme Court tried to strike God and prayer from the public schools. There have been several attempts to pass an amendment to the Constitution which would allow prayer in public schools – despite opposition from the Supreme Court. As Illinois Senator Everett Dirksen said years ago, "I'm not going to let nine men say to 190 million people, including children, when and where they can utter prayers." Though none have been successful to date, momentum is shifting toward such an amendment.

There have also been repeated attempts to challenge the conclusions of the Supreme Court's rulings from the state legislatures and the U.S. Congress. Alabama challenged the Court by instituting a "moment of silence" to meditate or pray, but it was later struck down by the Supreme Court in *Wallace v. Jaffree*. And Congress passed the Equal Access Act in 1984, which said that any school which allows non-religious student groups to meet on school grounds after hours cannot deny religious groups from also meeting on school grounds after hours.

Despite these minor victories, however, the essence of the Supreme Court's opposition to voluntary prayer in public schools has never been reversed – despite the consistent and overwhelming public support for a restoration of prayer to our schools.

In fact, virtually every study since 1962 has demonstrated that the Supreme Court is thwarting the will of the American people on the school prayer issue. From Gallup and Associated Press to NBC and CBS to the *New York Times*, time after time the polls have shown that around 80%, or four out of every five Americans, *support a school prayer amendment*. Despite the overwhelming support for school prayer, the Supreme Court has consistently sided with opponents of prayer like the American Civil Liberties Union (ACLU) and has helped drive God and religion from our lives.

STRIKING GOD FROM OUR LIVES

Sadly, there are powerful groups in the United States that oppose rights for the vast number of religious Americans in our country. The well-funded American Civil Liberties Union is at the vanguard of those who seek to stamp out our religious rights. Opposition to school-sponsored prayer is a bedrock principle for the ACLU. As national board policy #81(a) states in part:

"The ACLU believes that any program of religious indoctrination – direct or indirect – in the public schools or by use of public resources is a violation of the constitutional principle of separation of church and state and must be opposed."

The policy states further that the ACLU:

"Opposes the infusion of other types of religious practices and standards into the public schools. These include such practices as baccalaureate exercises in the form of religious services, prayer meetings at athletic events, the taking of religious census of pupils ... and the profession of religious observance or belief as a consideration in the evaluation and promotion of teachers".

The ACLU contends that public schools which allow religion would "indoctrinate impressionable young people into an officially endorsed religion. What is tyranny, if not that?"

Tyranny? The ACLU is actually calling voluntary prayer in public schools tyranny? If anyone is being a tyrant, it is the ACLU itself for denying children the right to pray to God during school.

At the cornerstone of these tyrant's plans to abolish God and prayer from our lives once and for all is the massive misinformation campaign being mounted by the opponents of religious freedom.

Just read the following mean-spirited excerpts from a pamphlet published by the Freedom From Religion Foundation:

"When religion has invaded our public school system, it has singled out the lone Jewish student, the class Unitarian or agnostic, the children in the minority. Families who protest state/church violations in our public schools invariably experience persecution. It was commonplace prior to the court decisions against school prayer to put nonreligious or nonorthodox children in places of detention during bible-reading or prayer recitation. The children of Supreme Court plaintiffs against religion in schools, such as Vashti McCollum, Ed Schempp and Ishmael Jaffree, were beaten up on the way to and from school, their families subjected to community harassment and death threats for speaking out in defense of a constitutional principle. We know from history how harmful and destructive religion is in our public schools. In those school districts that do not abide by the law, school children continue to be persecuted today."

This group keeps on talking about children and families being "persecuted". But who are the persecuted ones here? Are they the one or two children who may have been ostracized by private citizens for their beliefs? Or are they the vast majority of children and families who are prevented from exercising their right to pray by the United States government? I think the answer is clear, but not to opponents of prayer. Their pamphlet goes on:

> *"Proponents of the so-called 'voluntary' school prayer amendment are admitting that our secular Constitution prohibits organized prayers in public schools. Otherwise, why would an amendment to our U.S. Constitution be required? The nation must ask whether politically motivated Newt Gingrich & Co. are wiser than James Madison, principle author of the Constitution, and the other founders who engineered the world's oldest and most successful constitution! The radical school prayer amendment would negate the First Amendment's guarantee against government establishment of religion. Most distressing, it would be at the expense of the civil rights of children, America's most vulnerable class. It would attack the heart of the Bill of Rights, which safeguards the rights of individuals from the tyranny of the majority."*

There are too many outright lies here to rebut them all. But even they must know that no one who supports a school prayer amendment is stating that the Constitution already bans prayer in school. An amendment to the Constitution has become necessary because the Supreme Court, with the full support of opponents of prayer, has hijacked the First Amendment and denied our right to pray to God in school. And if you have any doubt of that, the pamphlet continues:

> *"Student-Initiated Prayer is a ruse proposed by extremist Christian legal groups. Religious coercion is even worse at the hands of another student, subjecting students to peer pressure, pitting students in the majority against students in the minority, treating them as outsiders with school complicity. Imposing prayer-by-majority-vote is flagrant and insensitive abuse of school authority. Such schools should be teaching students about the purpose of the Bill of Rights, instead of teaching them to be religious bullies. Some principals or school boards even have made seniors hold open class votes on whether to pray at graduation, leading to hostility and reprisal against those students brave enough to stand up for the First Amendment."*

Based on these writings, one can conclude that the arguments against prayer in school are based on nothing other than an irrational and hateful opposition to religion. The arguments in favor of prayer in school are much more clearly thought out.

STANDING UP FOR VOLUNTARY PRAYER IN SCHOOLS

An amendment to the Constitution to permit voluntary school prayer is desperately needed if opposition to religion in public life is to be overcome. There are many good reasons for such a Constitutional amendment, and Dr. Norman Geisler, Dean of the Southern Evangelical Seminary in Charlotte, NC outlined ten of the most critical for the *Charlotte Observer*:

1) Our government was based on religious principles from the very beginning. The Declaration of Independence says: "We hold these truths to be self-evident, that all men are created equal, that they are endowed by God with certain unalienable rights..." Indeed, it speaks of God, creations, God-given moral rights, the providence of God, and a final Day of Judgment - all of which are religious teachings. Indeed, the Supreme Court affirmed (Zorach, 1952) that "We are a religious people whose institutions presuppose a Supreme

Being." And school prayer has been an important part of our religious experience from the very beginning.

2) The First Amendment does not separate God and government but actually encourages religion. It reads: "Congress shall make no law respecting the establishment of religion, nor prohibiting the free exercise thereof." The first clause merely declares that the federal government cannot establish one religion for all the people. It says nothing about "separation of church and state." In fact, five of the 13 states that ratified it had their own state religions at the time. The second clause insists that the government should do nothing to discourage religion. But forbidding prayer in schools discourages religion.

3) Early congressional actions encouraged religion in public schools. For example, the Northwest Treaty (1787 and 1789) declared: "Religion, morality, and knowledge being necessary for good government and the happiness of mankind, schools and the means of learning shall forever be encouraged." Thus, religion, which includes prayer, was deemed to be necessary.

4) Early presidents, with congressional approval, made proclamations encouraging public

prayer. President Washington on October 3, 1789, declared: "Whereas it is the duty of all nations to acknowledge the providence of Almighty God, to obey His will, to be grateful for His benefits, and humbly to implore His protection and favor; and Whereas both Houses of Congress have, by their joint committee, requested me 'to recommend to the people of the United States a day of public thanksgiving and prayer..."

5) Congress has prayed at the opening of every session since the very beginning. Indeed, in a moment of crisis at the very first Continental Congress, Benjamin Franklin urged prayer and observed "In the beginning of the Contest with G. Britain, when we were sensible to danger, we had daily prayer in this room for Divine protection - Our prayers, Sir, were heard, & they were graciously answered... And have we now forgotten that powerful Friend? or do we imagine we no longer need His assistance? ...I therefore beg leave to move - that henceforth prayer imploring the assistance of Heaven, and its blessing on our deliberations, be held in this Assembly every morning before we proceed to business, and that one or more of the clergy of this city be requested to officiate in that service." Congress has begun with prayer ever since. If the government can

pray in their session, why can't the governed pray in their (school) sessions?

6) Public schools had prayer for nearly 200 years before the Supreme Court ruled that state-mandated class prayers were unconstitutional (Engle, 1962). The fact that prayer was practiced for nearly 200 years establishes it by precedent as a valid and beneficial practice in our schools.

7) Since the court outlawed prayer, the nation has been in steady moral decline. Former Secretary of Education William Bennet revealed in his cultural indexes that between 1960 and 1990 there was a steady moral decline. During this period divorce doubled, teenage pregnancy went up 200%, teen suicide increased 300%, child abuse reached an all-time high, violent crime went up 500% and abortion increased 1000%. There is a strong correlation between the expulsion of prayer from our schools and the decline in morality.

8) Morals must be taught, and they cannot properly be taught without religion. There cannot be a moral law without a moral Law Giver. And there is no motivation for keeping the moral law unless there is a moral Law Giver who can enforce it by rewards and punishments.

9) Forbidding prayer and other religious expressions in public schools establishes, in effect, the religion of secularism. The Supreme Court has affirmed that there are religions, such as "secular humanism", which do not believe in God (Torcaso, 1961). Justice Potter (Abington, 1963) rightly feared that purging the schools of all religious beliefs and practices would lead to the "establishment of a religion of secularism." In fact, the beliefs of secular humanism are just the opposite of the Declaration of Independence. By not allowing theistic religious expression, the courts have favored the religious beliefs of secular humanism, namely, no belief in God, God-given moral laws, prayer and a Day of Judgment.

10) To forbid the majority the right to prayer because the minority object, is to impose the irreligion of the minority on the religious majority. Forbidding prayer in schools, which a three-quarters majority of Americans favors, is the tyranny of the minority. It is minority rule, not democracy. Why should an irreligious minority dictate what the majority can do? The majority wishes to preserve our moral and spiritual values and, thus, our good nation.

America is a Christian nation, socially and historically. Though constituted without an official religion, America is populated largely by Christians and has laws based on Christian tenets and views of the world and the nature of mankind. Since a country's laws inevitably reflect the conscience of its people, America's laws must allow for the religious expression of its people.

It is, therefore, obvious to conclude that the First Amendment was never intended to ban prayer from public schools. Indeed, James Madison himself, who proposed the Amendment, said that "he apprehended the meaning of the words to be, that Congress should not establish a religion, and enforce the legal observation of it by law, nor compel men to worship God in any manner contrary to their conscience."

Of course, the meaning of the First Amendment was always clear to those who understood the history of the United States. Great Britain, against which the colonies rebelled, had an established religion – the Anglican church. The Founding Fathers did not want the government to force anyone to worship in a particular way, as the British Crown did. (In fact, many of the original American colonists, including the Pilgrims, set sail for America to have freedom to worship how they felt was right.) Therefore they included in the First Amendment the establishment clause which prevented the government from sponsoring any particular religion.

Just because the First Amendment forbids the government from sponsoring one or another particular religion, it does not mean that the government has to actively oppose all religion. But when the Supreme Court banned prayer in public schools, that is exactly what resulted. And subsequently, our society has suffered greatly.

THE BATTLE TODAY

Since the *Engel* case in 1962, there have been several attempts to pass an amendment to the Constitution which would specify that voluntary prayer in schools was allowable. Major attempts to pass a school prayer amendment occurred in 1964 (reaction to the *Engel* and *Abington* Supreme Court rulings), 1980 (after several stalled legislative attempts in the 1970's), 1983 (when Ronald Reagan pushed for it), and 1993 (led by Senator Jesse Helms). Unfortunately, each effort resulted in failure due to the concerted opposition from liberal Congressmen and anti-religious groups like the ACLU.

More recently, there was a serious push to restore voluntary prayer to our schools with the Religious Freedom Amendment, sponsored chiefly by Congressman Ernest J. Istook, Jr. The proposed text reads as follows:

"To secure the people's right to acknowledge God: The right to pray or acknowledge religious belief, heritage or tradition on public property, including public schools, shall not be infringed. The government shall not compel joining in prayer, initiate or compose school prayers, discriminate against or deny a benefit on account of religion."

Congressman Istook said that:

"This amendment is the only way we can end 30 years of court decisions that turned First Amendment rights upside-down. Courts have gone far beyond outlawing prayer in many public school settings. They have aided a systemic campaign to strip religious symbols, references and heritage from public view, as part of the attack on the underlying values which mean so much to most Americans. This is our peaceful answer to those who continue to attack faith and religion in the public square."

When announcing his amendment, Congressman Istook cited many examples of religious oppression. In one such case a court ordered a cross that has stood in a San Francisco park for

63 years to be removed. Crosses were also ordered off of city seals in Ohio and Oklahoma by court order. And Congressman Istook also noted the notorious case where Judge Roy Moore was ordered to remove a copy of the Ten Commandments from his Alabama courtroom.

"Under the pretense of promoting tolerance, religious expression is being singled out for censorship. All other types of language, conduct, nudity, and even sex acts are being given special protection, while religion and our values are being censored. We must reverse this topsy-turvy and terrible trend," added Congressman Istook, "or we will lose the bedrock values upon which America was founded and has prospered. The only way left is to pass a Constitutional Amendment."

Though Congressman Istook's Religious Freedom Amendment failed to pass in Congress, it was just the latest major attempt to overcome the barrier between church and state erected by the ACLU and other anti-prayer liberals. But pro-prayer grassroots groups have sprung up across the country to fight for our religious rights. Rallies have been held across the country – from California to Colorado to Kentucky to Pennsylvania to Washington, D.C. – in support of school prayer and posting the Ten Commandments on public property.

The growth and organization of religious groups which support voluntary prayer in public schools and display of the Ten Commandments on public property has strengthened the forces supporting our religious rights. And, of course, opinion poll sampling has shown that a large majority of Americans –- to 80% in some cases – favor allowing prayer in school. If momentum continues to build across the nation, it is just a matter of time before we finally restore all of our religious rights. But if the momentum stalls, and we fail in our task to restore God and prayer to our nation, the United States will fall from God's grace and be destroyed. It's as simple as that.

IV. THE TRUE MEANING OF THE FIRST AMENDMENT

The Founding Fathers intended the citizens of the United States to have constitutionally guaranteed religious freedom. But over the last 40 years, our religious freedom has been systematically curtailed. How did this happen? Well, it all started when the secular humanists began to corrupt the true meaning of the First Amendment to the United States Constitution.

Proverbs 14:34
Righteousness exalteth a nation: but sin is a reproach to any people.

The First Amendment is the most often quoted and sometimes the most misunderstood amendment in our Bill of Rights. The First Amendment is fundamental to the principles of freedom upon which our nation was founded and what we believe about America. Before we get into a full discussion regarding the true meaning of the First Amendment, let's take a brief historical look at the American Revolution, the founding of our nation and the Bill of Rights which will allow us to understand how all of these are truly and forever intertwined.

THE AMERICAN REVOLUTION — WHY WE FOUGHT

Simply stated, we fought the American Revolution to get out from under an oppressive government (Great Britain) that controlled the fate of its citizens by not allowing any personal or economic freedoms for the average citizens. The government of Great Britain was a monarchy where the Royal Family was everything and the average person was nothing. The idea of "getting ahead" was not even a thought for the average person.

By contrast, our founders established America upon the principles of personal and economic freedom for its citizens. These freedoms were to be facilitated by a government that was to be for the people and by the people. In addition to a government that provided freedom for its people, the new nation of America provided economic opportunity through the free enterprise system and did not limit its citizen's opportunities, as do socialist societies or monarchies.

Free speech, freedom of press, the right to peaceably assemble, the right to seek a redress of grievances from the government and the freedom of religion were obviously top priorities in the minds of our founders. After all, these freedoms are part of what we see as a natural law, but were simply not part of the law for the citizens of Great Britain.

These particular freedoms were of such great importance to our founders that they addressed them in the very First Amendment of our Bill of Rights. Make no mistake, these specific freedoms were first upon the minds of our founders when they wrote our Constitution. Freedom of religion was FIRST in the FIRST Amendment because our Founding Fathers found religious freedom to be the first thing on their minds when they wrote the First Amendment.

The American Revolution was fought for the right to exercise our freedom and the right to life, liberty and the pursuit of happiness. One of the most important rights guaranteed to our people was the right to the free exercise of religion, or more accurately, to freely chose your denomination. When we consider the freedoms our forefathers fought for, against seemingly insurmountable odds, perhaps none are so fundamentally important, nor often discussed as the freedoms spelled out and provided by the First Amendment. Most will agree that America, the land of the free, was founded as a nation that was dedicated to the fact that all men are equal and have certain rights. In fact, the Declaration of Independence states that we are equal in the Laws of Nature and Nature's God ... and that we are endowed by our Creator with certain unalienable rights, that among these are Life, Liberty and the Pursuit of Happiness. In other words, America was founded by a burning desire for freedom.

To assure a clear understanding of our freedoms the founders developed the Bill of Rights and listed some of the most important, specific freedoms intended for all citizens. At the same time, the Bill of Rights also placed restraints upon the Federal Government by stating specific actions they are NOT allowed to take. At the time the Bill of Rights was enacted, states rights were considered to be important, but nothing was more important than individual rights, AS GUARANTEED BY THE CONSTITUTION.

THE BILL OF RIGHTS

The Bill of Rights is truly a remarkable document. It consists of the first Ten Amendments, represents the heart of our constitutional freedoms, is virtually all-inclusive, and precisely written. Yet all ten of these amendments can be printed upon less that two pages of an average size book.

The Bill of Rights was passed by the U.S. Congress on December 15, 1791. Some of the specific freedoms provided in the Bill of Rights include, free speech, free press, free exercise of religion; the right to keep and bear arms; freedom from unreasonable search and seizure; the right not to testify against yourself; the right to not be deprived of life, liberty or property without due process of law; the right to not be subjected to double jeopardy; the right to just compensation for any property taken for public use; the right to a speedy and public trial by an impartial jury; the right to be informed of the nature and cause of the accusations; the right to have the assistance of counsel for your defense; the right to freedom from excessive bail and fines; the right to freedom from cruel and unusual punishment; and the freedom of each state to assume responsibilities for their own constitutions.

As you can see, the Bill of Rights is the heart of our American freedoms that are so often taken for granted. The Constitution as a whole and the Bill of Rights specifically must be protected to insure that we know what the rules are, to refer back to whenever our courts must make tough decisions, and yet do so with impartiality, common sense and fairness according to these rules and the law of the land.

The First Ten Amendments To The Constitution As Ratified By The States:

THE BILL OF RIGHTS.

Amendment I

Congress shall make no law respecting an establishment of religion, or prohibiting the free exercise thereof; or abridging the freedom of speech, or of the press; or the right of the people peaceably to assemble, and to petition the Government for a redress of grievances.

Amendment II

A well regulated Militia, being necessary to the security of a free State, the right of the people to keep and bear Arms, shall not be infringed.

Amendment III

No Soldier shall, in time of peace be quartered in any house, without the consent of the Owner, nor in time of war, but in a manner to be prescribed by law.

Amendment IV

The right of the people to be secure in their persons, houses, papers, and effects, against unreasonable searches and seizures, shall not be violated, and no Warrants shall issue, but upon probable cause, supported by Oath or affirmation, and particularly describing the place to be searched, and the persons or things to be seized.

Amendment V

No person shall be held to answer for a capital, or otherwise infamous crime, unless on a presentment or indictment of a Grand Jury, except in cases arising in the land or naval forces, or in the Militia, when in actual service in time of War or public danger; nor shall be compelled in any criminal case to be a witness against himself, nor be deprived of life, liberty, or property, without due process of law; nor shall private property be taken for public use, without just compensation.

Amendment VI

In all criminal prosecutions, the accused shall enjoy the right to a speedy and public trial, by an impartial jury of the State and district wherein the crime shall have been committed, which district shall have been previously ascertained by law, and to be informed of the nature and cause of the accusation; to be confronted with the witnesses against him; to have compulsory process for obtaining witnesses in his favor, and to have the Assistance of Counsel for his defence.

Amendment VII

In suits at common law, where the value in controversy shall exceed twenty dollars, the right of trial by jury shall be preserved, and no fact tried by a jury, shall be otherwise reexamined in any Court of the United States, that according to the rules of the common law.

Amendment VIII

Excessive bail shall not be required, nor excessive fines imposed, nor cruel and unusual punishments inflicted.

Amendment IX

The enumeration in the Constitution, of certain rights, shall not be construed to deny or disparage others retained by the people.

Amendment X

The powers not delegated to the United States by the Constitution, nor prohibited by it to the States are reserved to the States respectively, or to the people.

THE ORIGINAL INTENT OF THE FIRST AMENDMENT

The purpose of the First Amendment, like all of the amendments that make up the Bill of Rights, were written amidst fears that certain privileges needed to be spelled out concerning as the rights of the people. People living in various states wanted their rights spelled out in regard to certain things. They wanted to know that government had restrictions and that they were protected from the government.

This First Amendment not only gives us the right to free speech, freedom of press and the freedom to peaceably assemble, it also guarantees us the right to the free exercise of religion. The First Amendment begins with the phrase, "Congress shall make no law respecting an establishment of religion, or prohibiting the free exercise thereof …". In other words, the First Amendment guarantees our right to freedom OF religion. Unfortunately many people today argue that the First Amendment means freedom FROM religion.

While the First Amendment provides citizens with some of our most important rights and freedoms, it also restricts Congress by placing specific limits upon their power. In other words, our Bill of Rights guarantees certain rights to our citizens and at the same time, places certain limitations upon our government.

The First Amendment is short, to the point and easy to understand. The First Amendment specifically guarantees citizens the right to the free exercise of religion AND places specific limitations upon Congress in regard to the establishment of religion. The First Amendment begins, "Congress shall enact no law respecting an establishment of religion." Congress is restricted by the First Amendment which does not allow them to enact any law regarding the establishment of religion. That phrase, *establishment of religion*, is the so-called "establishment clause," which is so often quoted as precedence in court cases involving the issues that revolve around the freedom of religion.

The truth of the matter is, from the time the states ratified the First Amendment, until just about 40 years ago, the rulings made by our courts were based upon a literal interpretation of the First Amendment. The First Amendment was applied exactly as it was written and exactly as our founders intended. However, the original well intended meaning of the First Amendment has been traded in for an argument that is perverse and completely the opposite from what our founders intended.

RELIGION VS. DENOMINATION

One of the misinterpretations of the First Amendment revolves around the meaning of the word "religion". The word "religion" as it was used in the First Amendment has been determined to mean denomination. We know this because at the time our nation was established there were many denominations, but all of these denominations were Christian in one form or another.

One of the reasons we fought the American Revolution was that in Great Britain the government had established only one state denomination, legally recognized by the British government. That is, in England the government had established the Church of England as the only church allowed in that nation. However, since they did not want any one denomination to be declared America's only acceptable denomination, the Founding Fathers wrote into the First Amendment the words, "Congress shall make no law respecting the establishment of religion (denomination)".

When our Founding Fathers talked about the free exercise of religion, they meant the free exercise of any chosen Christian denomination. To understand that this is true we need only to think back to the fact that our founding fathers came to America, partly for religious freedom, because in England the government had decided and proclaimed that there was but one acceptable Christian denomination and that denomination was represented by the Church of England. In other words, the government of England had made a law that chose one denomination as the ONLY legal, accepted denomination in the entire nation of England. In effect, all other denominations were declared to be illegal because the government had chosen the Church of England to be the only Christian denomination allowed in their country.

Therefore when our founders put the "establishment clause" into our First Amendment, it was their intention to prevent our government from ever choosing one Christian denomination over another. They had seen what England had done when they endorsed one denomination at the exclusion of all others. Our founders wanted to be certain that we always had the freedom to choose our own denomination. So the intent of the First Amendment was to protect the people from the state. We did not want the government to be able to choose any one denomination and declare that denomination to be the only state approved church, like the Church of England.

THE MYTH: SEPARATION OF CHURCH AND STATE

Possibly the most misunderstood phrase in regards to our constitutional rights is *separation of church and state.* In fact, the very phrase, separation of church and state, cannot be found anywhere in our Preamble, Constitution, Bill of Rights, Declaration of Independence or any other official document of the United States.

Unfortunately, there are a number of anti-Christian groups, like the ACLU, who have repeatedly said that separation of church and state is a law. Today, many believe that the "law" of separation of church and state is real. IT IS NOT.

Others believe that we have a law of separation of church and state in the First Amendment of the Constitution. WE DO NOT. The so-called "law" of separation of church and state just simply does not exist even though people often repeat that it does.

We have all heard media reports that say you can't publicly display the Ten Commandments, nor any other sign of your Christian faith, because of the "law" of separation of church and state. There is no such law on the books anywhere in America. The "law" of separation has become widely accepted as truth because of a misunderstanding about the wording and a twisted ACLU argument about the original intent of the First Amendment. Some courts have even given credence to this "new", albeit incorrect, interpretation of the First Amendment.

From the ratification of the First Amendment and for more than the170 years following the adoption of the First Amendment, the phrase separation of church and state was NEVER mentioned in connection with the First Amendment. Today, the phrase separation of church and state is often mentioned, incorrectly, in the same breath as the First Amendment. The argument, is simply disingenuous.

During the years when the First Amendment was interpreted literally, none of today's court cases which attack Christianity would have stood a snow ball's chance in hell. In fact, although there were a few cases that dealt with Religious Freedom before the 1960's, they were dealt with firmly by judges who interpreted the Constitution literally, exactly as it was written.

Let me remind you what is restricted by this Amendment — the GOVERNMENT. In America, people are still free to make their own choices. This amendment does not place any limitation upon citizens, collectively or individually. Therefore, it is the people who are being protected against the power of our government.

All this changed suddenly in 1962, when the anti-Christian ACLU group of so-called freedom fighters convinced our Supreme Court that the First Amendment meant something altogether different than was ever intended by our Christian patriotic founders.

HOW DID THEY DO THAT?

Today the First Amendment plays a significant role in lawsuits involving religion, but that has not always been true. In the 1962 case of Engle v. Vitale, the ACLU was able to convince the Supreme Court that the First Amendment meant something that no other court had ever said before. The ACLU's perverted misinterpretation of the First Amendment became responsible for today's myriad of new and frivolous lawsuits. The purpose of these lawsuits is to attack Christianity in America and remove every trace of God from public view in America.

Since our Founding Fathers were Christians, freedom of religion meant the freedom to exercise the *religion of your chosen denomination.* Any other interpretation or argument is without the support of any historical fact, and without any reasonable foundation.

The freedom of religion, free speech, freedom of press and the right to peaceably assemble were obviously the top priorities for our founders. Therefore, they addressed these issues in the FIRST Amendment. Freedom of religion was First in the FIRST Amendment, not the 200th amendment.

When we read about court cases that involve questions of school prayer, hanging the Ten Commandments in public places, or allowing nativity scenes, or other "religious" displays, it is the phrase of the First Amendment that is frequently called the "establishment clause" which is referred to in newspaper articles reporting these cases. We frequently read that the ACLU is contending that a public display of the Ten Commandments is a violation of the "establishment clause" and is therefore UNCONSTITUTIONAL. Obviously they are reading from a different book.

The First Amendment guarantees *freedom of religion.* Although our founders were thinking of freedom for each denomination, because they were all Christians, today, the ACLU has convinced our courts that the First Amendment means *freedom from religion.* But how in the world did they ever do that?

The ACLU convinced the court that the words religion or denomination really meant Christianity. (Notice that Christianity is at the center of the ACLU's attack) Then the ACLU said that the word Congress did not mean Congress. Instead, the ACLU said that the word CONGRESS supposedly meant any tax supported organization such as a school, courthouse or library. Next they said that any action like displaying the Ten Commandments, by any tax-supported organization (schools, court houses, or libraries) was exactly the same as if it had been done by the Congress. And lastly they argued that if a court house hung the Ten Commandments it was exactly the same as if CONGRESS PASSED A LAW THAT REPRESENTED THE ESTABLISHMENT OF RELIGION.

This is an outrage and is unbelievably mind-boggling. There is no truth in this argument and it is clear that the victims of this atrocity are America's people of faith.

In 1962, the ACLU claimed its first victims. The US Supreme Court decided that if elementary school children were allowed to say a morning prayer, they were doing the same thing as if Congress passed a law establishing one denomination as our national denomination. It was quite remarkable that when it became time for the Supreme Court to site the precedents upon which this decision was based, they were not able to cite even one precedent. But that was because there were none. They had no former court case that ever ruled this way, and they had to look OUTSIDE OF ALL PRIOR CASES EVER RULED UPON BY THE SUPREME COURT FOR A REASON TO EXPLAIN THEIR ACTION! After searching for something to hang their hats upon, they came up with the phrase "Separation of Church and State".

WHERE DID SEPARATION COME FROM?

The phrase law of separation of church and state is nowhere to be found in our Declaration of Independence, Constitution, First Amendment, nor any other official document of the United States government. It was coined by Thomas Jefferson in a personal letter he wrote to a group of Baptists in Danbury, Connecticut. They had asked if there was to be a national denomination and Jefferson wrote back to assure them that this would never happen because of the First Amendment had created a wall of separation of church and state.

The ACLU and other anti-Christian organizations love to talk about the law of separation of church and state. They gleefully point to the "law" separation of church and state mentioned in Thomas Jefferson's letter. However, they fail to quote Jefferson when he said, "No power over the freedom of religion is given to the United States, by the Constitution." It is also interesting to note that when the Bill of Rights was written, Thomas Jefferson played no role in drafting the documents. He was not in the country at the time.

UNGODLY PRINCIPLE

As a Christian the separation of church and state is not only a flawed legal argument, but it is also an ungodly principle. First, it is nearly impossible to separate people from anything they have chosen to believe and is a part of their very make up. If a man has high ideals and they are a part of him, how can you separate him from those ideals and expect him to not allow his deep-rooted thoughts and values to accompany him to school, work or the grocery store? The state (e.g. the government) is made up of men and women. Does God want to separate men and women (the state) from the church? I think not.

The ACLU argued that the establishment clause (Congress shall enact no law regarding the establishment of religion) meant that if a tax supported court house displays the Ten Commandments, that action is exactly the same as if Congress enacted a law and was establishing a religion — in this case, Christianity. And that, according to the ACLU's version of the First Amendment establishment clause, was prohibited and therefore unconstitutional.

The literal interpretation of the establishment clause should lead the court to ask a simple question: Did Congress enact any law regarding that established a religion? The answer is clearly, no, they did not. Case dismissed!

Not only is that clear from the deep researching of the times, but since there were only Christians of different denominations in America at the time, the Founding Fathers obviously were not thinking about Buddhists in Japan who were literally a world away. When we allowed the ACLU to deny the literal interpretation of our Constitution, we gave up the principles of our founders, the principles of our Christian Heritage, and the principles that soldiers in two world wars fought to defend.

AS A RESULT ...

As a result of the ACLU's relentless attack upon Christianity and their attack upon what is simply morally right, we have seen a huge change in our nation. Since 1962, divorce rates, teenage pregnancies and violent crimes have skyrocketed.

We no longer uphold truth, honesty and morality. Instead, we now champion concepts such as, there is no right or wrong, there are no absolutes, morality is whatever each us determines for ourselves, sex is just a biological act, and lying to further your own agenda is acceptable.

The rules of society that created this great nation have now given way to a society where there are no rules. Unfortunately, that very concept has brought us to the place of deprivation we find ourselves in today.

Prior to the ACLU's twisted series of attacks upon the very moral fiber of America, we were a nation that played by the rules and respected one another. We understood that freedom and success came from operating within the guidelines of generally accepted principles. Somehow those ideas have been replaced with the idea that freedom comes only when you have no rules. If it feels good, do it. Instant gratification seems to be more important than someone else's well being, or even more important than the consequences you yourself may face. As a result, we now have school shootings, metal detectors in public buildings, "hooking up," drug sniffing dogs, drive by shootings, abortion upon demand, no fault divorce, condoms handed out by public schools to teenagers without their parents consent, and homosexual propaganda being taught to our children in elementary schools.

V. SECULAR HUMANISM

Throughout this book, secular humanism has been referenced as the guiding philosophy behind those seeking to destroy Christian America. The founding document of the secular humanism movement is the Humanist Manifesto. The Humanist Manifesto was first published in the 1930s. In 1973, an updated edition was published, Humanist Manifesto II. Here are the five basic tenets of humanism, based on the Human Manifesto II:

Isaiah 5:20
Woe unto them that call evil good, and good evil; that put darkness for light and light for darkness; that put bitter for sweet, and sweet for bitter.

Tenet I: Atheism

"Religious humanists regard the universe as self-existing and not created. We find insufficient evidence for belief in the existence of a supernatural; it is either meaningless or irrelevant to the question of the survival and fulfillment of the human race. As nontheists, we begin with humans, not God, not nature, not deity. Nature may indeed be broader and deeper than we now know;

any new discoveries, however, will but enlarge our knowledge of the natural...but we can discover no divine purpose or providence for the human species. While there is much that we do not know, humans are responsible for what we are or will become. No deity will save us, we must save ourselves."

Tenet II: Evolution

"Humanism believes that man is a part of nature and that he has emerged as a result of continuous process...Holding an organic view of life, humanists find that the traditional dualism of mind and body must be rejected...Humanism recognized that man's religious culture and civilization, as clearly depicted by anthropology and history, are the product of gradual development due to his interaction with his environment and with his social heritage. The individual born into a particular culture is largely molded to that culture...science affirms that the human species is an emergence from natural evolutionary forces. As far as we know, the total personality is a function of the biological organism transacting in a social and cultural contest."

Tenet III: Amorality

"We affirm that moral values derive their source from human experience. Ethics is autonomous and situational, needing no theological or ideological sanction. Ethics stem from human need and interest. To deny this distorts the whole basis of life. In the area of sexuality, we believe that intolerant attitudes, often cultivated by orthodox religions and puritanical cultures, unduly repress sexual conduct. The right to birth control, abortion, and divorce should be recognized. While we do not approve of exploitative, denigration forms of sexual expression, neither do wish to prohibit, by law or social sanction, sexual behavior between consenting adults. The many varieties of sexual exploration should not in themselves be considered "evil." Without countenancing mindless permissiveness or unbridled promiscuity, a civilized society should be a tolerant one. Short of harming others or compelling them to do likewise, individuals should be permitted to express their sexual proclivities and pursue their life-styles as they desire. We wish to cultivate the development of a responsible attitude toward sexuality, in which humans are not exploited as sexual objects, and in which intimacy, sensitivity, respect, and honesty in interpersonal relations are encouraged. Moral education for children and adults is an important way of developing awareness and sexual maturity."

Tenet IV: Individual Autonomy

"Human life has meaning because we create and develop our futures. Happiness and creative realization of human need and desires, individually and in shared enjoyment, are continuous themes in humanism. We strive for the good life, here and now. The goal is to pursue life's enrichment despite debasing forces of vulgarization, commercialization, bureaucratization, and dehumanization...Reason and intelligence are the most effective instruments that humankind possesses. There is no substitute; neither faith nor passion suffices in itself. The controlled use of scientific methods, which have transformed the natural and social sciences since the Renaissance, must be extended further in the solution of human problems...To enhance freedom and dignity the individual must experience a full range of civil liberties in all societies. This included freedom of speech and the press, fair judicial process, religious liberty, freedom of association, and artistic, scientific, and cultural freedom. It also includes a recognition of an individual's right to die with dignity, euthanasia, and the right to suicide.

We oppose the increasing invasion of privacy, by whatever means, in both totalitarian and democratic societies. We would safeguard, extend, and implement the principle of human freedom evolved from the Magna Carta to the Bill of Rights, the Rights of Man, and the Universal Declaration of Human Rights…The preciousness and dignity of the individual person is a central humanist value. Individuals should be encouraged to realize their own creative talents and desires. We reject all religious, ideological, or moral codes that denigrate the individual, suppress freedom, dull intellect, dehumanize personality.

We believe in maximum individual autonomy consonant with social responsibility. Although science can account for the causes of behavior, the possibilities of individual freedom of choice exist in human life and should be increased."

Tenet V: Socialistic One-World View

"We deplore the division of humankind on nationalistic grounds. We have reached a turning point in human history where the best option is to transcend the limits of national sovereignty and to move toward the building of a world community in which all sectors of the human family can participate. Thus we look to the development of a system of world law and a world order based upon transnational federal government. This would appreciate cultural pluralism and diversity. It would not exclude pride in national origins and accomplishments nor the handling of regional problems on a regional basis. Human progress, however, can no longer be achieved by focusing on one section of the world, Western or Eastern, developed or underdeveloped. For the first time in human history, no part of human kind can be isolated from any other. Each person's future is in some way linked to all. We thus reaffirm a commitment to the building of world community, at the same time recognizing that this commits us to some hard choices...The problem of economic growth and development can no longer be resolved by one nation alone; they are worldwide in scope. It is the moral obligation of the developed nations to provide – through an international authority that safeguards human rights – massive technical, agricultural, medical, and economic assistance, including birth control techniques, to the developing portions of the globe. World poverty must cease. Hence extreme disproportions in wealth, income, and economic growth should be reduced on a worldwide basis.

The principle of moral equality must be furthered through elimination of all discrimination based upon race, religion, sex, age, or national origin. This means equality of opportunity and recognition of talent and merit. Individuals should be encouraged to contribute to their own betterment. If unable, then society should provide means to satisfy their basic economic, health, and cultural needs, including, wherever resources make possible, a minimum guaranteed annual income."

These tenets are for all intents and purposes a repudiation of God and his laws! And since the terrible *Engle vs. Vitale* case in 1962, these tenets have slowly crept into our society's laws. As a result, we've seen a devastating decline in lawfulness, morality and decency in our nation. In the next chapter, we will see exactly what this immoral philosophy has wrought here in America.

Kip at age 23 at airport with President John F. Kennedy, Senator Albert Gore, U.S. Congressman Richard Fulton, Gov. Frank Clement, in summer of 1963 prior to th assassination of the President.

Kip, at age 24, as a business and property owner-developer and state finance chairman, Young Citizens for Governor Frank Clement 1964 U.S. Senate campaign, presenting a certificate to local business person.

Age 37, Kip was a major financier and fund-raiser for longtime friend and Gubanatorial candidate, Bob Clement. Pictured here with Clement, later to become U.S. Congressman and John J. Hooker—founder Minnie Pearl Fried Chicken Systems, 1970, Democratic nominee for Governor of Tennessee and nationally known political figure. Entertaining over 1900 registered guests for one evening at Grassland, raising over $100,000, a fair amount for that period of time.

Kip with Lamar Alexander, Governor of Tennessee 1978-1986, Director of Education in Cabinet of President George Bush, and candidate for President of the United States, 1996.

Kip with Ned Ray McWhorter, Tennessee Governor 1986-1994 and Jake Butcher, the democratic Nominee for Governor 1978 and founder of the largest failed banking empire in history to that point in time. This major collapse was the forerunner of the S&L debacle of the eighties, the banking collapse of that era, brining into existance a new era of bank regulations and mergers that spelled the end of credit and real estate leverage as his generation once knew. Kip and his girlfriend flew to Knoxville with Jake in his private jet, where he was founder of the World's Fair and stayed in his palatial estate. He was hailed as a great American hero, just prior to the banking collapse.

Age 29, with girlfriend Sue Barnhart, pilot, and Alabama football coach, Paul "Bear" Bryant, presenting the trophy in a sailing regatta of Mobile Bay.

Kip Caudill with Pastor Don Swarthout, President of Christians Reviving America's Values. Kip and Don have worked together for years promoting American patriotism and Christian values.

VI. THE ACLU'S FORM OF FREEDOM

America is a nation that was built upon the tenants of freedom. Our Declaration of Independence, in the first paragraph, states that we as a People (nation) are entitled to a decent Respect in the Opinions of Mankind and that respect is based upon the Laws of Nature and of Nature's God. The Declaration of Independence also says "WE hold these Truths to be self-evident, that all Men are created equal, that they are endowed by their Creator with certain unalienable Rights, that among these are Life, Liberty and the Pursuit of Happiness.

Proverbs 29:2
When the righteous are in authority, the people rejoice: but when the wicked beareth rule, the people mourn.

Our Declaration of Independence states that we have a God given right to certain freedoms. Our Constitution was written to define these rights and how they are to be protected. In effect, our Constitution is a list of rules that were agreed upon to create an orderly society. The

Declaration states our principles of freedom, while the Constitution clarifies the rules that allow freedom to operate in our society. It is these rules of society that level the playing field and give us the best shot at equality that man has so far devised. It means that you are free to live your life as you see fit *within the rules*. You are given the opportunity to make choices in you life as long as you follow a certain set of guidelines, rules or laws. You can go to college, pursue your chosen field of work, get married, move freely about the country, earn a living and have the opportunity to achieve success to the best of your ability. Freedom means that you are to be respected by your government and have the opportunity to make choices in your life, *within the law*. Freedom requires a set of rules so that we all know what will happen when you make certain choices. If you choose to go become a computer programmer, your choice is based upon certain expectations about working in that field. If you commit a crime you are going to jail. It is the same with a free society, your choices have consequences, some good, some not so good.

Freedom means choices. You can make bad choices and because of the rules there may be bad consequences. It is not OK to murder your neighbor. Would you choose a brand of freedom where murder is acceptable? Freedom is based upon a moral code that is based upon the Laws of Nature and Nature's God. The Natural Law is based upon certain concepts that are universally accepted. Behavior like murder, rape, stealing and lying in court, would represent crimes against the Natural Law.

Some would disagree with these concepts, but rules or laws against murder, rape and robbery enhance freedom. Freedom is enhanced because the consequences for committing these crimes creates a sense of living in a secure, predictable society wherein everyone plays by the same rules.

Rules are required for an orderly society and an orderly society is required if you want true freedom. That idea may seem contradictory at first, that rules equal freedom, but remember how you first felt following the terrorist attack against the World Trade Center and the Pentagon. Most Americans felt violated because freedom was under attack. Why? The simplest of rules, one of Nature's Laws, had been violated ... innocent people were the victims of aggression and were murdered by some terrorist group that does not believe in following any part of Nature's Law.

Was freedom enhanced or was freedom hindered by this horrific act of total disregard for human life? The answer is obvious. America lost some of it's freedom because of these attacks against us. And ultimately the perpetuators of this horrific act will lose all of their freedoms.

The terrorists who attacked the World Trade Center live in a "No Rules" society. As a result of their attack Americans became afraid to fly, to invest in the stock market or go to concerts, plays and sporting events. Many faced the loss of their own dignity and the ability to support their own families because of the loss of jobs. We lost our feelings of security about the economy and the safety of our lives and the lives of our families. In other words, freedom was lost by an act that was the result of a 'No Rules" type of Freedom. We can and do suffer a loss of freedom when there are no rules, or when the rules of an orderly society which protect our freedom are violated. But as we shall see in this chapter, there are some who believe that freedom means "No Rules."

THE WAR IN AMERICA

There is a war being fought in America. The New War Against Terrorism is raging and we certainly cannot underestimate its importance. The very tenants of freedom in America and the rights of people all over the world depend upon the outcome. The war on terrorism is a war we must win for the future of America and the world depends upon the outcome. However, there is a second war going on in America that is perhaps even more dangerous. This more dangerous war is an ideological war. This is a battle that comes against our way of life. It is a battle for control over the way we think in America and it is a war for the control over the minds of the rest of the world as well.

In this ideological war there are two opposing sides, with two very distinct patterns of thought and with two distinct world-views. While there are just two world-views involved in this tug-of-war, within each group there are several subgroups that can be defined with crystal clarity. These subgroups fit together with one or the other of the larger groups like the pieces of a jigsaw puzzle.

Whether you know it or not, we are involved in a battle that will define what freedom really means in America and the entire world. We are in a battle over a philosophical question regarding the rules of society and the concepts of right versus wrong and good versus evil. One side supports what I call the

"No Rules" World-View and the other supports the "Orderly Society" World-View.

Some people seem to think that a society with no rules is a free society. The people and groups who support this thinking would say: that man is his own authority; there is no God (no higher spiritual authority than man); there are no absolutes; no right or wrong; sex is nothing more than a biological function; and morality is whatever you may determine it is at the moment. These people argue that Freedom equals no rules and no consequences.

The proponents of a "no rules society" see abortion as a woman's right to choose, homosexuality as an alternate lifestyle that should be taught to your children in public schools, handing out condoms to your children without your approval is preferable to teaching abstinence in sex education classes, protecting so-called endangered species is more important than protecting people, it is an "artist's" right to receive tax dollars for the displaying of whatever obscenity he or she may choose, and it is their right to remove your right to recognize God in public places.

The other pieces which complete the "no rules" puzzle are tolerance, pacifism, one world government, radical environmentalism, no free enterprise, no rewards for individual accomplishment, no sovereignty for America, a redistribution of America's wealth, and morality left to each person.

The American Civil Liberties Union (ACLU) is a strong proponent of the "no rules" philosophy in America.

Those who subscribe to the Orderly Society World View believe that there is a Natural Law which comes from God or a spiritual source of an authority that is higher than mankind. They believe that freedom comes from an orderly society where everyone knows and follows a set of common rules.

The Orderly Society Group believes in a higher authority, there are absolutes, right and wrong, abortion is murder, homosexuality is a behavior and it does not deserve special rights any more than a murderer, abstinence should be taught in sex education classes, obscene art supported by tax dollars is unconstitutional, people are more important than wolves, and my right to recognize God is specifically guaranteed by the Constitution of the United States.

Other tenets of the Orderly Society World View are following acceptable standards, breaking the rules of society is not tolerated, when someone attacks your nation without provocation you can hit back, the sovereignty of nations, free enterprise, ingenuity and hard work are rewarded, we need to control our environment (not the other way around) and morality consists of what is simply right and wrong as determined by the Law of Nature and Nature's God —The Natural Law.

Patriotic Christians best represent the "orderly society" group.

THE AMERICAN CIVIL LIBERTIES UNION

The ACLU was founded in 1920 by Roger Baldwin, for the purposes of "defending" the "rights" of citizens from the "totalitarian" American government.

Baldwin, a proponent of the Human Manifesto, knew exactly how he was going to attack America and our institutions. The following quote is a revealing insight regarding exactly how the ACLU has gone about achieving their goals. In order to achieve their goals Baldwin said, "The courts are the vehicles we use to assert our interpretation of the US Constitution." This statement reveals an admission that the ACLU's a view of our own Constitution is a different interpretation than the view held by most Americans. It also reveals the ACLU is attacking America from the inside by using our very own courts and governmental systems.

Does this sound familiar? Former USSR leader Nakita Khruschev once said, "We will bury you!" When asked if he was saying that Russia would destroy us militarily, he said, "No, we will destroy you from the inside out."

Now forty plus years later, an enemy of freedom has infiltrated our nation, hijacked our own planes and used them as weapons against our own people and against the tenants of freedom. These terrorists claim that they are "religious." But, no true religion encourages mass murder as part of their doctrine or fundamental practices. Terrorism, by definition is an act of those who are against the generally accepted thinking of an orderly society.

While the terrorist attack upon the World Trade Center was appalling enough, it was not the first attack that came from inside our nation and used our own institutions. The first terrorist attack that came from the inside, and used our own facilities and institutions against us, was launched long ago by the ACLU.

In fact, we have the ACLU to thank for their type of freedom that led to the very disasters that we saw on September 11, 2001 at the World Trade Center and the Pentagon. The destruction of buildings and the mass murder of thousands of innocent people is the ultimate result of a world view that champions no rules, no consequences and no moral conscience.

On the other side of the coin, listen to what James Madison, known to be the Architect of our Constitution said, "We have staked the whole future of American civilization, not upon the power of government, far from it. We have staked the future of all of our political institutions upon the capacity of mankind for self government; upon the capacity of each and all of us to govern ourselves, to control ourselves, to sustain ourselves according to the Ten Commandments of God." (A set of rules)

French statesman, Alexis de Tocqueville, who studied America at great length in an attempt to determine what made America great said, "America is great because America is good, and if America ever ceases to be good, America will cease to be great." This speaks very well to the concept of what is right about our great nation.

TOLERANCE, PACIFISM AND THE AMORAL SOCIETY

During the days immediately following the terrorists destruction of the World Trade Center and the Pentagon, a good deal of discussion was heard regarding what we should do and where our actions would lead us. Some of the common topics of these discussions were Tolerance, Pacifism, and World Peace. In order to bring all of this into one big picture, let's look at these topics in an to attempt to find out how they fit together and whether they serve the best interests of America or the world.

Tolerance: The ACLU and others frequently demand tolerance. Immediately following the senseless killing of our friends and neighbors who worked in the World Trade Center, many shouted for a display of tolerance. While I understand the concept they are suggesting, the word tolerance means to tolerate. If I tolerate something, then I am putting up with something I disagree with. For example if you murdered my sister I doubt that I would be inclined to tolerate that very well because I would disagree with you.

Perhaps I would be more understanding if instead of tolerance we said, "We need to love people, with the love of Jesus Christ." Maybe it is only semantics, but I have a hard time with those who stated that if we attacked the terrorists who had just murdered thousands of us, it will only cause the terrorists to kill more people. I have a hard time with the fact that these attackers killed thousands of US citizens in an unprovoked attack and now you want me to wait and see whether they will do it again and again.

Tolerance is the exact attitude that allowed these terrorists the freedom to come across our borders, live in our country, attend our flight instruction schools, and then hijack our airplanes and blow up buildings killing thousands. This is a perfect example of the type of freedom that the ACLU and other groups champion. Tolerating terrorists from around the world in our own back yard has resulted in the killing and maiming of thousands and now you say we should continue to tolerate that type of behavior? I DON'T THINK SO!

Apart from the issue of tolerating the terrorist murderers of the world, the ACLU frequently calls for tolerance in the arena of homosexual rights and the homosexual agenda calling for the teaching of our children about the homosexual lifestyle in our public, tax supported schools. At the same time the ACLU says that they cannot tolerate prayer in schools or any other public place.

Apparently it is OK for the ACLU to demand tolerance for some people and call it well and good, but they cannot tolerate anyone else's freedom of speech.

Special rights for homosexuals is truly unacceptable. When we look at this logically, homosexuals are not a racial group, a religious group, nor people of a certain creed, nor a certain color. Homosexuality is a behavior. Murder is also a behavior. Should murderers be given "special" rights? Maybe we should teach elementary aged school children that mass murderers are simply living an alternative life style. If we are going to allow the public schools, supported with tax dollars to teach your second grader to be tolerant and accepting of the homosexual lifestyle, why don't we teach them that mass murderers are simply people who live a different lifestyle and that we should accept and tolerate their lifestyle of killing people?

Pacifism: It would be great if we all got along perfectly here on earth. Unfortunately, there will always be people who are good and people who are bad. Some think that when bad people do bad things to good people we should just turn, take it and perhaps even turn the other cheek. When the Bible tells us to turn the other cheek, I believe it is saying we should forgive others and give them another chance. However, there has to be a limit to how many opportunities even God will give to the one rotten apple in the bunch.

Ultimately, complete pacifism leads to bad people doing more bad things to more good people. Perhaps the bad things they do may include murdering those good people. In the case of the World Trade Center attack, the lack of defending our nation would most certainly invite further unprovoked destruction of American buildings and the heart of our freedom. And while that by itself is bad enough, if we do not stop these terrorists are you willing to accept the blame for additional deaths that will almost certainly occur? Will you have the blood of thousands upon your hands?

It would be wonderful if pacifism worked, but then these terrorists renegades who are somehow bad or evil by some quirk of nature would surely control our world. People who are pacifists are bound by an allegiance toward saving plants and animals, but they don't seem to have much concern for defending the principles of freedom, democracy, free enterprise or the principles of defending human life. Pacifists have a good idea, they want us all to love one another. *That is a good idea, but it just does not work.*

An Amoral Society: The ACLU has spent years calling for a brand of freedom that is diametrically opposed to everything that has helped make America great. They have spent millions of dollars to win a battle for a brand of freedom that does not accept any rules, regulations, laws, right or wrong — a brand of freedom that champions the minority opinion against the opinion of the moral majority. They seem to believe that freedom is equal to a society that has no rules, no consequences and the exaltation of the most vile, degrading, filthy amoral people that live in our society and the rest of the world's society.

The ACLU seems to always represent the reprobates of our society. They never seem to be on the side of a person or an organization that is basically good. They did not represent the Boy Scouts, they represented homosexuals who want to be around your young boys. The ACLU favors lowering the age of sexual consent to twelve or even ten. They favor the legalization of marijuana, and they represented a man in Adams County Ohio who wanted to place a six foot tall penis right next to a Ten Commandments monument. The ACLU represents groups like the North American Man Boy Love Association (NAMBLA) whose stated goal is to encourage the seduction of young boys into the homosexual lifestyle. The ACLU believes that it is OK to display extremely vulgar forms of "art" using your tax dollars, but they are against any public recognition of God as is clearly written in the First Amendment. The ACLU is against tax dollars being used to teach abstinence in public school sex education classes, but they are in favor of using tax dollars to hand out condoms to your children without your knowledge or your parental consent!

Are you understanding my point? The ACLU has a perverted sense of what freedom truly means, and they are using our courts to impose this perverted interpretation of our Constitution to further their agenda and to stop your agenda. The ACLU has a history of representing the seedier side of life. They also believe that true freedom comes from a "No Rules" type of society and they have dedicated their millions of dollars to enforce this thinking upon America. It is the type of freedom that the ACLU represents that is directly responsible for just the type of tragedy we just saw in Washington DC and New York City.

One World Government: Those who favor a "No Rules" Society generally believe in the principles of a One World Government. It is their feeling that if we had such an organization, everybody would be equal.

Equality sometimes sounds like a good idea, but good ideas are frequently not all they are cracked up to be. For example, a world where everyone is completely equal holds an appeal for some people. They may think that total equality would be the one way to create a world that treats everyone fairly. But when you consider that inmates in a prison are about as equal as you can get, the idea somehow loses some of it's luster.

We all are for a better world. Individuals are born with different skills and talents. The good news is that there is a place for your particular talent. The bad news is that some talents seem to be rewarded more than others, but that is the way of life in a free enterprise system. If we had a One World Government, it would want the United States to give up it's right to own property, the sovereignty of our government in favor of a committee who would decide what is best for the world and then tell our nation what to do!

Those who favor a One World Government also favor the redistribution of the world's wealth. The end result they desire is for the nations and people of the world to be treated exactly the same. The theory is that all nations and all people would become totally equal. However, I can assure you that the poor, third world nations will not improve up to the level of America, but rather America will be forced down to the level of these poor and unfortunate nations! The United Nations has already dismissed the United States as a member from it's Humanitarian Committee and yet Sudan is a member of that committee.

The rest of the world would love to control America. We are, after all, the greatest nation in the history of mankind. It is natural to look at our prosperity and our power and want to control such a great nation. However, they seem to forget that we have earned our position in the world because of our Christian Heritage. And they seem to have forgotten how many times the United States has come to the aid of various nations, militarily and financially.

The down side to all of this is that under a One World Government run by committee there would be no Super Power to take a stand for nations in true need. The United States would be expected to give up its sovereignty and the control of the greatest military power in the world to the discretion of this committee.

The result of all of this might be that there would just not be anyone to help when help is needed and desired. It is hard to believe that we would have a better world if there was suddenly no one strong nation to lead the rest of the world.

Can you imagine a One World Government made up of socialistic thinking? A One World Government that has the authority to assess and collect taxes and control your property? It is hard enough for the United States to run it's own affairs, imagine how a government that is many times larger would operate. A One World Government would collect taxes and then redistribute the wealth of the world in attempt to create complete equality. The results of this idea would most assuredly be that the United States would become a greatly diminished nation.

If equality between the citizens of the world were ever to be attained it would not be because the other nations lifted themselves up to the level of the United States, but rather that the United States would give up it's sovereign nation status, it's position of world leadership, control of it's own military, control of it's own wealth and the America would be reduced to the level of the other nations in the world. Perhaps I would like that idea if I lived in Afghanistan, but I do not.

PHONY FREEDOM

The ACLU holds itself out to be the great defender of all freedom. Isn't it interesting that their major location for operations is in the land of the free. Why are they not in Afghanistan fighting for the freedom of the Taliban? If you want to insure that all people are treated fairly and that all people are truly free wouldn't you go to those nations that are the most oppressive?

One of the ACLU's most frequent battle calls is a call for freedom of speech. The ACLU defends clients who want to call obscenity "art." They also claim that the Constitution allows the lowest of the low to express themselves in the most vile, filthy ways imaginable and that this is a right protected by the freedom of speech clause mentioned in the First Amendment.

If a crucifix in a jar of urine is "art," then I suppose that blowing up an airplane is just another form of free speech which the ACLU approves and defends. The ACLU's brand of freedom says that there is no right or wrong.

They frequently say the First Amendment guarantees the right to display vulgar, sexually explicit "art," as a matter of free speech, but they do not believe that the Ten Commandments can be displayed under that same free speech banner.

Imagine that you are about to watch the college national championship basketball game and just before the game starts someone grabs the microphone and says, "This is the ACLU and we have just won a huge victory for true freedom. We just came from the Supreme Court and they have issued an injunction against there being any restrictions or rules in the game of basketball. Finally we are all truly free. You may now do whatever you want to your opponent without any consequences. Have at it and enjoy your freedom."

Would No Rules then equal freedom? Or, would the game be ruined by those who begin to shove, trip, punch or even shoot the members of the other team? It is exactly the same with society. We must have rules or society is ruined and there is then NO FREEDOM.

We must keep the brand of freedom for which our forefathers and our fathers were so willing to fight for and to defend for future generations. We must keep the ideals of the American form of freedom in the front of our minds. We cannot allow any good sounding arguments that truly represent nothing more that a form of treason to become a "phony freedom." The idea of a "No Rules" society or that freedom equals "No Rules" leads down a slippery slope wherein the end of the path is a society with a phony freedom that in reality is no freedom at all.

The destruction of the World Trade Center and the murder of thousands of people is the result of the type of freedom that the ACLU and others believe brings real equality to the world. Unfortunately for those who were murdered, quite the opposite is true.

VII. CONCLUSION

I hope this book has been many things to readers like you. I hope it has been educational. I hope it has been informative. I hope it has been persuasive. And most of all, I hope it has been inspirational to you.

> **Psalms 118:8**
> It is better to trust in the Lord than to put confidence in man.

Why is inspiration of utmost importance? Because the reason I wrote this book was to raise Americans of faith out of their complacency! If Americans of faith aren't shaken awake soon, there won't be an America to defend!

My friend, it is clear that Christian America is under assault. And if Americans of faith don't wake up to the danger right now, the glorious, God-given heritage we've been given as citizens of the United States will be lost forever. Wake up, America!

Wake up and take action to help avert this disaster.

Wake up and rededicate yourself to living the way God wants us to live. Pray to God to give us the strength we need to be good and just and moral in our lives. Pray for our leaders to be good and just and moral. And even pray to God that our enemies are shown the error of their ways and come back to the divine plan.

Wake up and fight for your right to religious liberty. Demand that your children have the right to pray in school. Let your local school board, your congressman, your senators, your governor and all of your elected leaders know that you demand your constitutional right to religious freedom!

Wake up and educate other Americans to the danger that awaits our nation. Warn them about the secular humanists and their devious plan to bring down Christian America.

Wake up and find out which leaders are Godly men, and which side with the secular humanists. Vote for the men of God. Campaign against the secular humanists. Don't let passivity set in.

'Remember the old phrase, "All that is necessary for evil to triumph is for good men to do nothing".

Please, for the love of all that is good and just in the world, don't be one of the people that does nothing while evil takes over our nation.

Thank you very much, and God bless America.

APPENDIX
INVOCATIONS OF GOD IN PRESIDENTIAL INAUGURATIONS

George Washington, 1789

"... the benign Parent of the Human Race ... has been pleased to favor the American people with opportunities" for "the security of their union and the advancement of their happiness ..." "The success of this Government must depend" upon "His divine blessing".

John Adams, 1797

Invoking the Supreme Being, "Patron of Order, Fountain of Justice, and Protector in all ages ... of virtuous liberty" to continue "His blessing upon this nation ... and give it all possible success and duration consistent with the ends of His providence."

Thomas Jefferson, 1801

"May that Infinite Power which rules the destinies of the universe lead our councils to do what is best ... for peace and prosperity."

Jefferson, 1805

Beseeched "that Being in whose hands we are ... who has covered our infancy with His providence and our riper years with His wisdom and power" ... so that "He will so enlighten ... your servants, guide their councils" so they shall do "your good" and secure "the peace, friendship, and approbation of all nations."

James Madison, 1809

Beseeched "the guidance of that Almighty Being whose power regulates the destiny of nations, whose blessings" have enriched "this rising Republic."

James Monroe, 1817

Invoked "the Almighty that He will ... continue ... that protection ... He has already so conspicuously displayed."

Monroe, 1821

"... firm reliance on the protection of Almighty God ..."

John Quincy Adams, 1825

Invokes the Lord's favor and "His overruling providence."

Andrew Jackson, 1829

Expressed reliance on "that Power whose providence mercifully protected our nation's infancy, and has since upheld our liberties" and beseeched Him to "continue to make our beloved country the object of His divine care."

Jackson, 1833

Beseeched "that Almighty Being" to "overrule all my intentions and actions and inspire the hearts of my fellow citizens that we may be preserved from dangers ... and continue forever as a united and happy people."

Martin Van Buren, 1837

Beseeched "His providence to bless our beloved country with honors and with lengths of days."

William Henry Harrison, 1841

Expressed "profound reverence to the Christian religion," convinced that "sound morals, religious liberty, and just a sense of religious respectability are essentially connected with all true and lasting happiness" and commends us to "that good Being who has blessed us by the gifts of civil and religious liberty."

James K. Polk, 1845

Invokes "that Divine Being" who has protected us and beseeched his continued "benedictions."

Zachary Taylor, 1849

Invokes "the goodness (and protection) of Divine Providence."

Franklin Pierce, 1853

Invokes "the kind Providence" which enabled us to preserve our blessings.

James Buchanan, 1857

Invokes "the blessings of Divine Providence."

Abraham Lincoln, 1861

Speaking of opponents dissatisfied with the Government, Lincoln called for "Intelligence, patriotism, Christianity, and a firm reliance on Him who has never yet forsaken this favored land ..."

Both sides in the conflict "read the same Bible and pray to the same God, and each invokes His aid against the other. It may seem strange that any men should dare to ask a just God's assistance in wringing their bread from the sweat of other men's faces, but let us judge not, that we be not judged. The prayers of both could not be answered. That of neither has been answered fully. The Almighty has His own purposes. 'Woe unto the world because of offenses [and] woe to that man by whom the offense cometh.' If we shall suppose that American slavery is one of those offenses which, in the providence of God, must needs come, but which, having continued through His appointed time, He now wills to remove, and that He gives to both North and South this terrible war as the woe due to those [who commit the offense], shall we discern therein any departure from those divine attributes which believers in a living God always ascribe to Him? Fondly do we hope, fervently do we pray, that this mighty scourge of war may speedily pass away."

"With malice toward none, with charity for all, with firmness in the right as God gives us to see the right, let us strive to finish the work we are in, to bind up the nation's wounds, to care for him who shall have borne the battle and for his widow and his orphan, to do all which may achieve and cherish a just and lasting peace among ourselves and with all nations."

Ulysses S. Grant, 1869

Invokes "almighty God" to heal the nation.

Rutherford B. Hayes, 1877

Invokes "guidance of that Divine Hand by which the destinies of all nations and individuals are shaped" so that "'peace and happiness, truth and justice, religion and piety, may be established among us for all generations.'"

James A. Garfield, 1881

"I reverently invoke the support and blessings of Almighty God" for the "welfare of this great people."

Grover Cleveland, 1885

Invokes aid and blessings of "Almighty God, who presides over the destiny of nations ..."

Benjamin Harrison, 1889

"God has placed upon our head a diadem and laid at our feet power and wealth beyond definition or calculation," a beacon of hope for the freedom of all peoples.

Cleveland, 1893

"A Supreme Being who rules the affairs of men and nations ... will not turn from us now if we humbly and reverently seek His powerful aid."

William McKinley, 1897

Swore "before the Lord Most High;" to seek by "constant prayer" to discharge "my solemn responsibilities".

Theodore Roosevelt, 1905

No reference.

William H. Taft, 1909

Sought the "aid of Almighty God in the discharge of my responsible duties."

Woodrow Wilson, 1913

"I summon all honest men, all patriotic, all forward-looking men, to my side. God helping me, I will not fail them ..."

Wilson, 1917

He invoked "God's Providence" to purge fractional divisions of party and private interests and "I pray God I may be given the wisdom and prudence to do my duty."

Warren G. Harding, 1921

Spoke of "the God-given destiny of our Republic," was "answerable to God and country," and implored the "favor and guidance of God in His Heaven." I have taken the oath on "that passage of Holy Writ: 'What doeth the Lord require of thee but to do justly, and to love mercy, and to walk humbly with thy God?' This I plight to God and country."

Calvin Coolidge, 1925

"America seeks no earthly empire built on blood and force ... The legions which we send forth are armed, not with the sword, but with the cross ... all mankind [is] of divine origin. She cherishes no purpose save to merit the favor of Almighty God."

Herbert Hoover, 1929

"I ask the help of Almighty God."

Franklin D. Roosevelt, 1933

Asks "the blessing of God ... May He guide me in the days to come."

Roosevelt, 1937

Asks "Divine guidance to help us each and every one ..."

Roosevelt, 1941

"As Americans, we go forward, in the service of our country, by the will of God."

Roosevelt, 1945

"The Almighty God has blessed our land [and has given us] a faith which has become the hope of all peoples in an anguished world. So we pray to Him [for] the achievement of His will."

Harry S. Truman, 1949

"Steadfast in our faith in the Almighty, we will advance toward a world where man's freedom is secure ... With God's help, the future of mankind will be assured in a world of justice, harmony, and peace."

Dwight D. Eisenhower, 1953

In this "century of trial" we pray to 'Almighty God."

John F. Kennedy, 1961

Asking "His blessing and His help ... knowing that here on earth God's work must truly be our own."

Lyndon B. Johnson, 1965

"But we have no promise from God that our greatness will endure ... democracy rests on faith [and] the judgment of God is harshest on those who are most favored."

Richard M. Nixon, 1969

"As the Apollo astronauts flew over the moon's gray surface on Christmas Eve ... we heard them invoke God's blessing on [the earth's] goodness ... let us go forward, firm in our faith [and] sustained by our confidence in the will of God and the promise of man."

Nixon, 1973

"Sustained by our faith in God who created us, and striving always to serve His purposes."

Gerald Ford (not elected, no inauguration)

Jimmy Carter, 1977

No reference, but took oath of office on Bible opened to passage "What does the Lord require of thee, but to do justly, and to love mercy, and to walk humbly with thy God."

Ronald Reagan, 1981

"With God's help, we can and will resolve" our problems. "God bless you."

Reagan, 1985

We stand today "One people under God ..." We have moved "toward the 'brotherhood of man' that God intended for us." "... may He continue to hold us close ... one people under God, dedicated" to freedom. "God bless you and may God bless America."

George Bush, 1989

"My first act as President is a prayer. I ask you to bow your heads: Heavenly Father, accept our thanks for the peace that yields this day ... Make us strong to do Your work, willing to heed and hear Your will ... We are given power not to advance our own purposes ... There is but one just use of power, and it is to serve people.

Help us to remember it, Lord. Amen."
"God bless you and God bless the United States of America."

Bill Clinton, 1993

"The Scripture says, 'And let us not be weary in well-doing.'" "With God's help, we must answer the call ... God bless you all."

Clinton, 1997

"May God strengthen our hands for the good work ahead, and always, always bless our America."

George W. Bush, 2001

"I know this is in our reach because we are guided by a power larger than ourselves who creates us equal in His image."

SOURCE: U.S. Government Printing Offices' *Inaugural Addresses of Presidents of the United States* (Washington to Nixon) and White House Archives.

How you can help

This book was not published by one of the big publishing houses in New York. It was published by my friends at CRAVE, and they have been kind enough to pay for distribution of this book. But we need funds to continue to print and distribute copies of *Wake Up America!* and to promote the work of this foundation, which is to restore America to her position of greatness by returning to the foundation and principles of God in Christ.

You can order more copies of this book by sending donations of $5.95 per book, plus $2 shipping and handling, to:

The Caudill Foundation
P.O. Box 649
Goodlettsville, TN 37070

The Caudill Foundation is a 501c3 charitable foundation. Your donations are tax deductible. I urge you to consider a donation to help this work continue.

LANCEDRAGON
AU FLEUVE NOIR

La trilogie des Chroniques de Lancedragon
1. Dragons d'un crépuscule d'automne
2. Dragons d'une nuit d'hiver
3. Dragons d'une aube de printemps
4. Dragons d'une flamme d'été (grand format)
par Margaret Weis et Tracy Hickman

La trilogie des Légendes de Lancedragon
1. Le temps des jumeaux
2. La guerre des jumeaux
3. L'épreuve des jumeaux
par Margaret Weis et Tracy Hickman

Rencontres de Lancedragon I
1. Les âmes sœurs
par Mark Anthony et Ellen Porath
2. L'éternel voyageur
par Mary Kirchoff et Steve Winter
3. Cœur sombre
par Tina Daniell

Rencontres de Lancedragon II
4. La règle et la mesure
par Michael Williams
5. La pierre et l'acier
par Ellen Porath
6. Les compagnons
par Tina Daniell

Les Préludes de Lancedragon
1. L'Ombre et la Lumière
par Paul B. Thompson
2. Kendermore
par Mary Kirchoff
3. Les frères Majere
par Kevin Stein
4. Rivebise, l'Homme des Plaines
par Paul B. Thompson et Tonya R. Carter
5. Sa Majesté Forgefeu
par Mary Kirchoff et Douglas Niles
6. Tanis, les années secrètes
par Barbara et Scott Siegel

Trilogie des Agresseurs

1. Devant le masque
   par Michael et Teri Williams (septembre 1998)
2. L'aile noire
   par Mary Kirchoff (octobre 1998)
3. L'Empereur d'Ansalonie
   par Douglas Niles (novembre 1998)

LES COMPAGNONS

par

TINA DANIELL

Couverture de
CLYDE CALDWELL

FLEUVE NOIR

Titre original :
The Companions
Traduit de l'américain par
Isabelle Troin

Collection dirigée par
Patrice Duvic et Jacques Goimard

Représentation en Europe :
Wizards of the Coast, Belgique, P.B. 34,
2300 Turnhout, Belgique. Tél : 32-14-44-30-44.
Bureau français :
Wizards of the Coast, France, BP 103,
94222 Charenton Cedex, France. Tél : 33-(0)1-43-96-35-65.
Internet : www.tsrinc.com.
America Online : Mot de passe : TSR
Email US : ConSvc@aol.com.

ISBN : 2-265-06457-2

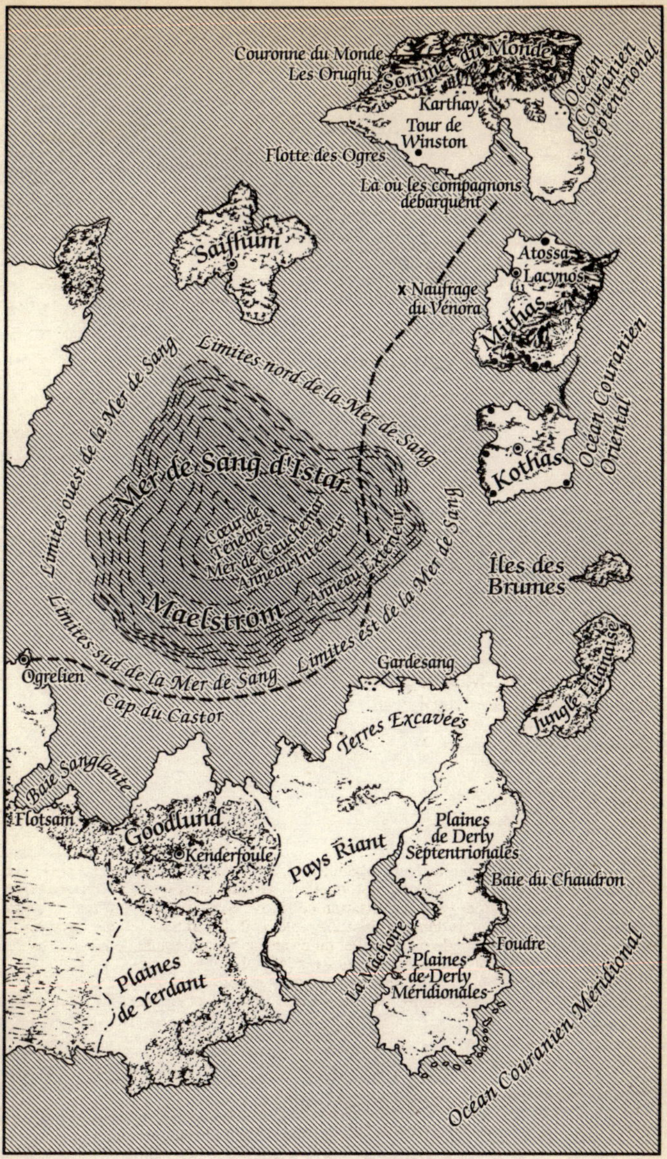

Couronne du Monde
Les Orughi
Sommet du Monde
Océan Couranien Septentrional
Karthay
Tour de Winston
Flotte des Ogres
Là où les compagnons débarquent
Saifhum
Atossa
Lacynos
x Naufrage du Vénora
Mithas
Limites nord de la Mer de Sang
Limites ouest de la Mer de Sang
Océan Couranien Oriental
Kothas
Mer de Sang d'Istar
Cœur de Ténèbres
Mer de Cauchemar
Anneau Intérieur
Anneau Extérieur
Limites est de la Mer de Sang
Îles des Brumes
Maelström
Jungle Éliaise
Ogrelien
Limites sud de la Mer de Sang
Gardesang
Cap du Castor
Terres Excavées
Baie Sanglante
Flotsam
Goodlund
Kenderfoule
Pays Riant
Plaines de Derly Septentrionales
Baie du Chaudron
La Mâchoire
Foudre
Plaines de Derly Méridionales
Plaines de Yerdant
Océan Couranien Méridional

CHAPITRE PREMIER

Tasslehoff Racle-Pieds était seul. Ayant exploré entièrement le *Vénora*, il avait battu en retraite dans la cabine qu'il partageait avec Sturm de Lumlane et Caramon Majere. Le capitaine n'avait pas caché son soulagement. Tass ne comprenait pas pourquoi l'homme lui criait toujours après : n'avait-il pas tenté de l'aider en abattant les voiles ? Les gens étaient parfois d'une ingratitude...

La cabine était un cagibi étroit muni de trois couchettes superposées. Assis en tailleur sur le sol, Tass examinait le contenu de ses sacoches et des innombrables bourses qu'il portait toujours à la ceinture. Il écarquillait les yeux comme s'il découvrait chaque objet pour la première fois. Ses souvenirs lui disaient qu'il les avait « trouvés » quelque part ; où et dans quelles circonstances, il n'aurait su le dire.

Autour de lui étaient éparpillés une petite licorne en porcelaine, une plume multicolore, des cailloux brillants et quelques gemmes, une ficelle, un parchemin enrubanné, une flûte en bois, des cartes jaunies, une poignée de boutons, l'écusson terni d'un forestier et un morceau de fourrure grise mangée aux mites que Tass chérissait tendrement. C'était un souvenir de sa rencontre avec le dernier mammouth à poil laineux, jurait-il à qui voulait l'entendre.

Une chose en particulier retint son attention. Tass la ramassa et l'examina sous la maigre lumière dispensée par la lampe à huile. A travers le hublot, le kender voyait les eaux bleues du Détroit de Schallmer danser sous le soleil de la fin d'après-midi.

— Tiens, je ne me rappelle pas de ce truc, marmonna-t-il en tripotant un objet ratatiné. On dirait une oreille d'ogre, sauf que je ne crois pas en avoir jamais coupé. C'est peut-être Flint qui m'en a fait cadeau...

Il haussa les épaules, reposa son bien et continua à passer en revue ses trésors. Il s'était lancé dans cette tâche monumentale avec un but précis qui lui était aussitôt sorti de la tête. Soudain, un sourire illumina son visage ridé. Il tendit la main vers une bouteille de verre au long col.

— Ah ah! s'exclama-t-il, satisfait.

Après l'avoir inspectée, il l'installa sur une étagère assez large pour servir de bureau, où reposaient déjà une plume et un morceau de parchemin. Puis il entreprit de ranger ses possessions, selon un ordre connu de lui seul.

*

* *

Caramon Majere était assis en tailleur sur le pont au milieu d'un groupe de marins. Le jeune homme avait le don de se faire des amis partout où il allait.

Sturm, Tass et lui avaient embarqué l'avant-veille à bord du sloop qui devait les ramener de Port-Ponant vers l'Abanasinie. Quarante-huit heures plus tard, Caramon tutoyait déjà tout l'équipage, du capitaine Murloch jusqu'au dernier moussaillon. L'après-midi touchait à sa fin et le petit groupe partageait un pichet de bière à l'arrière du *Vénora*.

Le crépuscule approchait ; une lumière orangée enflammait l'horizon. Il n'y avait pas un nuage dans le ciel, mais un vent léger poussait doucement le sloop. Aucun des marins présents n'était de garde cette nuit.

Attirés par la vitalité de Caramon comme par un aimant, ils l'écoutaient raconter ses nombreuses conquêtes féminines.

— C'est à Caergoth qu'on trouve les plus belles femelles de Krynn, intervint un marin robuste et moustachu.

— Sûr qu'elles sont girondes, approuva un de ses camarades aux petits yeux noirs. Mais je les préfère plus fines, comme celles de Flotsam.

— Je n'oublierai jamais Ravinia, soupira Caramon d'une voix déjà empâtée par l'alcool. Une serveuse de Port-Ponant. Elle était plutôt avare de ses baisers, contrairement à moi.

Le jeune homme cligna de l'œil. De grands éclats de rire saluèrent sa remarque. Il porta le pichet à ses lèvres et but longuement avant de le faire passer à son voisin. Le récipient fit le tour du groupe à une vitesse surprenante et fut bientôt de retour dans ses mains.

Ravi de l'impression qu'il produisait, Caramon repoussa une mèche de ses longs cheveux bruns avant de prendre une nouvelle rasade de bière. Il n'avait pas remarqué un détail : depuis un bon quart d'heure, il était le seul à boire.

*
* *

Sturm entendait à peine les rires avinés qui retentissaient à l'arrière du *Vénora*. Penché par-dessus le bastingage, le jeune homme qui voulait devenir Chevalier Solamnique contemplait pensivement les eaux du détroit. Aucune lumière ne se reflétait dans ses yeux bruns limpides.

Pendant de longues minutes, il resta immobile comme une statue. Il était de loin le moins sociable des trois compagnons ayant embarqué à bord du *Vénora*. Sa discrétion passait souvent pour de l'arrogance. Pourtant, aujourd'hui, sous la lumière fiévreuse du couchant, il semblait plus solitaire que fier.

Le voyage le mettait d'humeur maussade. Sa vie avait pris une tournure dramatique à bord d'un autre bateau, lorsque sa mère et lui avaient fui le château familial, laissant son père et une poignée d'hommes lutter contre la population en colère.

Tel était le prix à payer pour l'honneur. Aujourd'hui, Sturm était bien décidé à marcher sur les traces d'Angriff de Lumlane, et à suivre comme lui la Règle et la Mesure.

Comme pour refléter les pensées du jeune homme, une voûte de nuages noirs apparut à l'horizon. Un vent vif et frais se leva, arrachant Sturm à sa contemplation. Il leva la tête et aperçut la masse sombre qui fondait rapidement sur le *Vénora*.

On aurait dit une créature de légende, avec de grandes ailes et des serres redoutables. Sturm resta un instant immobile avant de se dire qu'il ferait peut-être bien de prévenir le capitaine Murloch, et de vérifier ce que faisaient Tass et Caramon.

*
* *

Dans la cabine, Tass s'appliquait à écrire une lettre à Raistlin Majere, le jumeau de Caramon. Il attendait cette occasion depuis longtemps : au moins depuis l'avant-veille, quand la bouteille magique s'était rappelée à son bon souvenir.

Des années plus tôt, il l'avait échangée contre des perles et du parfum à un marchand de Sanction. Ou peut-être à un cousin de Kenderfoule… C'était il y a si longtemps ! On le lui avait assuré : lancée dans l'océan, cette bouteille porterait un message à son destinataire où qu'il se trouvât sur le continent d'Ansalonie.

C'était le genre d'objet fabuleux dont oncle Chausse-Trappes parlait. Et Tass allait l'utiliser ! Son ami Raistlin était presque magicien (le Conclave l'avait déjà invité à passer l'Epreuve), et il apprécierait sûrement ce mode de communication original.

Le kender fronça les sourcils. Qu'allait-il pouvoir raconter ? Raistlin était souvent d'humeur maussade, pour ne pas dire sinistre. Un message dans une bouteille magique amènerait peut-être un sourire sur ses lèvres minces. Tass se lança enfin :

Cher Raistlin,

N'est-ce pas fabuleux ? Je t'écris dans une cabine du Vénora, *où nous avons embarqué il y a deux jours. Caramon est sur le pont, en train de prendre du bon temps avec ses nouveaux copains, et Sturm doit errer quelque part avec un air tragique... Tu connais Sturm. Et Caramon aussi, je suppose.*

Au fait, salut, Tanis !

Après notre arrivée en Ergoth Méridional, nous avons rejoint la côte sans incident. Nous avons trouvé l'herboriste minotaure recommandé par Asa, il nous a fourni la plante rare dont tu avais besoin pour ton sort. Je n'en doutais pas : comme tous les kenders, Asa est un maître cartographe, et c'est mon ami depuis des années. Ne t'inquiète pas. J'ai soigneusement rangé ta jalopine dans une de mes sacoches.

Tu as sans doute deviné que cette bouteille est magique. Je l'ai acquise par les moyens les plus honnêtes du monde durant ma période de vagabondite (du moins, je suppose), et en la retrouvant par hasard, je me suis dit que j'allais vous écrire à toi, Tanis et Flint.

Salut, Flint ! Tu te demandais si je ne t'avais pas oublié, n'est-ce pas ?

Si tout se passe bien, un pêcheur pauvre mais honnête récupérera cette bouteille, devinera son importance et l'apportera à Solace contre une généreuse récompense. Il te suffira alors de la déboucher pour qu'elle lise ce mes-

sage..., tu te rends compte ? A l'heure qu'il est, je suppose que oui.

Nous rentrons en Abanasinie à bord du sloop. Nous devrions être à Solace dans une semaine ou deux : cela dépendra des choses amusantes que nous rencontrerons en chemin. Tu sais combien Caramon aime à se reposer et à explorer les tavernes : il est donc probable que cette lettre te parviendra avant nous.

Notre petite expédition a été un franc succès. Caramon a beaucoup apprécié la ville de Hyssop — Asa avait aussi raison sur ce point-là — et il s'y est fait beaucoup d'amis. D'amies, surtout. Sturm lui tenait compagnie, ou il explorait le port de Hyssop, qui est bien plus petit que celui de Port-Ponant, mais propre et accueillant. A mon avis, très peu d'étrangers s'y arrêtent. Je crois que Sturm a bien aimé le coin, mais avec lui, c'est difficile à dire.

J'ai fait de mon mieux pour garder un œil sur lui et sur ton frère, tout en menant mes propres explorations. Hyssop regorge de boutiques, mais on dirait que les marchands n'ont jamais rencontré de kender de leur vie. Quand je rentrais chez eux, ils s'excitaient tellement que Sturm a fini par me conseiller de rester avec lui et de ne pas approcher du quartier commerçant. Il a beaucoup insisté.

Il nous est arrivé quelque chose d'étrange durant ce voyage. C'est pourquoi je t'écris cette lettre, je n'allais pas gaspiller une bouteille magique pour te raconter nos périples.

Je n'avais encore jamais vu d'échoppe aussi étrange que celle du minotaure. D'abord, elle se dressait dans une caverne, et sans la carte d'Asa, nous ne l'aurions sans doute jamais trouvée : tu sais pourtant combien je suis bon en découvertes !

L'herboriste était très poli, et il sentait beaucoup moins mauvais que les autres minotaures. Sturm a même reniflé une odeur de savon sur lui. Il s'appelait Argotz, et...

Une violente secousse fit tanguer le navire, tandis qu'une rafale de vent ouvrait le hublot et s'engouffrait à l'intérieur de la cabine. Le kender bondit sur ses pieds pour regarder dehors. Par les dieux ! Une tempête se préparait. Tass ne s'était encore jamais trouvé en mer par temps d'orage, et il sentait qu'il allait bien s'amuser.

Il se rassit et commença à gribouiller plus vite pour achever sa missive avant de monter sur le pont.

*

* *

Sturm avait à peine fait trois pas quand les premiers grêlons s'abattirent sur lui. Le pont s'inclina sous ses pieds. Il faillit glisser, mais se retint au bastingage.

Levant les yeux, il vit que la masse de nuages noirs avait fondu sur le *Vénora* à une telle vitesse que le ciel, déchiré d'éclairs spasmodiques, était obscurci d'un bout à l'autre de l'horizon. Sturm se dirigea à grand-peine vers le poste du capitaine, à la poupe du navire.

Un instant plus tard, il fut presque aveuglé par une pluie cinglante. Il leva un bras pour se protéger et, agrippé de l'autre main au bastingage, reprit sa progression.

Devant lui, un groupe d'hommes mettaient une chaloupe à la mer. Son estomac se noua. Il voulut les rejoindre, mais une vague plus haute que les autres fit pencher le navire. Sturm s'étala sur le pont trempé.

Lorsqu'il se releva, les marins avaient disparu. D'autres, étreignant des bouées de sauvetage, sautaient déjà par-dessus bord. Le jeune homme se pencha pour les suivre du regard, mais il ne put distinguer que les vagues noires assaillant le *Vénora*.

La désertion de l'équipage était un acte aussi lâche qu'étrange. Les marins croyaient-ils leurs chances de survie meilleures s'ils abandonnaient le navire ? Non… Ou s'agissait-il d'une mutinerie ?

Sturm leva les yeux vers le gouvernail où se tenait généralement le capitaine Murloch et sa perplexité se mua en peur. Personne. Abandonnée à elle-même, la roue de bois tournait à une vitesse effrayante.

Pourtant, Murloch ne semblait pas du genre à s'enfuir au moindre problème. Sturm l'avait choisi à Port-Ponant à cause de son visage buriné trahissant des années d'expérience. Tass l'avait aussitôt surnommé « Face-de-Morse » à cause de ses deux dents de devant proéminentes.

Un craquement sinistre tira Sturm de ses réflexions. La moitié supérieure du mât central venait de se briser, et s'inclinait lentement vers la mer en furie. Personne ne s'était soucié de baisser les voiles à l'approche de la tempête, et maintenant, il ne restait plus un marin à bord…

Sturm se hâta de rejoindre le pont arrière, tandis que le *Vénora* entamait une danse sauvage sur les flots. Le sloop semblait décrire des cercles et la tête du jeune homme tournait. Fouetté par la pluie et le vent, il découvrit enfin Caramon allongé par terre, les yeux fermés, un pichet vide à la main.

Sturm secoua la tête, exaspéré. Son ami était encore soûl. Il respectait son courage et ses talents de guerrier… Il admirait même sa générosité, malgré les tours pendables qu'elle leur avait joués. Mais cette habitude de boire n'importe quoi, n'importe quand et avec n'importe qui...

Avisant la cabine la plus proche, il décida d'y traîner son compagnon pour le mettre à l'abri. Vu la corpulence de Caramon, ça n'allait pas être facile.

Sturm se pencha pour prendre son ami sous les aisselles, et remarqua alors que ses armes avaient disparu. De plus en plus étrange…

Avant qu'il puisse en tirer des conclusions, le jeune homme entendit un bruit étouffé. Il leva la tête. Trop tard. Quelque chose le frappa à la tempe et il bascula dans un précipice sans fond.

*
* *

Tass était si occupé à finir sa lettre à Raistlin qu'il en avait oublié la tempête. Quand le roulis jeta sa lampe à terre, plongeant la cabine dans les ténèbres, le kender fut bien obligé de s'interrompre. Par réflexe, il tendit une main pour empêcher la bouteille magique de tomber.

— Pas moyen d'être tranquille cinq minutes, grommela-t-il.

Il enroula le parchemin et le glissa dans le goulot, puis replaça le bouchon et vit son message émettre une lueur dorée avant de disparaître. Se dressant sur la pointe des pieds, il jeta la bouteille dans l'océan déchaîné.

Des éclairs déchirèrent le ciel. Tass en profita pour récupérer ses sacoches (pas question d'abandonner un de ses trésors derrière lui !) et saisir son bâton à fronde, l'arme favorite des kenders. Entre les grondements du tonnerre, il crut entendre quelque chose sur le pont.

— Je parie que Sturm et Caramon s'amusent comme des petits fous, dit-il à voix haute. Ils doivent être impatients que je les rejoigne.

Tout guilleret, Tass emprunta l'étroit passage qui conduisait à l'escalier, puis monta sur le pont. Il fut très déçu de ne pas y recevoir l'accueil chaleureux auquel il s'attendait. Ni Sturm, ni Caramon, ni le capitaine Murloch n'étaient en vue.

Grâce à l'agilité légendaire des kenders, Tass n'avait aucun problème d'équilibre. Il regarda autour de lui. Le mât central était brisé, les voiles attachées à son tronçon claquaient dans la tempête. Mais où étaient passés les marins ?

Tass sentit un mouvement derrière lui. Il fit volte-face et se retrouva nez-à-nez avec le vieux Face-de-Morse, qui grimaça.

Tant mieux, se dit joyeusement le kender. *J'aime les gens qui restent de bonne humeur en toutes circonstances.*

— Bonjour, capitaine Murloch, cria-t-il pour se faire entendre malgré le vent et la pluie. Ça secoue drôlement, pas vrai ? Si vous voulez, je peux vous aider. (Sa voix se chargea de reproche.) Vous auriez quand même dû me laisser abattre les voiles. Vos hommes n'ont pas l'air de prendre leur travail très au sérieux. Heureusement que mon ami Flint n'est pas là, sinon, il...

Absorbé par son babillage, Tass ne vit pas la massue qui s'abattait sur son crâne.

— Maudits kenders ! Même au milieu d'un ouragan, ils piaillent à vous en faire tomber les oreilles, grommela le capitaine Murloch en regardant le corps immobile de Tass.

Il saisit ce dernier par sa queue-de-cheval et le traîna vers ce qui restait du mât principal, près de l'endroit où gisaient déjà Sturm et Caramon. Puis il ligota les trois amis conformément aux instructions qu'il avait reçues, et recula pour admirer son œuvre.

Il avait rempli sa part du marché. La généreuse rétribution versée par son commanditaire compenserait la perte du *Vénora* et les risques. Mais comme beaucoup de vieux loups de mer, Murloch adorait son navire, et il ne s'en séparait qu'à regret.

— Adieu, mon vieux, murmura-t-il, passant la langue sur ses lèvres. On faisait une sacrée équipe, tous les deux.

Il saisit une bouée de liège, l'enfila et l'attacha autour de sa taille à l'aide d'une corde. Puis il jeta un dernier regard aux trois hommes inconscients, avant de sauter à la mer. Il s'était déjà éloigné d'une bonne centaine de pieds quand les nuages fondirent sur le *Vénora*, le soulevèrent et l'entraînèrent au cœur d'un vortex traversé d'éclairs.

*
* *

Murloch arriva en vue du rivage Abanasinien une demi-journée plus tard, porté par les courants maritimes. Il était épuisé et à demi mort de faim, mais satisfait. Une vie de luxe et d'oisiveté l'attendait à terre.

Un son étrange lui fit lever la tête. Le soleil brillait si fort qu'il dut mettre une main en visière. On eût dit que des taches blanches dansaient devant ses yeux. A moins que...

Bouche bée, le capitaine vit un essaim d'insectes volants fondre sur lui. Son cœur se serra, et un bourdonnement menaçant emplit ses oreilles. Il leva les bras dans un vain effort pour se protéger ; un cri étranglé sortit de sa gorge.

Il était trop tard. Des milliers d'abeilles s'engouffrèrent dans sa bouche et son nez, lui piquèrent les yeux et les oreilles, le recouvrirent jusqu'à former une couverture vivante jaune et noire.

Quelques secondes plus tard, l'essaim reprit son vol, abandonnant derrière lui le cadavre du capitaine Murloch. Le visage du marin était constellé de piqûres rouges, sa langue avait quintuplé de volume et pendait hors de sa bouche.

Le courant poussa le corps vers le rivage.

*
* *

Des milliers de lieues plus loin, sur une terre couverte de sel, brûlée par le soleil, balayée par les vents et cernée par la mer, une silhouette trapue se pencha pour examiner les objets brillants disposés devant elle.

Il lui avait fallu une demi-journée de marche pour atteindre le plateau de montagne où, deux fois par semaine, la créature venait communier avec son dieu. Elle leva la tête pour observer la manière dont le soleil matinal se reflétait sur les bouts de verre coloré : les prismes, les cristaux et les fragments de miroir.

Derrière elle se tenaient ses trois plus fidèles disciples, les Très-Hauts. Autrefois, elle avait fait partie de leur petit groupe ; un jour, l'un d'eux lui succéderait. Les Très-Hauts étaient entourés de dizaines d'acolytes aux traits monstrueux, dont les armes meurtrières étincelaient. Leurs visages animaux ne trahissaient aucune émotion et un voile glauque couvrait leurs grands yeux ronds.

Au-delà se massait une foule de gardes et de soldats, loyaux à leur maître et n'attendant qu'un signal de lui. Quoi qu'il leur demande, ils s'exécuteraient, car ils ne vivaient que pour le servir.

Le Maître de la Nuit marcha autour des objets brillants, se penchant pour les examiner uns à uns. Des plumes et de la fourrure ornaient son crâne cornu. Des clochettes tintaient au moindre de ses mouvements. Dans ses mains énormes, il portait un long bâton d'encens qui répandait un parfum douceâtre.

Les signes étaient troublants. Il devait prendre des précautions, achever certains préparatifs, se débarrasser des gêneurs et des intrus. Rien ne devait interférer avec le lancement du sort.

Sargonnas attendait.

Le Maître de la Nuit observa le jeu de la lumière sur les perles de verre et sut que le moment approchait.

CHAPITRE II

— Vingt à cinq, dit Tanis, morose, en gravant le nouveau score dans une petite table de l'atelier de Flint.

L'air réjoui, le nain fit rouler une pierre noire vers un cercle tracé à la craie sur le sol. Au moment où elle entra en contact avec les autres cailloux du cercle, Flint bondit et en attrapa un maximum avant qu'ils ne s'éparpillent.

— Huit, annonça-t-il avec satisfaction. Mais nous ne sommes pas obligés de compter les points, mon garçon. Après tout, ce n'est qu'un jeu stupide, ajouta-t-il en s'efforçant de dissimuler son sourire.

— Vingt-huit à cinq, s'obstina Tanis, barrant le score précédent et inscrivant le nouveau.

Flint s'était mis en semi-retraite et n'ouvrait plus sa boutique que quand l'envie lui en prenait. Il entretenait encore son matériel, pourtant certains de ses outils n'avaient pas servi depuis des semaines.

Le nain n'éprouvait plus pour la métallurgie la passion qui avait fait de lui un maître-artisan, recherché jusqu'au Qualinesti. Cette passion était à l'origine de sa rencontre avec Tanis, à l'époque où le demi-elfe n'était encore qu'un jeune garçon.

Flint avait proposé une partie de rostreballe à son ami, dans l'espoir de le divertir, mais il n'obtenait pas le succès escompté. Tanis pensait à Kitiara, qui avait quitté Solace trois mois plus tôt sans lui dire où elle se rendait.

Depuis, le demi-elfe boudait.

Quant au nain, son moral n'aurait pu être meilleur : l'insupportable kender, Tasslehoff Racle-Pieds, avait quitté la ville depuis plusieurs semaines.

Tout était si paisible en son absence, songea Flint avec satisfaction.

Tanis se leva et se dirigea vers le cercle de craie. Il réarrangea les cailloux, puis recula et jeta la pierre noire d'un gracieux mouvement de poignet. Mais le projectile manqua sa cible : aucun des cailloux ne parvint à sortir du cercle.

— Quel dommage, dit Flint en fronçant les sourcils.

Malgré son air compatissant, une lueur amusée dansait dans ses yeux. Tanis ne fut pas dupe.

— C'est bon, tu as gagné, capitula le demi-elfe. Tu as tellement d'avance qu'il est inutile de continuer.

— Comme tu veux, dit Flint en se baissant pour ramasser les cailloux.

Il était très content de lui-même, ce qui ne l'empêchait pas d'éprouver de la sympathie pour son jeune compagnon.

— Tout ça pour une femme, grommela-t-il assez fort pour que Tanis l'entende.

Il replaça la chope sur une des nombreuses étagères garnissant les murs de son atelier.

— Depuis plus d'un siècle que je te connais, c'est la première fois que je te vois dans cet état. Toi qui as vaincu des ogres et des géants, je ne croyais pas que tu succomberais devant une femelle...

Flint jeta un regard en coin à Tanis pour surprendre sa réaction. Assis sur un tabouret, les bras croisés sur sa poitrine, le demi-elfe semblait perdu dans ses pensées.

— Tu me dois une pièce de cuivre, annonça le nain en désespoir de cause.

Tanis poussa un soupir et plongea la main dans sa bourse. Flint s'empara de la pièce d'un air cupide et l'examina soigneusement comme s'il craignait qu'elle fût fausse.

On frappa à la porte. Le nain alla ouvrir et se retrouva face à Moya, un gamin d'une dizaine d'années, qui lui tendit un parchemin plié en quatre.

— Message pour Flint Forgefeu, déclara-t-il d'un air important.

Le nain prit le parchemin. Avant qu'il puisse le lire, Moya le lui arracha des mains.

— Ça fera une pièce de cuivre, déclara-t-il, péremptoire.

— Une pièce de cuivre ! s'étrangla Flint. C'est du vol !

— Non : juste le prix de la course, rétorqua le gamin.

— Une pièce de cuivre ! insista Flint. Et je ne sais même pas ce qu'il y a dedans ! Si ça se trouve, c'est une mauvaise nouvelle. Je ne vais quand même pas payer pour qu'on m'apporte des mauvaises nouvelles !

Moya refusa de céder. A contrecœur, le nain lui remit la pièce qu'il venait de gagner à Tanis, puis lui claqua la porte au nez. A la façon dont était plié le parchemin, il savait déjà que le message émanait de Raistlin, le frère jumeau de Caramon. Il le déplia et lut :

Flint,

J'ai de bonnes raisons de croire que Caramon, Sturm et Tasslehoff courent un grave danger. Retrouve-moi à l'endroit habituel près du Lac de Cristalmir. Amène Tanis.

Raistlin

Le demi-elfe, qui avait lu par-dessus l'épaule de son ami, fronça les sourcils. Il ne savait que penser de cette missive. En l'absence de Caramon et de leur demi-sœur Kitiara, Raistlin était devenu très taciturne. Il n'avait pas l'habitude de se trouver seul, privé de l'ombre protectrice de son jumeau.

Quelques jours plus tôt, Tanis et Flint avaient rencontré le jeune mage à l'*Auberge du Dernier Refuge*. Pour une fois, c'était Raistlin qui semblait inquiet au sujet de Caramon.

« — Il avait dit que le voyage prendrait deux semaines. Ça ne lui ressemble pas de s'absenter aussi longtemps sans me prévenir », avait expliqué le jeune homme.

« — Ouais, mais c'est bien du genre de Tasslehoff, avait marmonné Flint en vidant sa chope de bière. A mon avis, c'est ce maudit kender qui dirige l'expédition, comme d'habitude.

« Il fait croire aux autres qu'il les suit… En fait, il les mène par le bout du nez. Il a dû se mettre en tête de visiter l'Ergoth Méridional, ou quelque chose dans le genre. Ne te fais pas de mauvais sang : il finira par réapparaître, et ton frère avec. »

C'était un des discours les plus longs que Tanis ait jamais entendu sortir de la bouche de Flint. Raistlin n'avait pas répondu, se contentant de fixer la cheminée du regard.

Et maintenant, ce message…

— Qu'en penses-tu ? demanda Tanis à Flint.

Le nain avait l'air ennuyé, et regrettait amèrement sa pièce de cuivre. Trois mois s'étaient écoulés depuis le départ de Caramon, de Sturm et de Tass. Finalement, Raistlin avait peut-être raison...

— Je suppose qu'on ferait mieux de se dépêcher, soupira Flint.

Comme autrefois avec Tanis, le nain avait pris les jumeaux sous son aile après la mort de leur mère. Le demi-elfe avait appris à les connaître et à les apprécier, avec quelques réserves. Caramon était loyal et toujours de bonne humeur, mais il se laissait parfois emporter par son goût pour la boisson et les femmes. Quant à Raistlin, impossible de savoir ce qu'il pensait vraiment.

Les deux amis sortirent de l'échoppe de Flint et se dirigèrent vers le Lac de Cristalmir. Si les habitants de Solace n'avaient pas eu l'habitude de les voir ensemble, sans doute leur auraient-ils jeté des regards curieux. Petit et large, le nain devait presque courir pour ne pas se laisser distancer par son compagnon, qui se déplaçait avec la grâce et l'agilité de sa race du côté maternel, les elfes du Qualinesti.

Pourtant, l'humeur de Tanis était sombre. Il ne se préoccupait pas tant de Raistlin et Caramon que de leur demi-sœur Kitiara, dont le visage rieur et les yeux bruns étincelants hantaient ses rêves chaque nuit. Pourtant, ils ne s'entendaient guère et passaient le plus clair de leur temps à se quereller.

Quelques semaines auparavant, Kitiara avait informé Tanis qu'elle partait dans le nord rejoindre une bande de mercenaires rassemblés par un mystérieux seigneur dans un but aussi secret qu'illégal. Le demi-elfe avait protesté qu'une telle expédition était indigne de la jeune femme, mais celle-ci avait répondu :

« — Ça vaudra toujours mieux que de mourir d'ennui à Solace ! »

Tanis avait changé de tactique et proposé de l'accompagner. Kitiara avait éclaté de rire.

« — Tu n'as pas ce qu'il faut pour ce genre de travail », avait-elle dit d'une façon assez insultante.

Le matin suivant, Tanis s'était levé de bonne heure pour assister à son départ. En arrivant aux écuries de Solace, il avait trouvé la jeune femme déjà en selle. Elle s'était penchée vers lui, avait déposé un baiser sur ses lèvres et était partie sans lui dire un mot.

— Flint, demanda soudain Tanis, as-tu déjà été amoureux ?

— Si j'avais dû l'être, j'aurais mieux choisi l'objet de mon affection que toi, répliqua le nain.

— Que veux-tu dire ? protesta Tanis.

— Je veux dire, jeune chiot, que Kitiara Uth Matar ne correspond pas à mon idéal féminin, ni à celui de n'importe qui possédant deux sous de jugeote, expliqua Flint sans se laisser démonter. Je vois bien la façon dont tu la regardes, et crois-moi, ça n'a rien à voir avec la sienne.

— Tu n'as pas répondu à ma question, fit sèchement remarquer Tanis.

— Eh bien..., dit Flint en s'arrêtant au milieu du chemin, il y a eu quelqu'un, autrefois. Une naine des collines, comme moi. Mais je ne sais pas si on peut appeler ça de l'amour. Ça ressemblait plus à une... romance.

Un peu de couleur monta aux joues du nain, qui baissa le nez vers ses chaussures.

— Et alors ? le pressa Tanis. Que s'est-il passé ?

— C'était la fille d'un chasseur, répondit Flint. Nos familles nous avaient promis l'un à l'autre.

Le nain secoua la tête, comme pour chasser ses souvenirs.

— Ah, c'était quelqu'un, soupira-t-il. Elle s'appelait Lolly, Lolly Ockenfels. Elle venait d'un clan très respectable. Seulement, les temps étaient durs à Soucolline. Ça n'a d'ailleurs pas beaucoup changé depuis. Je pensais que ce n'était pas le bon moment pour fonder une famille, et je la connaissais à peine. On s'est donné rendez-vous pour en parler, et là, j'ai découvert qu'on se ressemblait beaucoup. Elle était comme moi...

Tanis haussa les sourcils d'un air interrogateur.

— Une vraie tête de cochon, tu veux dire ?

— Elle avait du caractère, riposta Flint, irrité. Et pas plus envie que moi de sacrifier à la tradition. Mais...

— Mais quoi ? demanda Tanis, avide de connaître la suite.

Pour une fois qu'il arrivait à faire parler son vieil ami !

— Tu poses beaucoup de questions, je trouve, dit Flint. Je ne sais pas pourquoi je te raconte tout ça.

Il se remit en marche d'un pas résolu ; Tanis lui bloqua la route.

— Mais quoi ? répéta-t-il.

Les épaules du nain s'affaissèrent.

— Comme on était seuls tous les deux, on a pas mal discuté, et j'ai appris à la connaître, soupira-t-il. Elle était plutôt jolie. Elle avait des couettes, des épaules solides et des yeux marron, euh, vraiment profonds.

La voix du nain mourut.

— Et puis ? le pressa Tanis.

Flint serra les dents.

— Et puis je t'en ai assez dit. Raistlin nous attend.

Le demi-elfe comprit qu'il ne tirerait rien de plus de son ami.

*
* *

Lorsque les deux compagnons atteignirent enfin le lieu du rendez-vous, leur humeur avait radicalement changé. La perspective d'une aventure avait ragaillardi Tanis, tandis que Flint, attristé par ses souvenirs, ne cessait de maudire Tasslehoff.

L'été rayonnait sur la région. Des fleurs pourpres écarlates et dorées bordaient le chemin, des saules se penchaient vers la surface du lac. Il n'y avait pas un seul nuage dans le ciel et les eaux placides s'étendaient à perte de vue.

Assis sur un gros rocher, Raistlin attendait ses amis. Les jumeaux Majere adoraient le Lac de Cristalmir. Enfants, ils y avaient joué un tour pendable à deux de leurs camarades qui ne cessaient de tourmenter Raistlin... Encore aujourd'hui, le jeune mage venait souvent là pour méditer.

Entendant Tanis et Flint, il se leva et vint à leur rencontre.

— Que se passe-t-il ? demanda Tanis. Et pourquoi tous ces mystères ? Ne pouvions-nous pas nous rencontrer chez Otik ?

Le sourire grave de Raistlin s'évapora.

— Non, dit-il en secouant la tête. Personne d'autre que nous ne doit être au courant.

D'une poche de sa robe couleur de rouille, il sortit une bouteille de verre à long goulot. Tanis haussa un sourcil.

— Je ne vois pas ce que ce truc a d'extraordinaire.

Raistlin lui jeta un regard perçant ; comme toujours, le demi-elfe eut l'impression que les iris bleu pâle du jeune mage pouvaient lire au fond de son âme.

— Une petite minute…

Raistlin ôta le bouchon. De la bouteille s'échappèrent des effluves d'air iodé. Les parois de verre brillèrent, tandis que des papillons de lumière se formaient à l'intérieur. Pareils à de minuscules étoiles, ils s'assemblèrent pour former la silhouette de Tasslehoff Racle-Pieds. La voix reconnaissable du kender s'éleva du goulot :

Cher Raistlin,

N'est-ce pas fabuleux ? Je t'écris dans une cabine du Vénora, *où nous avons embarqué il y a deux jours. Caramon est sur le pont, en train de prendre du bon temps avec ses nouveaux copains, et Sturm doit errer quelque part avec un air tragique. Tu connais Sturm...*

Le trio écouta en silence la première partie du message.

— Incroyable, balbutia enfin Tanis. Où l'as-tu trouvée ?

— Un kender en bouteille, marmonna Flint. Ça n'est pas une mauvaise idée...

— Chut ! intima Raistlin. On arrive au passage intéressant.

... L'herboriste était très poli, et il sentait beaucoup moins mauvais que les autres minotaures. Sturm a même reniflé une odeur de savon sur lui. Il s'appelait Argotz, et il avait bien de la jalopine.

On a un peu marchandé : je dois être sacrément doué pour ça car, rentrant à l'auberge, je me suis aperçu que ma bourse contenait deux fois plus d'herbes que je n'en avais payés.

Mais ce n'est pas ça le plus étonnant, bien qu'on ne rencontre pas tous les jours des minotaures herboristes terrés au fond d'une caverne. Du moins, c'est ce qu'a dit Asa, et je crois que toi aussi...

— Ce maudit kender n'est pas là, et il réussit quand même à me donner la migraine avec son bavardage, grommela Flint.

Non, le plus bizarre, c'est ce qui s'est passé ensuite. Ai-je précisé que quand nous lui avons rendu visite, Argotz était en train de plier bagage ? Il avait l'air très pressé de se rendre quelque part. Sur le coup, nous n'y avons pas prêté attention.

Mais deux jours plus tard, le matin où nous avions prévu de quitter Hyssop, un homme est arrivé en courant à l'auberge. Il disait que la caverne du minotaure herboriste avait explosé. Nous nous sommes aussitôt rendus sur place pour vérifier. Il y avait un gros trou dans le flanc de la montagne, et les affaires d'Argotz étaient éparpillées un peu partout.

« Argotz a sans doute mélangé les herbes qu'il ne fallait pas », a affirmé un voisin.

— Vraiment ? ai-je répondu. Alors pourquoi sa tête est-elle plantée sur une pique au bord du chemin ?

Sturm et Caramon m'ont dit que je me mêlais de ce qui ne me regardait pas.

Alors, nous nous sommes rendus à Port-Ponant où nous avons engagé le capitaine Murloch. Il me fait beaucoup penser à Flint, bien qu'il soit humain et qu'il ait encore plus de ventre. Il pense savoir tout faire et n'apprécie pas que je lui donne mon avis.

Bref, c'était l'histoire du minotaure herboriste et de la jalopine, j'espère que tu l'aimeras, vu qu'elle me coûte cette bouteille magique. Je dois me dépêcher à présent, car une grosse tempête se prépare. Le ciel est tout noir et vraiment menaçant, je n'en ai encore jamais vu de pareil.

Bien à toi,

Tasslehoff Racle-Pieds de Kenderfoule,
et dernièrement de Solace

P.S. : Quiconque découvrira cette bouteille et la débouchera entendra ce message, mais ça n'est pas grave. Merci de l'apporter ensuite à Raistlin Majere de Solace, qui donnera au moins cinquante pièces de cuivre (peut-être plus, parce qu'il est généreux et ne se soucie pas de l'argent). Demandez en ville : tout le monde le connaît.

Raistlin reboucha la bouteille et la rangea dans sa poche.

— Où l'as-tu trouvée ? répéta Tanis, les yeux plissés.

— Un colporteur l'a repêchée dans le port de Vengeance, sur la côte abanasinienne. Après avoir entendu le message, il a décidé de me l'apporter. De toute façon, il avait prévu de se rendre à Solace. Il est arrivé hier et a demandé à l'*Auberge du Dernier Refuge* si quelqu'un me connaissait. Otik me l'a envoyé, je lui ai donné soixante-quinze pièces de cuivre pour prouver que Tass n'avait pas menti.

— Soixante-quinze pièces de cuivre ! s'étrangla Flint, notoirement près de ses sous.

— Bah, cette bouteille les vaut bien, dit Tanis en haussant les épaules. Mais je ne comprends pas ton inquiétude, Raistlin. Certes, le passage sur le minotaure est un peu bizarre...

— Le problème n'est pas là, coupa le jeune mage. Le colporteur était passé à Port-Ponant quelques semaines plus tôt, et on y racontait que le *Vénora* s'était perdu en mer au cours d'une violente tempête. Ça n'était pas la première fois que le brave homme visitait Port-Ponant. Il connaissait le capitaine Murloch de vue, et il jure avoir aperçu certains membres de son équipage dans une taverne. Ils payaient leurs libations en pièces minotaures.

— Etrange, murmura Tanis en passant la main dans ses cheveux roux.

— Et il y a mieux : le cadavre de Murloch a été retrouvé sur une plage, reprit Raistlin. Son corps était boursouflé, ses traits presque effacés, son visage couvert de piqûres et de brûlures. Quand ils l'ont trouvé, ses marins ont ramassé l'argent et se le sont partagés avant de disparaître…

Tanis s'assit sur un rocher, tandis que Flint fronçait les sourcils.

— Ça fait plus de sept semaines que le *Vénora* a quitté Port-Ponant, ajouta Raistlin.

Le nain poussa un soupir. Sturm et Caramon… Ces deux-là n'étaient que de grands gamins. Pas moyen de les laisser seuls trois jours sans qu'ils se fourrent dans le pétrin. Alors, avec Tass...

— Bon, ils ont quelques semaines de retard. Ce n'est peut-être pas dramatique, dit Flint sans conviction.

Raistlin s'assombrit.

— Il y a autre chose ; j'aurais dû m'en rendre compte depuis le début. Je me trouvais avec Tass le jour où Asa lui a dit qu'un minotaure herboriste vendait de la jalopine en Ergoth Méridional. J'avais trouvé dans un des grimoires de Morath un sort extrêmement intrigant. Je n'avais pas réussi à le déchiffrer entièrement, mais la jalopine figurait au nombre de ses composants.

Tanis dévisagea Raistlin. Il sentait que le jeune mage ne leur disait pas tout.

— Bref, comme il est impossible d'en obtenir en Abanasinie, Tass s'est porté volontaire pour faire le voyage. Sturm et Caramon ont proposé de l'accompagner.

— On sait, grommela Flint, impatient d'en finir.

Sans se départir de son calme, le jeune mage joignit ses doigts devant son menton.

— Après avoir reçu le message de Tasslehoff, je me suis rendu à Fondemare pour consulter Morath. Il m'a dit que la jalopine poussait en abondance sur l'île de Karthay, un coin désolé du royaume des minotaures.

« Selon les lois de ce peuple, elle ne peut pas être exportée : ils la considèrent comme sacrée. Autrement dit, celui qui a assassiné l'herboriste a peut-être suivi Caramon, Sturm et Tasslehoff pour les tuer… »

Tanis bondit sur ses pieds.

— Nous devons nous rendre à Vengeance, retrouver ces marins et les forcer à nous dire ce qui s'est passé à bord du *Vénora*, déclara-t-il vivement. Si nécessaire, nous nous rendrons à Port-Ponant pour chercher des indices.

Une expression horrifiée se peignit sur le visage de Flint.

— A Port-Ponant ? répéta le nain.

Certes, il s'inquiétait pour ses amis, et il avait prévu de prendre des vacances, mais plutôt près d'une jolie montagne que dans une ville portuaire bruyante et agitée.

— C'est inutile, intervint Raistlin. Dix jours se sont écoulés depuis le passage du colporteur à Vengeance. Le temps que nous nous y rendions, il ne restera plus la moindre piste.

— Ça tombe sous le sens, approuva Flint.

— Souvenez-vous que les marins étaient en possession de pièces minotaures. A mon avis, ce n'est pas dans l'ouest que nous trouverons les réponses à nos questions, mais du côté de la Mer de Sang et des îles minotaures, déclara Raistlin.

Flint devint livide et dut s'asseoir pour encaisser le choc.

— La Mer de Sang ? balbutia-t-il.

— Les îles minotaures ? renchérit Tanis. Mais elles se trouvent à des milliers de lieues. Il nous faudra plusieurs mois pour nous y rendre ! Si Caramon, Sturm et Tass sont en danger, nous n'arriverons jamais à temps pour les sauver !

— De toute façon, fit remarquer Flint, je ne vois pas comment ils auraient pu couvrir en aussi peu de temps la distance entre le Détroit de Schallmer et la Mer de Sang.

— Je l'ignore, admit Raistlin. Probablement par magie. Mais s'ils sont toujours vivants, je suis sûr qu'ils se trouvent là-bas, et je n'ai pas l'intention de les y laisser. Voulez-vous m'accompagner, oui ou non ?

— Comment comptes-tu te rendre dans les îles minotaures ? insista Tanis.

Les yeux de Raistlin brillèrent.

— Morath m'a parlé d'un Oracle qui vit près du Sombrebois. Il connaît un portail qui pourrait nous transporter à Ogrelien, sur la côte de la Mer de Sang.

— Ogrelien ! se lamenta Flint.

— De là, il nous suffirait de trouver un bateau pour faire la traversée, acheva Raistlin.

Le nain leva les mains.

— Pas question que je traverse la Mer de Sang ! s'écria-t-il. Déjà, il me faudrait une sacrée bonne raison pour naviguer sur le Lac de Cristalmir !

Il arpenta la rive, donnant des coups de pied aux cailloux. Raistlin l'ignora et se tourna vers Tanis, qu'il étudia de son regard pénétrant.

Le demi-elfe s'agita, mal à l'aise. Il ne doutait pas de la loyauté de son ami, mais son petit doigt lui disait que le mage leur cachait quelque chose. Après une longue minute de silence, il hocha enfin la tête.

— Sturm et Caramon risqueraient leur vie pour nous ; je pense que nous leur en devons autant.

Une idée lui traversa la tête.

— Et Kit ? Ne crois-tu pas que nous devrions la contacter ?

— Je lui ai déjà envoyé un message, répondit Raistlin. Ne t'inquiète pas pour elle. Si elle peut nous rejoindre, elle le fera.

— Mais où se trouve-t-elle ? insista le demi-elfe. Peut-être que...

Un regard appuyé de Raistlin le fit taire. Les deux jeunes gens se tournèrent vers Flint qui, debout près du rivage, faisait des ricochets pour se calmer. Toutes ses pierres coulaient au bout de deux rebonds… Un mauvais présage, il en était sûr.

Le nain rejoignit ses amis et secoua la tête en soupirant.

— Très bien, grogna-t-il. Je viens. Mais que les choses soient bien claires : je le fais pour Caramon et pour Sturm, pas pour cette andouille de kender !

CHAPITRE III

Depuis six jours, les hommes de Nellthis cherchaient la piste du leucrotta. A en croire la rumeur, la bête attaquait les habitants de la forêt à l'est de Lemish, au pied d'une petite chaîne de montagnes.

De toutes les créatures étranges d'Ansalonie, le leucrotta était l'une des plus rares. Nellthis avait envoyé à sa recherche une douzaine d'hommes conduits par son meilleur chasseur, Ladin Elferturm. Il ne pouvait tolérer que ce monstre vagabonde en lisière de son royaume.

En présence de dames, ou au cours de rassemblements mondains, Elferturm pouvait passer pour un rustre au cerveau un peu lent. Mais dans les bois, il était dans son élément, ses sens percevaient jusqu'au moindre son, jusqu'à la moindre odeur. Et nul, à part Nellthis, n'était plus habile que lui avec un arc long…

Trouver le leucrotta, s'il existait, n'était pas simple. Ses sabots laissaient les mêmes empreintes que ceux des cerfs, dont regorgeaient les bois.

Pourtant, dès le second jour, de nombreuses carcasses à moitié dévorées avaient persuadé Ladin Elferturm qu'il se trouvait bien face à un redoutable prédateur. Le quatrième jour, le chasseur se sentit capable de reconnaître ses traces.

Le matin du sixième jour, il sépara ses hommes en deux groupes et leur ordonna de se poster aux extrémités d'un étroit ravin où il pensait avoir acculé la bête. Puis il envoya chercher son seigneur.

Nellthis arriva moins de quatre heures plus tard, accompagné de sa nièce Kitiara Uth Matar et de plusieurs de ses suivants. Tous portaient des justaucorps de cuir et étaient armés pour la chasse. Avec ses courts cheveux noirs, Kit aurait facilement pu se faire passer pour un homme…

Nellthis aboya des ordres. Les chasseurs se hâtèrent de gagner leur poste. Puis, accompagné de deux hommes et de sa nièce, dont les joues s'empourpraient de plaisir, le seigneur descendit dans le ravin, laissant Elferturm surveiller les opérations.

Le second de Nellthis ne fut pas étonné qu'on l'abandonne ainsi, mais il était déçu. Il pensait, à tort, être meilleur archer que son maître, et il aurait voulu impressionner Kitiara en tuant le leucrotta devant elle. Poussant un soupir, il suivit la jeune femme du regard jusqu'à ce qu'elle disparaisse entre les buissons.

*
* *

Suivis par deux hommes qui portaient leur équipement, Nellthis et Kitiara firent descendre leurs montures dans la gorge étroite. L'oncle de Kit mit pied à terre et examina les empreintes dans le sable. Puis il fit signe aux autres d'attacher leurs chevaux et de le suivre aussi discrètement que possible.

Nellthis de Lemish ne portait que son arc favori, fait d'if et de chanvre, ainsi qu'un carquois contenant des flèches empoissonnées ornées de plumes d'oie.

Les quatre compagnons se faufilèrent entre les rochers, faisant de leur mieux pour rester discrets. Nellthis et Kitiara se séparèrent, emmenant chacun un chasseur, et se placèrent des deux côtés du ravin.

Au loin, les autres étaient déjà en place. Kit sentait l'impatience de son oncle. Nellthis avait juré de réunir les trophées de toutes les créatures de Krynn, et plusieurs mois s'étaient écoulés sans qu'il ait pu ajouter une merveille à ses murs.

Nellthis était un curieux personnage. Petit et grassouillet, il arborait une ridicule moustache dont les extrémités s'enroulaient sur ses joues. Comme une femme gâtée, il passait des heures à choisir la couleur et l'étoffe de ses vêtements, et il avait même engagé une couturière à temps plein pour s'assurer d'être toujours à la dernière mode.

Kit savait que les gens se moquaient de lui à cause de son caractère volcanique, de sa gloutonnerie, de sa façon de trop boire et de trop dormir. Nellthis était assez riche pour s'offrir les mets les plus fins, ainsi qu'une vie de luxe et d'oisiveté.

Kitiara détestait la paresse, mais elle respectait le pouvoir de son oncle qui lui permettait de satisfaire ses caprices. Et elle chérissait le lien qui les attachait : Nellthis n'avait-il pas épousé la sœur de Gregor Uth Matar, son père ?

Kit n'avait jamais connu sa tante, morte en donnant le jour à un fils qui n'avait pas survécu plus de deux jours. Mais elle savait que Nellthis était resté en contact avec Gregor, auquel il avait parfois prêté de l'argent pour subvenir aux besoins de sa petite famille.

Après la disparition de son beau-frère, Nellthis avait continué à prendre des nouvelles de Kitiara. Quand Solace et la présence de Tanis lui étaient devenues insupportables, la jeune femme s'était naturellement tournée vers lui.

Nellthis avançait d'un pas prudent, plaqué à la paroi de la gorge. Kit s'émerveilla de le voir si bon archer malgré son style de vie décadent. Soudain, un craquement fit sursauter la jeune femme. Imitant son oncle, elle encocha une flèche.

Ils aperçurent au même moment l'ouverture de la caverne. Elle formait une plaie sombre à la surface ocre de la falaise.

Deux yeux rouges brillants se posèrent sur les chasseurs.

D'instinct, Kit s'accroupit.

L'immense créature sortit de sa cachette comme pour mettre les humains au défi. Elle mesurait huit pieds de haut et autant de long. Son corps était celui d'un cerf, sa tête celle d'un blaireau, sa queue touffue celle d'un lion. Sa gueule grande ouverte révélait deux rangées de crocs pointus. Un filet de bave dégoulinait sur son menton... Bien qu'elle se trouvât de l'autre côté du ravin, Kit crut sentir son haleine fétide.

Nellthis fit signe à son escorte. L'homme qui accompagnait Kit dégaina son épée, l'autre se mit à plat ventre et se dirigea vers le leucrotta, traînant un filet. La créature le vit approcher, mais ne chargea pas. Elle aurait pu s'échapper en quelques bonds, pourtant elle attendait, immobile, que ses adversaires prennent l'initiative.

Nellthis et Kit tirèrent presque en même temps, tandis que l'homme au filet se relevait et bondissait. Tous furent en retard d'une demi-seconde sur le leucrotta, qui avait déjà choisi sa proie. Avec une rapidité surprenante, il se porta à la rencontre de l'homme au filet. Celui-ci tenta de battre en retraite... La créature ouvrit ses mâchoires puissantes et le décapita. Le corps du chasseur s'effondra dans la poussière ; son sang éclaboussa Nellthis.

La flèche du seigneur s'était plantée dans le flanc gauche de la créature, celle de Kit avait manqué sa cible. Pendant qu'oncle et nièce encochaient un deuxième projectile, le leucrotta bondit derrière un buisson épineux. Il ouvrit la gueule et produisit un son strident, presque douloureux.

— Que fait-il ? chuchota Kitiara à Nellthis.

— Il nous provoque, répliqua son oncle à voix basse. Il se vante du nombre de ses victimes.

— Tu comprends sa langue ? s'étonna Kitiara.

Une lueur amusée dansa dans les yeux ronds de Nellthis.

— Non. Je ne fais que deviner.

Le leucrotta poussa un second cri inintelligible. Au-dessus de lui, Kit vit les archers se mettre en position. Ils ne tireraient qu'en cas d'absolue nécessité. La proie appartenait à leur maître.

— A mon avis, il a dit : « Je vais d'abord manger le gros, et je garderai la femelle pour dessert », souffla Kit.

Un concert de cris fit écho à ceux du leucrotta. La jeune femme écarquilla les yeux, persuadée que la bête avait une compagne. Nellthis sursauta, leva la tête. Le monstre lui-même hésita.

De son poste, en haut de la falaise, Ladin Elfertrum, très fier de son imitation, fit signe à son maître de profiter de la diversion. Mais le leucrotta s'était repris plus vite que ses adversaires ; il jaillit de sa cachette avant que Kit ou Nellthis puissent réagir.

Nellthis pivota pour décocher une flèche au monstre qui bondissait. Il tira, se jeta à terre, roula sur lui-même avec une agilité surprenante. Au passage, une griffe du leucrotta lui déchira le dos. Il lutta pour se relever et, adossé à la paroi du canyon, encocha une nouvelle flèche.

Il n'eut pas besoin de tirer. Déjà, la bête gisait sur le flanc, en proie aux spasmes de l'agonie. Un sang gluant à l'odeur âcre dégoulinait d'une plaie béante, sur son ventre. La flèche de Nellthis était plantée dans son estomac offert, une autre, sans doute tirée par Kit, dépassait de son cou.

Après s'être assuré que sa nièce n'avait rien, Nellthis se dirigea vers le leucrotta. Il avait mal au dos, mais rien n'aurait pu lui gâcher le plaisir d'achever la bête. Il l'étudia quelques instants, savourant son triomphe, puis lui décocha une flèche dans la tête. L'animal poussa son dernier soupir et s'immobilisa.

Kit s'approcha de son oncle tandis que le chasseur survivant levait son chapeau en signe de victoire.

— Je te remercie de m'avoir sauvé la vie, dit Nellthis à regret.

— Je ne crois pas que ma flèche l'ait tué seule, corrigea Kit. C'était l'effet des deux.

Nellthis dévisagea la jeune fille. Elle avait une expression grave, et il comprit qu'elle n'avait pas dit ça pour lui faire plaisir.

— Sans doute, conclut-il avec satisfaction.

Elfertrum rejoignit son maître.

— Beau travail, dit-il en hochant la tête.

Nellthis fronça les sourcils.

— Ça n'est pas grâce à toi ! aboya-t-il. La prochaine fois que tu te mêles de stratégie, demande mon avis avant…, ou tu ne chasseras plus jamais au Lemish !

Elfertrum s'empourpra de colère tandis que Kit et son oncle s'éloignaient.

Une heure plus tard, après avoir halé la créature hors du ravin et enterré sa malheureuse victime, Nellthis, Kit et les chasseurs reprirent le chemin du château. Ils entrèrent en triomphe dans la cour centrale, où domestiques et écuyers se rassemblèrent pour féliciter leur maître. Nellthis ordonna qu'on prépare un banquet et louangea Kit devant l'assemblée.

Un peu en retrait, la jeune femme observait son oncle avec amusement et affection. Elle allait remonter dans sa chambre lorsqu'elle vit une silhouette cachée derrière un rideau faire signe à Nellthis. Celui-ci prit aussitôt congé de sa cour, se dirigea vers la porte du château et disparut à l'intérieur.

Ce n'était pas la première fois que Kit le voyait se comporter ainsi. Nellthis était un homme plein de mystère, surtout ces derniers temps. Parfois, il disparaissait plusieurs jours d'affilée. Kitiara l'avait interrogé, sans succès. C'était une des choses qu'elle préférait chez son oncle : ses mines de conspirateur.

— C'est ta flèche qui a tué le leucrotta, dit Ladin Elfertrum en touchant le bras de la jeune femme.

Kit se dégagea.

— C'étaient les deux en même temps, répliqua-t-elle, sévère. Et même si Nellthis n'était pas mon oncle, je trouverais déloyal de ta part de dire ça dans son dos.

Elle voulut s'éloigner, mais Elfertrum lui saisit le poignet pour la retenir.

— Qu'as-tu ? chuchota-t-il d'une voix rauque. Je croyais... qu'il y avait... quelque chose entre toi et moi.

Une fois de plus, il avait du mal à trouver ses mots. Il se sentait si maladroit devant cette jeune femme à la langue bien pendue ! Kit allait répliquer vertement quand quelqu'un attrapa Elfertrum par le col de sa veste et l'obligea à pivoter. C'était Kurth, le forgeron du château.

— Je t'ai déjà dit de ne plus embêter Kitiara, gronda-t-il. Elle est à moi : elle n'a que faire d'un imbécile dans ton genre.

Elfertrum se raidit.

— J'en ai assez de tes menaces, cracha-t-il.

Les deux hommes se toisèrent, leurs yeux lançant des éclairs. Secouant la tête, Kitiara les laissa à leur dispute. De toute façon, elle était lassée de l'un et de l'autre. Elle venait de disparaître à l'intérieur du château quand le poing de Kurth s'écrasa sur le menton d'Elfertrum.

*
* *

Dans les profondeurs de son château, au fond de la petite cave où on gardait les vins les plus chers, Nellthis de Lemish présidait une réunion. A la table éclairée par une bougie étaient assises trois silhouettes enveloppées de capes sombres.

Le premier inconnu était grand et mince. Un foulard drapé autour de sa figure ne laissait voir que ses yeux verts. Il avait une voix profonde, indubitablement mâle. Nellthis et lui dirigeaient les débats.

Le deuxième inconnu était si recroquevillé sur lui-même qu'on aurait pu le croire bossu. Il ne parlait guère, se contentant de lâcher parfois un mot dans un dialecte nordique que Nellthis ne comprenait pas.

Le troisième était le plus étrange. Les deux autres semblaient à la fois l'étudier et le craindre. L'inconnu portait une longue robe noire, une capuche et un masque. Une bosse dans son dos indiquait la présence d'un appendice. Ses yeux brillaient d'une lueur rouge ; une salive à l'odeur de souffre dégoulinait en grésillant sur son menton.

Nellthis prit son temps pour étudier les messages et les rapports étalés sur la table. Il les lut soigneusement pendant que ses invités s'agitaient sur leur siège. Enfin, avec un geste théâtral, il y apposa sa signature, les enroula et les rendit au premier inconnu.

— Notre maîtresse sera très satisfaite, dit l'homme sans la moindre trace d'émotion. Vous recevrez bientôt votre récompense.

— Ma récompense, répliqua Nellthis, grand seigneur, est de la servir.

Les inconnus s'inclinèrent. Nellthis se leva, se dirigea vers un des casiers et tira sur deux des bouteilles de l'étagère supérieure. Le meuble glissa sur le côté en silence, révélant un étroit tunnel qui passait sous la cour du château, se prolongeant sur plusieurs lieues avant de déboucher au cœur de la forêt. Les trois silhouettes s'y engagèrent sans un adieu.

*

* *

Allongée sur son lit, dans une chambre luxueuse, au sommet de la tour nord, Kitiara contemplait le plafond.

Cela faisait trois mois qu'elle se trouvait au Lemish et elle s'ennuyait déjà. Elle avait livré un duel, pris trois ou quatre amants, appris à manier l'arc long et le fouet...

Mais elle ne s'était guère aventurée hors du domaine de Nellthis.

C'était à des moments comme celui qu'elle se surprenait à penser à Tanis. Maudits soient le demi-elfe et ses principes ! Pourquoi ne parvenait-elle pas à l'oublier ?

En outre, Kitiara s'inquiétait pour son oncle. Il avait connu Gregor du temps où leurs familles vivaient côte à côte. Les deux hommes avaient été impliqués dans une affaire illégale qui avait failli mal se terminer. C'était avant que Nellthis, poussé par son audace et sa soif de pouvoir, n'aille s'installer au Lemish.

Il y avait chez l'oncle de Kit quelque chose d'insaisissable et d'intrigant. Il possédait une demeure luxueuse et d'innombrables domestiques, pourtant, il ne travaillait pas, et ses champs ne produisaient qu'une modeste récolte de maïs et de grain. D'où sortait son argent ?

Ces derniers temps, il avait pas mal voyagé, effectuant de brefs séjours dans les villes et les villages voisins. A son retour, il était toujours accompagné d'un ou deux paysans, qui venaient rejoindre son personnel déjà pléthorique et ne semblaient pas faire grand-chose de leurs journées.

Parfois, Nellthis disparaissait dans son propre château : une vieille bâtisse aux couloirs labyrinthiques à laquelle étaient attachées de nombreuses dépendances. Kit partait à sa recherche et errait en vain pendant des heures, puis elle le découvrait brusquement au détour d'un couloir, grimaçant comme s'il l'attendait.

La curiosité démangeait la jeune femme, mais elle rongeait son frein. Nellthis avait toujours été bon pour elle. A plusieurs reprises, elle était arrivée chez lui sans s'annoncer, et jamais il ne lui avait refusé l'hospitalité.

Quelqu'un toqua à la porte de la chambre, tirant Kitiara de sa rêverie. La jeune femme bondit pour ouvrir. Elle s'attendait à trouver un de ses soupirants, l'œil poché et les vêtements en lambeaux. Mais elle découvrit un kender que surveillait Odilon, le maître d'hôtel de son oncle.

Le nouveau venu portait une longue queue-de-cheval qui pendait jusqu'à ses genoux. Les cheveux châtains, il était plus petit et plus âgé que Tasslehoff Racle-Pieds.

Kitiara ne le connaissait pas.

Rayonnant, le kender lui tendit un parchemin cacheté à la cire. La jeune femme fut très surprise qu'il ne l'ait pas déjà ouvert.

— Kitiara Uth Matar ? demanda le kender en gonflant la poitrine. Née à Solace, mais résidant temporairement à Lemish ? J'ai pour elle un message très urgent.

La jeune femme hocha la tête et, d'un geste vif, s'empara du parchemin. Le kender manœuvra pour s'introduire dans sa chambre, mais elle lui bloqua le chemin.

— Mission accomplie, pépia la petite créature. Je m'appelle Tremblefeuille, et je viens de parcourir trois cents lieues pour vous porter ce message, bien que j'aie des milliers de choses plus importantes à faire dans cette région du monde. Une de mes sœurs vit à une journée de voyage à l'est. En fait, ce n'est pas vraiment ma sœur, plutôt une cousine, mais je l'aime vraiment beaucoup.

« Et puis il y a la caverne hantée que j'ai toujours rêvé de visiter. Elle est indiquée sur une de mes cartes. C'est un endroit secret, mais je pourrais vous la montrer si vous me laissez lire cette lettre. Depuis le temps que je la porte, je me demande ce qu'elle peut bien contenir de si urgent... »

Parlant sans interruption, Tremblefeuille avançait, feintait et reculait, cherchant une ouverture. Odilon le saisit par le col et l'entraîna vers les escaliers. Le kender se débattit et brandit une gemme au-dessus de sa tête.

— Ne vous inquiétez pas : vous ne me devez rien. Le mage — du moins, il a dit qu'il était mage, mais ça m'étonnerait, parce qu'il avait l'air un peu jeune —, m'a donné un gros tas de pièces, et ce superbe collier très rare. J'espère qu'il est enchanté, mais avec les mages, on ne sait jamais. Certains ont un sens de l'humour très bizarre, et...

« Oups, je dois y aller ! Si vous me cherchez, je serai dans la cuisine, je vais manger un morceau avant de repartir. Je pourrai livrer un message à Solace, mais pas avant l'année prochaine, parce que... »

Kitiara referma la porte en grimaçant. Le collier avait appartenu à sa mère, et il n'était pas plus magique qu'elle. Jamais elle ne comprendrait cette affection que Raistlin portait aux kenders, ni pourquoi il leur faisait confiance. Pour une fois, pourtant, il semblait avoir eu raison.

Assise au bord de son lit, Kitiara entama sa lecture. Son demi-sourire devint très vite une expression consternée. Longtemps, elle resta immobile, sans réussir à trouver un plan.

*

* *

Lunitari baignait sa chambre d'une lueur argentée lorsque Kit se releva enfin, décidée à demander conseil à son oncle.

Pour une fois, elle le trouva dans ses appartements, assis à son bureau sous la lumière dorée d'une lampe à huile. Malgré l'heure tardive, Nellthis répondait à son courrier. Voyant entrer sa nièce, il posa sa plume. Il n'avait pas d'enfant, et appréciait beaucoup la compagnie de la jeune femme.

Kitiara lui dit qu'elle avait reçu une lettre de Raistlin, portée par le kender Tremblefeuille. Nellthis avait déjà entendu parler de lui : il s'était invité à souper au château. En bon commerçant, Tremblefeuille avait convaincu la cuisinière d'écrire à toute sa famille d'Ergoth Méridional : bien sûr, il se ferait un plaisir d'acheminer les missives jusqu'à leur destinataire, moyennant une somme ridicule. La pauvre femme étant presque illettrée, il avait dû lui prêter main-forte pour la rédaction de son courrier.

— A mon avis, il sera encore avec nous pour le petit déjeuner, gloussa Nellthis.

Le châtelain n'avait jamais rencontré Raistlin, bien qu'il s'intéressât beaucoup à lui. A chacune de ses visites, il demandait à la jeune femme des nouvelles des jumeaux.

Kitiara lui tendit la lettre, qu'il parcourut rapidement.

— Est-ce possible ? demanda-t-il, les sourcils froncés, en la reposant devant lui. Ton frère ne pourrait-il pas se tromper ?

— Je suppose que oui, répondit Kit, dubitative, mais il a la fâcheuse habitude d'avoir toujours raison. (Elle soupira.) Que puis-je faire ? J'avais l'intention de repartir pour m'engager dans une compagnie de mercenaires. La lettre contrarie mes projets.

L'agacement de la jeune femme ne parvenait pas à masquer sa réelle inquiétude. Elle avait pratiquement élevé les jumeaux, et ce qui leur arrivait la touchait aussi.

— Caramon donnerait sa vie pour moi. Je dois faire quelque chose, mais comment rejoindre les autres ? poursuivit-elle. Si Raistlin a vu juste, nous devons nous rendre à des milliers de lieues d'ici. Le voyage sera long et fastidieux à cheval… et bien plus dangereux en bateau.

Bouillant de frustration, la jeune femme fit les cent pas pendant que Nellthis pianotait sur son bureau, les lèvres pincées.

— Si seulement il y avait un moyen ! s'exclama Kit en tapant du poing dans sa paume ouverte.

— Il en existe peut-être un, répondit pensivement son oncle.

Kit s'arrêta et se tourna vers lui.

— Que veux-tu dire ?

— Il existe peut-être un moyen, répéta Nellthis, mais ça ne sera pas facile.

— Si c'est une question d'argent, j'en ai un peu et je peux en trouver plus. Ma parole constituera une garantie suffisante, déclara la jeune femme.

Nellthis fit un geste insouciant de la main.

— L'argent n'est pas un problème. Ce qu'il te faut, c'est du courage et de la chance.

Kit ne voyait pas ce que son oncle avait en tête, mais elle lui faisait confiance. Elle sourit.

— J'ai le courage nécessaire, si tu me cèdes un peu de ta chance. (Puis, plus sérieusement :) Je ferai ce qu'il faudra, et je te jure de te rembourser par tous les moyens.

Nellthis la dévisagea.

— Je n'attends rien que ta gratitude. Oh, et avant que j'oublie, ajouta-t-il tendant la main vers une petite fiole remplie de liquide transparent. Voici un souvenir de notre chasse au leucrotta. Je l'ai fait extraire spécialement pour toi par le taxidermiste.

— Qu'est-ce donc ? demanda Kit en plissant les yeux.

— La salive de la créature, répondit Nellthis. Selon la légende, elle constitue un antidote très efficace contre les philtres d'amour. A en juger par l'amusant épisode de tout à l'heure, tu en auras sans doute plus besoin que moi.

Sceptique, Kit hésita.

— Prends-la, insista son oncle. On ne sait jamais, ça peut toujours servir.

La jeune femme haussa les épaules et empocha la fiole.

— A présent, poursuivit Nellthis, nous devons nous dépêcher.

Il reprit sa plume et rédigea un message. Après avoir soufflé sur l'encre, il plia le parchemin et le rangea dans la poche de sa chemise. Puis il se leva.

— Nous avons des choses à faire. Je veux que tu rencontres des... amis à moi. Va préparer tes bagages, si tu veux partir avant le lever du soleil.

CHAPITRE IV

Caramon fut le premier à reprendre conscience.

Sa tête lui faisait horriblement mal… Avait-il rêvé ?

Il se trouvait au sommet d'une haute tour de pierre battue par les vents et trempée par une pluie cinglante. Sauf que ce n'était pas une tour, mais le plus grand arbre d'une forêt, qui se balançait dans la tempête tandis que le jeune homme s'accrochait aux branches.

Puis la foudre frappa l'arbre, qui se fendit par le milieu. Caramon se sentit tomber. Il pouvait se sauver : il lui suffisait d'agripper l'ancre du navire argenté qui le survolait, dansant à quelques pouces de ses doigts...

— Uh, grogna-t-il.

La bière des marins était encore pire que l'eau-de-vie des nains. Caramon voulut se masser les tempes, mais quelque chose l'empêchait de bouger ses bras. Il ouvrit les paupières avec difficulté et réalisa qu'il était ligoté à un poteau en compagnie de Tass et de Sturm, toujours inconscients.

Caramon ferma les yeux et se détendit. Ce n'était qu'un cauchemar, qui se dissiperait en même temps que les effets de la bière.

Peu à peu, les bruits de tempête s'estompèrent, pour être remplacés par les cris des goélands, le soupir du vent et le doux craquement d'un navire. Puis des grognements sourds, accompagnés de grattements et de couinements réguliers, montèrent vers Caramon.

Le jeune homme rouvrit les yeux. Où se trouvait-il ? Que s'était-il passé ? Pourquoi ses amis et lui étaient-ils attachés au mât du *Vénora* ? Sturm avait la bouche ouverte et la tête rejetée en arrière. Tass arborait une grosse ecchymose violette sur le front.

Caramon tourna la tête. Il n'y avait personne d'autre sur le pont du navire, qui se balançait au gré du courant. Il fouilla sa mémoire, essayant de se souvenir comment il s'était fourré dans un tel pétrin. Il se rappelait d'avoir partagé un pichet de bière avec quelques marins, puis plus rien.

Caramon leva la tête vers le ciel. Il avait l'impression étrange d'être en pleine journée, peut-être à cause de la chaleur et de l'humidité. Pourtant, le soleil ne se trouvait nulle part en vue. On eût dit qu'une épaisse couche de brume grise le cachait.

Les craquements se turent et furent remplacés par un bruit de pas et d'armes.

— 'Sque c'est ? marmonna Tass en ouvrant un œil.

Le brouillard se dissipa un peu. Caramon vit des mains agripper le bastingage du *Vénora.* Des silhouettes se hissaient à bord. A pas prudents, les inconnus s'approchèrent des compagnons.

— Sturm, réveille-toi ! chuchota Caramon d'une voix pressante.

Il sentit son ami bouger près de lui et se concentra sur les nouveaux venus : plusieurs humains, quelques ogres, une phalange de minotaures et une mystérieuse créature enveloppée dans une cape, qui se tenait un peu en arrière. De temps en temps, elle sifflait un ordre.

Caramon reporta son attention sur les ogres. Ils lui semblèrent plus petits et plus gras que les spécimens habituels. Leurs cheveux blonds étaient sales, leur peau grise, leurs mains et leurs pieds palmés.

Le jeune homme s'étonna de les voir en telle compagnie. Autrefois, les minotaures avaient été les esclaves des ogres ; les deux races se considéraient comme ennemies.

Les humains portaient des haillons colorés ; ils étaient minces et brunis par le soleil. Des coutelas pendaient à leur ceinture.

Du coin de l'œil, Caramon vit Sturm relever la tête. Il sentit Tass essayer de défaire ses liens. Sans succès.

Se frayant un chemin parmi le groupe d'abordage, les minotaures se dirigèrent vers les trois compagnons. Ils n'étaient que cinq, mais les autres semblaient les craindre.

Un gros anneau ornait leur museau. Leur corps était couvert d'une fourrure rousse, leur front orné de cornes massives. Deux d'entre eux s'arrêtèrent à quelques pas des prisonniers.

— Tu crois que ce sont les bons ? souffla le premier.

— Bien sûr ! Le Maître de la Nuit ne commet jamais d'erreur.

L'odeur puissante dégagée par les créatures agit sur Caramon comme des sels, achevant d'aiguiser ses perceptions. *Le plus grand doit être le chef,* se dit le jeune homme. Autour de son cou musclé pendait un collier de pierres polies ; à sa ceinture, il portait un fléau.

— Ils semblent si pathétiques, reprit le premier. Quelle menace peuvent-ils représenter ?

— Je ne fais qu'exécuter les ordres du maître, Dogz. Je ne lis pas dans ses pensées.

— A ton avis, lequel est-ce ?

— C'est ce que nous allons découvrir.

Les autres membres du groupe s'étaient disposés en cercle autour du mât, comme des loups n'osant pas s'approcher d'un feu de camp. Caramon se tortilla pour regarder derrière les minotaures, qui, avec leurs sept pieds de haut, lui bloquaient la vue. Il crut apercevoir un autre navire dans le brouillard non loin du *Vénora.*

— Que se passe-t-il ? demanda Sturm, encore mal réveillé.

— Des minotaures et des brigands humains, chuchota Tass.

— Des pirates, renchérit Caramon.

— Silence ! aboya le chef des minotaures en brandissant son fléau d'un air menaçant. Nous ne sommes pas des pirates, imbécile !

Son compagnon et lui revinrent vers la silhouette encapuchonnée et conversèrent quelques instants avec elle.

Pendant ce temps, les autres membres du groupe se rapprochaient des prisonniers. Caramon lut dans leurs yeux une grande soif de sang.

— Où sommes-nous ? demanda Sturm, la voix pâteuse.

— J'espérais que tu pourrais répondre à cette question, dit Caramon.

— Si seulement je pouvais consulter mes cartes, soupira Tasslehoff.

Caramon ne répondit pas. Mieux valait garder le silence. Il avait le sentiment confus que la moindre faiblesse signerait leur perte.

Les deux minotaures revinrent vers les prisonniers. Celui qui s'appelait Dogz tendit des mains énormes et palpa Caramon de la tête aux pieds. Il cherchait quelque chose…

Le jeune homme se débattit, mais il n'était pas en position de résister. Faute de mieux, il cracha à la figure de Dogz. Le minotaure fit un bond en arrière. Ses camarades rirent.

Furieux, la créature flanqua un coup de pied dans la mâchoire de Caramon. Le jeune homme eut l'impression qu'une enclume venait de l'atteindre de plein fouet. Plié en deux par la douleur, il cracha une dent ensanglantée.

— Par mon honneur, vous regretterez cette méprisable attaque ! s'écria Sturm, vibrant d'indignation.

— Quand son frère entendra parler de vous, renchérit Tass, il vous changera en crapaud à cornes !

— Taisez-vous, haleta Caramon.

Les minotaures se moquaient des fanfaronnades de leurs prisonniers. Déjà, Dogz se penchait sur Sturm pour le fouiller à son tour.

Pas celui-là non plus, songea-t-il. Le Solamnique ne portait rien sur lui, ni arme ni bourse.

Dogz leva une main couverte du sang : la nuque de Sturm était poisseuse. Dégoûté, il gifla le jeune homme à la volée. Le Solamnique encaissa stoïquement.

— Cette fois, vous avez dépassé les bornes ! s'exclama Tass. Sturm n'a jamais frappé un adversaire désarmé de toute sa vie. Du moins, depuis que je le fréquente, et ça fait des années... Enfin, une ou deux. C'est la personne la plus noble et la mieux intentionnée que je connaisse..., moi mis à part.

La voix aiguë parut surprendre le minotaure, comme s'il remarquait Tass pour la première fois. Il recula pour parler à son chef.

— Le troisième est un kender, Sarkis.

— Et alors ?

Dogz grimaça.

— Les kenders sont malpropres. Ils arpentent le monde en vivant de rapines. On dit qu'en toucher un, c'est risquer le dégoût, ou pire, la maladie. Je ne crois pas qu'il soit nécessaire de le fouiller.

Derrière les deux minotaures s'éleva un sifflement furieux. Puis on entendit la voix indignée de Tass.

— Moi, malpropre ? Ça te va bien de dire ça, espèce de grosse vache ! Je te fais savoir que je me baigne régulièrement. Je me suis lavé la figure pas plus tard qu'hier, à condition qu'aujourd'hui soit le lendemain d'hier, ce dont je ne suis pas sûr parce que j'ai comme un trou de mémoire.

« D'ailleurs, en parlant d'hygiène personnelle, tu ferais mieux d'ouvrir les deux hangars à grain qui te servent de narines et de renifler tes aisselles ! »

Sturm se mordit la langue. Caramon leva les yeux au ciel. Les humains et les ogres gloussèrent.

Le minotaure nommé Sarkis se dirigea vers la silhouette encapuchonnée et parla avec elle dans une langue inconnue, faite de sifflements et de syllabes gutturales.

Caramon songea avec regret à Raistlin. Ensemble, il n'était guère de situations dont les jumeaux ne puissent se sortir. Qu'aurait fait le jeune mage à sa place ?

Sarkis se tourna vers Dogz.

— Les kenders n'ont aucun honneur, dit-il, méprisant. Mais ils sont de notoriété publique immunisés contre les maladies. Celui-là ne risque pas de te contaminer... Je vais le fouiller à ta place.

Tasslehoff vit les grandes mains du minotaure se tendre vers lui.

— Gros crétin moche ! Je ne suis peut-être pas aussi honorable que Sturm, mais deux fois, dix fois, cent mille fois plus que tes semblables à face de bœuf ! Et si je le voulais vraiment, je pourrais te transmettre n'importe quelle maladie, non mais ! Hé, arrête ça ! Ça chatouille ! Hi hi hi !

Il parle trop, songea Sturm.

Ayant saisi les bourses et les sacoches de Tass, le minotaure ricana. Il jeta à Dogz un regard féroce, puis revint vers la silhouette encapuchonnée et conféra avec elle pendant quelques secondes.

— C'est lui, annonça-t-il en se tournant à nouveau vers Dogz. Amène-le.

Le second minotaure se dirigea vers Tass, qui poussa un cri aigu. Sturm et Caramon bandèrent leurs muscles, mais ils ne pouvaient rien faire.

Dogz détacha le kender, le saisit par sa queue-de-cheval et le porta à bout de bras comme un lapin bavard.

— Aïe ! Tu me fais mal, espèce de grosse vache stérile ! Tête d'œuf ! On t'a déjà dit que tu sens l'ail ? Fais un peu attention ! Et d'abord, où m'emmènes-tu ?

Sous les yeux de Sturm et Caramon, Dogz passa le kender gigotant à deux humains, qui enjambèrent le bastingagc et disparurent. Avec une grimace satisfaite, le minotaure se tourna vers Sarkis.

Caramon vit la silhouette encapuchonnée battre en retraite à son tour, suivie par une partie des humains, les ogres et les trois autres minotaures.

— Et ces deux-là ? demanda Dogz à Sarkis.

Son chef haussa les épaules, l'air indifférent.

— Ils ne comptent pas. Jette-les par-dessus bord et mets le feu au navire.

Les quelques humains restants s'avancèrent. L'un d'eux, un géant à la barbe rousse qui portait une marque de corde autour du cou, jeta à Sarkis un regard avide. Le minotaure hocha la tête, puis, suivi par son second, il alla rejoindre le reste de l'équipage dans le canot qui les attendait.

Les humains fondirent sur les prisonniers, qu'ils rouèrent de coups de pied. Incapable de se défendre, Caramon ferma les yeux pour les protéger. Près de lui, Sturm poussa un gémissement lorsque les premiers coups l'atteignirent, puis il encaissa le reste en silence.

Le ruffian à la cicatrice tapa dans le tronçon de mât jusqu'à ce que celui-ci se détache. Aidé de ses camarades, il le porta près du bastingage. Toujours attachés, Caramon et Sturm se sentirent soulevés dans les airs et projetés par-dessus bord.

Ils tombèrent à l'eau dans une gerbe d'éclaboussures. Caramon se débattit, mais ses mains étaient liées trop étroitement. En temps normal, il était déjà piètre nageur… Il devait à Sturm de ne pas s'être noyé dans le Lac de Cristalmir trois mois plus tôt. Depuis, il s'était risqué à quelques brasses, mais sans résultat probant.

Sturm avait touché l'eau en premier ; il mit quelques secondes à refaire surface, toussant et crachant comme un phoque. Lui non plus ne pouvait pas se libérer ; il battit des jambes pour se maintenir à flot. Par bonheur, le tronçon de mât l'y aidait en partie.

— Ne te débats pas ! cria-t-il à Caramon. Tu vas épuiser toutes tes forces.

L'eau était tiède et boueuse : brune plutôt que bleue ou verte, et pleine de sédiments. Chaque coup de pied des deux jeunes gens soulevait des bulles et des algues gluantes. Une odeur de marécage flottait dans l'air.

Une violente explosion assourdit les deux guerriers. Une colonne de flammes et de fumée engloutissait le *Vénora*. Le courant avait déjà entraîné le navire loin d'eux. Quant à l'autre vaisseau, celui que Caramon avait aperçu dans la brume, il avait tout simplement… disparu.

Caramon et Sturm regardèrent brûler les restes du *Vénora*. Quand la dernière flamme s'éteignit, une obscurité grise enveloppa les deux compagnons.

Elle n'était pas plus sombre que leurs pensées.

Où se trouvaient-ils ? Pourquoi les avait-on agressés ainsi ? Comment pourraient-ils retrouver et délivrer Tasslehoff ? Et surtout, réussiraient-ils à survivre ?

*

* *

Ses amis lui manquaient, et il aurait bien eu besoin qu'on vienne le délivrer. Pourtant, Tasslehoff Racle-Pieds s'amusait comme un petit fou.

D'accord, on l'avait enfermé dans une minuscule cellule, à fond de cale. D'accord, les barreaux de fer avaient l'air solide, et le navire empestait davantage qu'un cimetière de putois. D'accord, il était prisonnier de minotaures, d'ogres aux mains palmées et de pirates humains qui pouvaient à tout moment décider de le mettre à mort.

Mais jusqu'à présent, il avait été plutôt bien traité. Sarkis lui avait rendu ses bourses et ses sacoches, avec une déférence telle qu'on eût pu les croire sacrées. Tass en avait profité pour dresser l'inventaire de ses possessions : pour une fois, rien n'était venu le distraire. Il regrettait juste d'avoir déjà utilisé sa bouteille magique pour envoyer une lettre à Raistlin.

Tass pouvait dormir tout son soûl, et ses geôliers le nourrissaient d'une sorte de ragoût gras et plein de grumeaux auquel il s'était habitué assez vite. Ses repas lui étaient apportés par de petits singes qui remplissaient la fonction d'aides-cuisiniers.

Le kender se fit un ami de l'un d'eux, une petite créature à poils longs et à l'estomac proéminent, qu'il baptisa Otik en souvenir d'un certain aubergiste.

Tass avait plein de visiteurs intéressants. Il était le premier kender qu'aient jamais rencontré la plupart des membres de l'équipage. Les marins aimaient l'observer, le provoquer ou lui jeter des trognons de pomme. Tass les renvoyait, mais il adorait se lancer dans des concours d'injures avec ses geôliers. Les humains, en particulier, connaissaient des expressions nouvelles qui stimulaient l'imagination du kender.

Les minotaures se comportaient plus dignement, même s'ils sentaient mauvais. Ils regardaient Tass avec une expression voisine du respect. Une fois, Sarkis passa plusieurs minutes à détailler le kender de la tête aux pieds, comme s'il voulait graver son image dans sa mémoire. Malgré tous ses efforts, Tass ne put lui arracher un mot.

Dogz était différent. Au début de ses échanges verbaux avec le kender, des commentaires désobligeants avaient fusé de part et d'autre. Puis la curiosité du minotaure avait pris le pas sur son arrogance. A présent, il arrivait presque à tenir des conversations amicales avec Tass, et il semblait avoir un peu peur de lui.

Dogz était le cousin de Sarkis, qu'il respectait et servait loyalement. Sarkis considérait ses relations avec le kender comme un signe de faiblesse, aussi Dogz devait-il se cacher pour rendre visite à Tass.

— Alors comme ça, tu aimes vraiment être un minotaure ? demanda un jour le kender, étonné par l'orgueil de son interlocuteur.

Lui trouvait Dogz fascinant, mais les hommes à tête de taureau étaient tenus en grand mépris sur Krynn.

— C'est un... honneur, répondit Dogz, hésitant.

— Je voudrais que tu m'expliques pourquoi. Je veux dire… en tant que kender, le monde entier est ma maison. J'ai des amis et des parents partout, sauf peut-être à Thorbardin parmi les Theiwars, et encore, je suis sûr que j'arriverais à les dérider si je m'y mettais vraiment. Je sais dessiner des cartes, j'ai une jolie queue-de-cheval...

Tass s'interrompit, conscient que Dogz ne parlerait pas s'il ne lui en donnait pas l'occasion. Après quelques instants, le minotaure répondit :

— Nous nous battons pour vivre, nous vivons pour nous battre. Nous ne nous inclinons devant personne. Notre destin est de régner.

Une puissante conviction se dégageait de ses paroles, mais Tass lut de la tristesse dans ses yeux.

— Un sacré fardeau, remarqua le kender, pensif.

Il fut tenté d'ajouter « même pour un bœuf », mais il se retint au dernier moment.

Une semaine plus tard, quand Tass réalisa qu'il n'avait pas vu Otik depuis trois jours, c'est au minotaure qu'il exprima son inquiétude.

Dogz désigna l'écuelle du kender.

— Ben, c'est du ragoût de singe. C'est pour ça qu'on garde à bord ces créatures dégoûtantes, pas pour les apprivoiser.

Tass en perdit l'appétit. Le minotaure s'en aperçut et demanda de sa voix la plus douce :

— Les kenders ne mangent pas de singe ?

— Pas que je sache, se lamenta Tass, inconsolable de la perte d'Otik.

— Alors que mangent-ils ?

— De tout, sauf du singe. Surtout quand ce singe est un ami.

— Oh. Je suis désolé.

— Moi aussi. (Tass pressa son petit visage contre les barreaux de la cellule.) Je pourrais toujours me dire que c'était du porridge. J'adore ça avec des mûres et du miel. Mais je suppose que vous n'en avez pas à bord ?

Dogz secoua la tête. Tass soupira et repoussa son écuelle. Plusieurs minutes s'écoulèrent avant que le minotaure demande timidement :

— Puisque tu ne finis pas ton ragoût, je peux peut-être... ?

Tass lui fit passer son écuelle entre les barreaux.

Les ogres aux mains palmées étaient très différents des minotaures. Tass apprit bientôt qu'on les appelait des orughis. Petits, gras et stupides, ils injuriaient le kender dans leur langue natale. Faute de mieux, Tass s'efforçait d'imiter leur ton et d'égaler leur puissance vocale.

Certains orughis, manquant d'esprit sportif, descendaient dans la cale le temps de crier une insulte bien sentie, puis remontaient en courant sur le pont. Quand ils restaient assez longtemps, Tass aimait à observer l'arme ancestrale que certains portaient sur l'épaule : un boomerang métallique muni d'une longue corde, le tonkk, qui servait à chasser les oiseaux. Le kender aurait voulu en essayer un, juste pour voir. Sarkis n'avait pas jugé bon de lui enlever son bâton, sans doute parce qu'il ne pouvait lui être d'une grande utilité dans sa cellule.

Un après-midi, le bateau ralentit et s'arrêta. Les marins s'agitèrent sur le pont et Tass les entendit décharger quelque chose. Pendant plusieurs heures, personne ne se soucia de rendre visite au kender. Il commençait à croire qu'on l'avait oublié quand Dogz et Sarkis descendirent enfin dans la cale. Ils portaient une petite cage de bois qui sentait le singe.

Les deux minotaures entrèrent dans la cellule de Tass, l'empoignèrent et le forcèrent à pénétrer dans la cage. Puis ils attachèrent celle-ci à deux perches qu'ils calèrent sur leurs épaules, avant de remonter sur le pont. Là, Tass aperçut pour la première fois la rive d'une des légendaires îles de Mithas. Il avait hâte de raconter ça à ses amis... Si on le laissait vivre assez longtemps.

Des dizaines de galions, de vaisseaux marchands et de bateaux de pêche se pressaient dans le port de Lacynos. Un système de cordes et de poulies permettait de décharger le bois et les autres marchandises indispensables en provenance du continent. Des esclaves humains l'actionnaient, surveillés par des minotaures qui n'hésitaient pas à faire claquer leur fouet si la cadence ralentissait. Marchands et pirates se disputaient sur les quais. Des algues et des détritus flottaient à la surface de l'eau.

La cité elle-même n'était guère plus propre. Dans les rues encombrées, la pluie avait changé la terre en boue. Les grossiers bâtiments de bois munis d'échelles extérieures étaient disposés en blocs.

Tass tournait la tête en tous sens pour ne rien manquer. Il y avait beaucoup d'humains... Sans doute avaient-ils un monopole sur les tavernes. Beaucoup ressemblaient à des brigands, avec leurs nombreux bijoux. Ils portaient des sabres ou des couteaux dentelés. Parfois, une bagarre éclatait entre l'un d'eux et les minotaures.

Dogz et Sarkis emmenèrent le kender vers un rassemblement d'échoppes, d'étals et de tentes où régnait une joyeuse cacophonie. Tass repéra des bijoux et des armes exotiques, de la laine et des vêtements, ainsi que de nombreux poissons fumés, en boîte, frais ou... moins frais.

— Notre place du marché, expliqua Dogz en penchant la tête vers le kender. On y trouve la plus belle argenterie des îles minotaures. Il faut être très prudent pour ne pas se faire rouler.

— Arrête de lui faire la conversation ! aboya Sarkis. C'est un prisonnier, pas un touriste.

Tass se mordit la langue pour ne pas répondre vertement.

Les minotaures traversèrent la place du marché et s'engagèrent dans une rue moins fréquentée. Ils se dirigèrent vers le plus grand bâtiment de Lacynos : la résidence saisonnière de leur roi. C'était un manoir aux colonnes de marbre, flanqué de nombreuses dépendances et de jardins spacieux. Perché sur une colline, il surplombait la cité bourdonnante d'activité.

Le petit groupe passa devant un contingent d'esclaves au visage couvert de sang séché. Les malheureux creusaient des tranchées sous la supervision de minotaures qui faisaient claquer des fouet au-dessus de leur tête. Beaucoup étaient décharnés et malades. Ils n'osèrent même pas jeter un regard au kender.

En arrivant devant la porte du palais, Tass aperçut des formations de soldats arpentant la cour principale. Des sentinelles étaient postées à intervalles réguliers le long des remparts : tous semblaient connaître Dogz et Sarkis.

Tass en avait assez d'être plié en deux dans sa cage, et il aurait bien aimé explorer les alentours. Il fut donc enchanté quand, après avoir pénétré dans un bâtiment et descendu un long escalier, Sarkis et Dogz le laissèrent enfin sortir. Hélas, il eut à peine le temps de s'étirer avant que Sarkis le pousse dans une autre cellule, sombre, mais plus spacieuse que la précédente.

Sans autre commentaire, le minotaure fit volte-face et s'en fut. Dogz le suivit du regard, puis se tourna vers le kender.

— Au revoir, ami Tass, dit-il tristement.

Il fit mine de partir.

— Attends ! s'écria le kender. Que va-t-il m'arriver ?

Dogz s'éloigna sans répondre.

Une heure ou deux s'écoulèrent. Tass s'ennuyait ferme. Il était maintenant habitué à l'odeur et à la saleté des cellules minotaures, mais l'ameublement se composait en tout et pour tout d'une paillasse et d'un seau, et il n'y avait personne pour faire de concours d'injures. A côté, son séjour à fond de cale ressemblait à une joyeuse rigolade.

Les événements se précipitèrent quand Sarkis revint accompagné de deux minotaures inconnus. L'un d'eux était vêtu d'un simple kilt. L'autre portait une cape écarlate et un mince diadème en or. Impassible, il s'approcha du prisonnier et fit un rictus qui découvrit ses dents jaunâtres. Son haleine méphitique manqua faire tomber Tass à la renverse.

— Ainsi, voilà le fameux mage kender, laissa-t-il tomber.

— Oui, mon roi, répondit Sarkis.

Mage kender ? songea Tass, stupéfait. *De quoi ces andouilles veulent-ils parler ?*

— Le Maître de la Nuit sera très content, dit le roi en tournant les talons et en remontant les escaliers.

— Quel Maître de la Nuit ? s'époumona Tass. Et d'abord, vous êtes roi de quoi ? Si c'est vous le taureau en chef, vous feriez mieux de me relâcher avant que mes amis découvrent où je suis ! Et j'en ai des tas ! Si on vous a choisi comme roi, c'est sans doute parce que vous avez l'haleine la plus ignoble de Lacynos, et même de Mithas ! Ou d'Ansalonie !

Si seulement il avait pu se servir de son bâton ! Si seulement il n'y avait pas eu de barreaux entre lui et les minotaures ! Le kender saisit son arme et la brandit d'un air menaçant. Sarkis et son compagnon au kilt le dévisagèrent sans réagir. A court d'imagination, Tass se tut.

— Je n'avais encore jamais vu de kender, grogna le minotaure au kilt, surpris. Et encore moins de mage kender.

— Oui, Cleef-Eth, répondit Sarkis avec déférence. Comme vous me l'aviez ordonné, je l'ai fait placer sous votre garde.

— C'est bien. Torturez-le jusqu'à ce qu'il nous révèle ses secrets. Mais ne le tuez pas, du moins, pas encore. Faites-lui juste assez mal pour qu'il comprenne que nous sommes sérieux.

Sarkis caressa le manche de son fléau.

— Avec grand plaisir, Cleef-Eth, dit-il en grimaçant.

CHAPITRE V

Des branches mortes couvertes d'une mousse spongieuse jonchaient le sol de la forêt. De soudaines coulées d'eau, trahissant la présence d'un torrent souterrain, faisaient parfois surface avant de disparaître à nouveau. Le sol montait en pente douce. Au loin, des pics et des promontoires rocheux jaillissaient entre les arbres. De-ci, de-là, quelques pâles rayons de soleil perçaient les épaisses frondaisons.

Les trois amis progressaient lentement. Tanis et Flint devaient utiliser leur arme pour se frayer un chemin dans la végétation. Le demi-elfe en concevait un certain mécontentement, alors que le nain était heureux de manier sa hache, fût-ce dans un but aussi peu noble.

Derrière eux, Raistlin attendait en silence chaque fois qu'ils s'arrêtaient. Pour marcher, le jeune mage s'aidait de la canne en cèdre que Flint lui avait fabriquée quelques mois plus tôt. Ses traits pâles étaient tirés par la fatigue, mais il supportait les retards avec plus de patience que ses compagnons.

Le Maître Mage leur avait donné des indications très précises. La caverne de l'Oracle était bien dissimulée, son emplacement connu d'un petit nombre de privilégiés… Par chance, elle était à une demi-journée de marche de Solace. Morath avait conseillé à Raistlin de se méfier : malgré des apparences trompeuses, l'Oracle possédait des pouvoirs fantastiques et il n'appréciait guère les étrangers.

Une fois sorti de Solace, le chemin de graviers qui conduisait vers le sud-est se divisait en deux sentiers : le premier s'enfonçait dans les montagnes, le second s'incurvait vers l'est. Suivant les instructions de Morath, les trois compagnons avaient pris ce dernier.

Puis le sentier se divisa à son tour en plusieurs pistes. Sans les conseils du Maître Mage, les voyageurs n'auraient jamais choisi la plus anodine : un simple ruban de boue et de poussière conduisant à un bois grouillant de végétation.

Pendant une demi-heure, les trois amis se frayèrent un chemin à la force du poignet avant de déboucher enfin à l'air libre. Ils durent encore contourner des rochers, sauter par-dessus des arbres morts et escalader une petite colline.

Raistlin faisait de son mieux pour ne pas ralentir les autres. Sa détermination à atteindre la caverne de l'Oracle impressionnait Tanis, qui avait banni Kitiara de ses pensées et se concentrait sur leur mission. Quant à Flint, il saisissait toutes les occasions de se plaindre.

— J'espère pour lui que ton mage sait de quoi il parle, grommela le nain en se tamponnant le front à l'aide d'un mouchoir souillé.

Raistlin lui jeta un regard peu amène.

— Si tu as le moindre doute, rien ne t'empêche de rebrousser chemin, dit-il d'une voix que la fatigue rendait cassante. Pour un aventurier comme toi, je croyais que cette petite expédition serait une promenade de santé.

Flint tourna le dos au jeune mage en marmonnant dans sa barbe quelque chose au sujet « des jeunes qui avaient perdu le respect de leurs anciens ». Tanis lui-même aurait aimé une explication, mais il vit une étincelle de colère dans l'œil de Raistlin et jugea préférable de se taire.

Enfin la piste déboucha sur une petite clairière envahie par les hautes herbes. A une des extrémités se dressait un énorme sapin, adossé à un éboulis de rochers. Des tentacules de brume sortaient d'une ouverture noire, à la base du tronc.

Flint et Tanis hésitèrent ; Raistlin avança jusqu'à la gueule de la caverne, faisant signe à ses amis de le rejoindre.

— Holà ! cria-t-il, se penchant vers les ténèbres béantes. Nous sommes trois compagnons qui venons de la part du Maître Mage Morath !

Le silence lui répondit. Des doigts de brume blanche s'enroulèrent autour de ses chevilles et remontèrent le long de ses jambes sans le toucher, pulsant comme s'ils répondaient à la chaleur de son corps.

Les yeux écarquillés, Tanis regarda Flint. Le nain hocha la tête et empoigna sa hache. D'un geste, Raistlin intima à ses amis de rester immobiles. Puis il baissa la tête et, sans hésitation, plongea dans la cavité. Tanis et Flint durent se hâter pour le rattraper.

A l'intérieur de la caverne, ils butèrent contre le jeune mage qui s'était arrêté, le temps que ses yeux s'habituent à la pénombre. Le brouillard blanc ondulait autour des trois compagnons. Même en utilisant sa vision elfique, Tanis n'y voyait pas grand-chose.

Des gémissements indistincts s'élevèrent des profondeurs de la caverne. Une odeur saumâtre planait dans l'air.

— Ça pue comme un cadavre de troll, chuchota Tanis à l'oreille de Flint, qui s'était plaqué un mouchoir sur la bouche.

— Silence ! siffla Raistlin.

Le jeune homme tendit sa canne vers le plafond et informa les autres qu'ils se trouvaient dans un tunnel. Les mains tendues devant lui, il avança avec prudence. Tanis et Flint lui emboîtèrent le pas.

Quelques minutes plus tard, alors que le passage décrivait une courbe, les trois compagnons arrivèrent en vue d'une lumière diffuse qui facilita leur progression. Elle s'intensifia peu à peu, jusqu'à ce qu'ils émergent dans une sorte de grotte ronde sans autre issue que le tunnel d'où ils arrivaient.

Bien qu'il n'y eût personne, l'endroit semblait habité, comme en témoignait la présence d'une chaise, d'une paillasse et d'un coffre. Un peu de soleil filtrait d'une fissure, éclairant le sol de terre battue.

A l'autre bout de la grotte, un liquide inconnu bouillonnait dans un énorme chaudron. La brume blanche avait battu en retraite et formait comme un nuage au-dessus du récipient. L'odeur putride planait toujours dans l'air, mais les gémissements s'étaient tus.

Tanis tendit la main pour toucher les murs veinés de lignes de couleur, et qui ne semblaient pas être en pierre.

— Une sorte de bois pétrifié, commenta Flint, plein d'admiration, caressant sa barbe poivre et sel.

Il flanqua un coup de coude au demi-elfe et lui indiqua Raistlin d'un signe de tête. Sans prêter la moindre attention à ses amis, le jeune mage s'était accroupi devant la paillasse et parlait au sol à voix basse.

— Nous ne venons pas en ennemis, murmura-t-il, les yeux baissés. Et même si c'était le cas, vous pourriez facilement nous vaincre, ô Chen'tal Pyrnee.

Se rapprochant, Tanis vit une musaraigne blanche tapie sous la paillasse. La petite créature semblait très agitée. Elle avait des yeux rouges perçants et couinait d'un air indigné en agitant les moustaches.

— N'ayez pas peur de nous, poursuivit Raistlin. Nous sommes venus vous présenter nos respects et solliciter une faveur. Je sais que nous nous sommes introduits dans votre domaine sans y être invités, mais écoutez-nous, je vous en prie.

« Si vous le souhaitez, vous pouvez nous bannir ou même nous détruire. Mon maître, Morath de Fondemare, m'a dit que vous en étiez capable, car vous possédez des pouvoirs extraordinaires. »

Une explosion retentit dans la petite grotte, suivie par un crépitement. La musaraigne disparut. A sa place, une très vieille ogresse se matérialisa près du chaudron. Elle saisit la louche et touilla son contenu, dévisageant Raistlin d'un œil violet et venimeux. Son autre paupière, cousue, laissait suinter un pus jaunâtre.

Tanis recula, sur la défensive. Flint saisit le manche de sa hache ; Raistlin se releva.

— Ah ! Je pourrais sucer vos os pour dîner, caqueta l'ogresse. Il me suffirait de lever le petit doigt ! (Elle inclina la tête.) Comment va ce vieux fou de Morath ? J'entends parler de lui quand il a besoin de me demander une faveur. Qui êtes-vous pour vous recommander de lui ?

Chen'tal Pyrnee était incroyablement laide. Personne n'aurait pu deviner son âge ou son poids. Elle portait plusieurs couches de vêtements amples et de foulards aux couleurs passées… Sa carrure était celle d'un ours. Elle emplissait la grotte, jetant une ombre menaçante sur les trois compagnons.

Son visage était constellé de verrues et de pustules. De longs poils frisaient sur son nez et son menton. Les dents qui lui restaient étaient noires et pourries. Une sorte de bonnet à carreaux recouvrait ses mèches de cheveux filasse… Elle dégageait une odeur encore pire que celle du chaudron.

— J'étais son élève, expliqua Raistlin en s'inclinant devant l'ogresse. Morath a confiance en moi, c'est la raison pour laquelle il m'a envoyé. Je n'avais ni le temps ni les moyens d'expédier un message pour vous prévenir de mon arrivée. Mes compagnons et moi effectuons une mission des plus urgentes.

Chen'tal Pyrnee souleva une louche pleine d'un liquide verdâtre, qu'elle goûta en fronçant les sourcils, sans quitter Raistlin de l'œil. Tanis s'émerveilla de l'assurance du jeune mage, qui ne flancha pas sous ce regard inquisiteur.

— Morath est un impudent, marmonna l'ogresse. Il passe son temps à m'envoyer ses élèves, dans l'espoir qu'ils réussiront à m'extorquer un sort. Les gamins font la queue devant ma caverne pour réclamer mon aide.

« Parfois, je prends pitié d'eux et j'accède à leur requête. Mais je transforme le plus grand nombre en porcs-épics ou en couleuvres. S'ils ne sont pas capables de reprendre leur apparence originelle, c'est qu'ils n'étaient pas dignes d'être des mages.

— Le maître m'a dit qu'il ne vous avait adressé personne depuis plusieurs années, fit remarquer Raistlin.

— Ah ! (Chen'tal Pyrnee remua les lèvres comme si elle mâchait quelque chose.) Peut-être, peut-être. Je perds le compte des jours. Ça ne te donne pas le droit de me contredire, jeune insolent. Et qui sont tes compagnons ? J'ai du mal à croire que Morath s'abaisse à prendre des elfes et des nains comme élèves.

Flint serra les dents. Il aurait bien assommé l'ogresse, mais Tanis le retint par la manche et jeta un regard interrogateur à Raistlin. D'un froncement de sourcils, celui-ci lui fit comprendre qu'ils devaient traiter Chen'tal Pyrnee avec respect.

Tanis baissa la tête, flanquant un coup de coude à Flint pour qu'il en fasse autant. Le nain s'exécuta à contrecœur. Raistlin avait expliqué à ses amis que le salut de Tass, de Sturm et de Caramon allait dépendre en grande partie de l'Oracle, ajoutant que celle-ci pouvait être très dangereuse si on la contrariait.

— Ce sont mes amis, dit le jeune mage.

L'ogresse ricana.

— Peuh ! Il est facile de reconnaître ses ennemis, mais plus encore de se tromper sur le compte d'un ami. Un ennemi se révèle par une seule action. Un ami doit sans cesse prouver qu'il est digne de confiance.

— Je suis d'accord avec vous, approuva Raistlin en hochant la tête.

Chen'tal Pyrnee plissa son œil droit d'un air soupçonneux. Sans crier gare, elle sortit à nouveau la louche du chaudron et projeta le contenu contre le mur de la grotte, si près de Raistlin que celui-ci dut faire un bond sur le côté pour ne pas être éclaboussé.

Le liquide verdâtre brûla le bois sur lequel il dégoulina en grésillant, mettant à jour des motifs de cuivre et de turquoise. Un bref instant, un flot de lumière multicolore inonda la grotte.

Tanis eut du mal à retenir Flint. Les traits tendus, Raistlin ne pipait mot. L'ogresse tentait de l'intimider… et elle avait réussi. Au fond de lui, il était terrifié. Morath l'avait mis en garde contre le tempérament versatile de Chen'tal Pyrnee, mais le jeune mage ne voulait pas montrer sa peur.

Un lourd silence tomba sur la grotte. Des volutes de brume planaient au-dessus du chaudron. L'ogresse touillait sa mixture, son œil violet se posant alternativement sur les trois compagnons. Enfin, elle prit la parole.

— Je pourrais vous faire des tours comme celui-là pendant toute la journée, se vanta-t-elle.

Malgré elle, elle était satisfaite par le comportement de l'improbable petit groupe. Soudain, elle lâcha sa louche et devint grave.

— Vous êtes pressés, je crois. Qu'est-ce qui vous amène chez la vieille Chen'tal ? Il vaudrait mieux pour vous que ce soit quelque chose d'important, ou au moins d'intéressant. Je n'aime pas me mettre en frais pour des invités ennuyeux. En tout cas, pas longtemps, gloussa-t-elle.

Raistlin fit un pas en avant. De son sac à dos, il sortit une épaisse roue de fromage bleu enveloppée dans du papier.

— Nous vous avons apporté un cadeau, dit-il poliment.

L'ogresse saisit l'offrande et la déballa avec avidité. Son œil unique brilla de plaisir. En la regardant, Flint s'aperçut tout à coup qu'il était affamé. Pourvu que Chen'tal Pyrnee ne puisse pas entendre les gargouillements de son estomac…

L'ogresse arracha un morceau de fromage et l'enfourna dans sa bouche, puis le mâcha férocement.

— Hum... J'adore ce goût de moisi, dit-elle en se léchant les babines.

Elle jeta le reste de la roue dans le chaudron. Quel gâchis… Malgré lui, Flint laissa échapper un gémissement. Tanis réprima un sourire, comme s'il avait lu dans les pensées du nain.

— Morath se rappelait combien vous l'aimiez, déclara Raistlin. (Il tendit à Chen'tal une bourse rebondie.) Voici le paiement de la faveur que nous sommes venus vous demander.

— A savoir ? s'enquit l'ogresse, curieuse.

Elle prit la bourse et la soupesa, faisant tinter les pièces qu'elle contenait. Un sourire satisfait découvrit ses chicots. Il y avait bien assez pour acheter les services qu'on lui demandait d'ordinaire.

— D'après le Maître Mage, expliqua Raistlin, vous possédez la clé d'un portail ouvrant sur Ogrelien, au bord de la Mer de Sang. Mon frère et deux de nos amis sont retenus prisonniers dans cette partie du monde, et nous craignons pour leur vie. Nous n'avons pas le temps de faire le voyage à cheval ou par bateau, aussi nous sommes venus vous trouver dans l'espoir que vous accéderiez à notre demande.

L'ogresse jeta au jeune mage un regard lourd de reproche.

— Morath ne devrait pas raconter ce genre de choses à n'importe qui. Il sait que ce n'est pas prudent.

Elle baissa la voix et, avec des mines de conspirateur, se pencha vers Raistlin. Son haleine était pire que celle d'un cheval.

— Les portails existent grâce à la seule bienveillance des Hulders. Ils fonctionnent grâce à une magie très puissante et ne doivent pas être utilisés à la légère. Les Hulders s'imposent un certain nombre de conditions.

— Je croyais que c'était un peuple de légende, protesta Tanis.

L'œil violet se tourna vers le demi-elfe, qui avait parlé sans réfléchir. Il se tendit, mais Chen'tal eut l'air plus amusée que froissée par son intervention. Elle se redressa de toute sa hauteur.

— Oh, je pense que les Hulders existent, caqueta-t-elle. Bien sûr, il n'y a pas de preuve, mais c'est aussi le cas pour de nombreuses choses que nous tenons pour acquises.

« On dit que les Hulders sont invisibles le jour et timides la nuit. Pourtant, je crois qu'ils sont toujours près de nous : ils nous surveillent et ils attendent. Il faut vivre selon ses convictions. (Elle haussa les épaules.) Une des miennes est que les Hulders existent. »

L'ogresse reporta son attention sur Raistlin. Son sourire disparut. D'un mouvement du poignet, elle renvoya la bourse dans la direction du jeune mage.

— Un chariot plein de pièces ne suffirait pas à me faire affronter la colère des Hulders, dit-elle. Ce serait risquer ma vie pour peu de choses. (Elle se pencha à nouveau vers Raistlin.) La magie, en revanche...

« Je ne dis pas que je sais où se trouve ce portail, et je ne dis pas non plus que je ne le sais pas. Si je le savais, je demanderais un artefact magique en échange de ma collaboration, et rien d'autre. Etant un élève de Morath, tu en possèdes peut-être un ? »

L'ogresse revint vers son chaudron et se remit à touiller sa mixture. Elle jeta à Raistlin un regard interrogateur. Les épaules du jeune mage s'affaissèrent ; il ouvrit la bouche pour dire quelque chose, puis se ravisa. Le silence devint oppressant.

— Raistlin ! chuchota Tanis en lui faisant signe de le rejoindre.

Flint, que l'ogresse dégoûtait, s'approcha pour écouter ce que disaient ses amis.

— Et la bouteille magique de Tass ? suggéra le demi-elfe. C'est bien un objet magique, non ?

— C'est vrai, admit Raistlin à contrecœur.

— Nous n'en avons plus l'usage, insista Tanis. Chen'tal la voudrait peut-être.

Le jeune mage secoua la tête.

— Tu ne comprends pas.

— J'entends ce que vous dites ! caqueta l'ogresse en portant une main en coupe à son oreille et en penchant la tête vers les trois compagnons.

Ces derniers battirent en retraite à l'autre bout de la grotte. Raistlin baissa la voix.

— Je ne tiens pas tant que ça à cette bouteille, expliqua-t-il, mais la donner à Chen'tal va à l'encontre de l'enseignement que j'ai reçu. L'ogresse traite avec quiconque peut s'offrir ses services. Elle s'est déjà alliée avec des créatures maléfiques, et elle le fera sans doute encore. Aucun artefact magique, si innocent soit-il, ne doit tomber entre ses mains.

— Elle en possède déjà au moins un, protesta Flint : la clé qui ouvre le portail. Ne serait-il pas acceptable de lui donner le nôtre en échange ? De cette façon, elle ne gagnerait pas vraiment de pouvoir.

— Pas bête, approuva Raistlin.

— Après tout, ajouta Tanis, la vie de Caramon est en jeu.

— Et celle de Sturm, fit remarquer Flint. Sans compter celle de Tasslehoff.

Raistlin fronça les sourcils.

— Je suppose que vous avez raison, dit-il.

Il se tourna vers Chen'tal Pyrnee, qui les observait en essayant de surprendre leur conversation. Plongeant la main dans son paquetage, il sortit la bouteille magique. L'ogresse s'en empara et la leva dans ses deux mains, les yeux brillant de convoitise.

— Une bouteille à message ! s'exclama-t-elle. Elle est si jolie ! Je n'en avais pas vu depuis des siècles ! Ce n'est pas très pratique : chaque propriétaire ne peut s'en servir qu'une fois, mais c'est parfois utile. J'espère qu'il y a un message amusant à l'intérieur, pour que je ne m'ennuie pas en attendant.

— Si vous aimez les kenders..., commença Flint avant que Tanis ne le bâillonne de la main.

Chen'tal jeta au nain un regard soupçonneux, mais Raistlin lui fit un signe de tête rassurant.

— C'est un kender qui nous l'a envoyée au cours d'un voyage en mer, et...

— Ooooh ! Un kender ! s'extasia l'ogresse, tout excitée. Ça ne pouvait pas mieux tomber. Ce sont de petites créatures si divertissantes ! Il y a quelques années, j'en avais engagé une pour nettoyer ma grotte et balayer, mais ça n'a pas duré, parce qu'un jour... Enfin, laissons tomber : c'est une trop longue histoire, et je crois me souvenir que vous êtes pressés.

A une vitesse surprenante, Chen'tal se dirigea vers le coffre et l'ouvrit, son large dos masquant le contenu à ses visiteurs. Elle fouilla dans ses affaires et se redressa soudain, triomphante. Dans sa main, une gemme noire pendait au bout d'une chaîne d'argent.

— La voilà ! clama l'ogresse en tendant le bijou à Raistlin. Elle est très puissante, faites appel à votre sagesse avant de l'utiliser.

— L'Amulette des Ténèbres, souffla le jeune mage en contemplant le joyau.

Flint s'approcha pour regarder. A ses yeux, la gemme était semblable à beaucoup d'autres. Il voyait bien que Raistlin semblait y attacher une grande importance.

— Bien sûr, ajouta Chen'tal, je n'ai jamais eu l'occasion de m'en servir personnellement. Je peux donc seulement vous suggérer le meilleur usage à en faire.

— Et moi qui croyais l'Amulette des Ténèbres perdue à tout jamais, murmura Raistlin.

— Perdue, peut-être, répliqua l'ogresse, mais pas à tout jamais. Et puis, je n'ai pas dit que c'était l'Amulette des Ténèbres. Ce que je garantis, c'est qu'elle vous emmènera de l'autre côté du portail, à Ogrelien. Pour le reste..., vous pouvez bien l'appeler Amulette de Tarte à la Rhubarbe, si ça vous chante.

— Comment l'active-t-on ? s'enquit Raistlin.

L'ogresse regarda autour d'elle, méfiante, puis se pencha pour chuchoter quelque chose à l'oreille du jeune mage. Celui-ci hocha la tête, indiquant aux autres qu'il était satisfait. Il empocha l'amulette.

— Où se trouve le portail ? demanda Tanis.

— C'est très simple...

Chen'tal Pyrnee énonça des instructions si longues et si embrouillées que la tête du demi-elfe lui tourna bientôt. Il était question de marcher vers l'est, de prendre à gauche après un certain rocher, de suivre la lisière des arbres jusqu'à un précipice et...

— Je connais cet endroit, déclara Flint.

L'ogresse s'interrompit pour dévisager le nain.

— J'ai traîné dans le coin pendant une bonne trentaine d'années, expliqua fièrement celui-ci. Il n'y a pas un pic que je n'ai escaladé ou au moins vu de loin.

— Dans ce cas, dépêchons-nous, dit Tanis, impatient.

Raistlin s'inclina devant l'Oracle.

— Merci encore de votre aide.

Les trois amis sortirent de la caverne à reculons, sans quitter du regard l'ogresse qui remuait sa mixture d'une main en contemplant l'artefact de l'autre.

— Merci à vous pour la bouteille ! cria-t-elle alors que ses invités disparaissaient dans le tunnel. Bonne chance avec le portail ! Et si vous croisez ce vieux sacripant de Morath, dites-lui de ne plus m'envoyer personne pendant les dix années à venir ! J'ai de quoi m'occuper en attendant !

*

* *

Ce soir-là, les compagnons étaient si fatigués qu'ils campèrent à quelques lieues de la caverne de l'Oracle. Tanis alla ramasser du bois mort pour le feu, tandis que Flint préparait un brouet d'herbes sauvages. Raistlin but sans un mot, le regard dans le vague et le visage livide. Puis, voyant que le nain ne cessait de marmonner dans sa barbe, il lança :

— Si tu veux rebrousser chemin, fais-le ! Toi aussi, Tanis ! Je suis capable de trouver le portail et de me rendre seul à Ogrelien !

— Je n'ai jamais dit que j'avais changé d'avis, protesta Flint, vexé. Je parlais seulement du chemin que nous devrons parcourir.

— Il faut grimper jusqu'à une corniche au sommet d'une falaise à pic, expliqua Tanis, plus diplomate.

— Se trouve-t-elle loin d'ici ? demanda Raistlin, l'air las.

— Pas très, répondit Flint. Ce n'est pas le problème. J'arriverai à l'escalader, et Tanis aussi. (Il étudia la silhouette frêle du jeune mage.) Mais elle n'est pas très, euh, praticable pour quelqu'un dans ta, euh, condition.

— Se trouve-t-elle loin d'ici ? répéta Raistlin, tendu.

— Non : à une heure de marche, peut-être deux, répondit Tanis.

— Bien.

— Comment savoir si l'Oracle nous a dit la vérité ? grommela Flint. Nous perdons peut-être notre temps.

Raistlin fit un geste insouciant.

— Elle a dit la vérité, ne t'en fais pas. D'après Morath, quand Chen'tal Pyrnee choisit de négocier, elle le fait toujours honnêtement.

— Admettons. Et la falaise ? insista Flint.

— Ne t'inquiète pas pour moi.

Raistlin pinça les lèvres, l'air obstiné, et le nain comprit qu'il n'en tirerait rien de plus.

Flint se fourra dans son sac de couchage : quelques minutes plus tard, ses ronflements sonores envahirent la petite clairière.

Lunitari et Solinari brillaient dans le ciel, leurs deux trajectoires jumelles ne se croisant pas à cette période de l'année. Des centaines d'étoiles piquetaient la voûte céleste.

L'été touchait à sa fin ; le feuillage des arbres s'éclaircissait. Des rochers aux formes torturées se dressaient sur le sol en pente. Au loin, la neige qui couvrait les montagnes brillait doucement au clair de lune. Seuls les cris de quelques créatures nocturnes venaient troubler la sérénité du lieu. Un vent léger effleurait les frondaisons comme une caresse.

Tanis inspira profondément. Il aimait cette odeur de pin, de terre et d'air de la montagne mêlés. Il jeta un coup d'œil à Raistlin… Perdu dans ses pensées, le jeune mage semblait si fragile que le moindre coup de vent aurait pu le renverser. Il poussa un soupir, se leva et fit les cent pas autour du feu de camp.

Tanis était conscient des limites physiques de Raistlin… Mais le jeune mage partait souvent à l'aventure avec Caramon, et à plus d'une reprise, il avait surpris dans son regard la flamme qu'il aimait tant chez Kitiara. Flint avait tort de le sous-estimer, songea le demi-elfe.

A cet instant, Raistlin leva la tête. Comme s'il avait lu dans les pensées de son ami, il lui jeta un regard plein de défi.

— Ce qui préoccupe Flint, expliqua gentiment Tanis, c'est la perspective de traverser la Mer de Sang. Il sait que tu arriveras jusque-là, mais il déteste l'eau depuis sa malheureuse aventure sur le Lac de Cristalmir.

Raistlin rit et se rassit. Ses épaules s'affaissèrent sous le poids des efforts consentis depuis deux jours.

— Peut-être, dit-il doucement.

Quelques mois plus tôt, Flint et Tasslehoff avaient organisé un tour du Lac de Cristalmir. Caramon et Sturm avaient bu les paroles du nain qui leur racontait ses aventures pendant que Raistlin cherchait sur la berge les herbes nécessaires à ses sorts. C'était là que Tasslehoff avait parlé pour la première fois de son ami Asa, et de l'herboriste minotaure résidant en Ergoth Méridional.

Un stupide incident avait failli gâcher cette sortie, une des premières du groupe. Ayant « trouvé » une barque, Tass avait persuadé les autres de l'accompagner dans une promenade nautique. Non loin du rivage, Caramon avait repéré un gros poisson verdâtre. Avec son impulsivité coutumière, il avait parié qu'il l'attraperait à mains nues… mais il s'était penché trop loin, faisant chavirer le bateau.

Tass et Sturm étaient parvenus à remettre l'embarcation à l'endroit. Flint avait plongé à la rescousse de Caramon qui, ne sachant pas nager, avait coulé comme une pierre.

Les minutes avaient passé. Enfin, n'y tenant plus, Tass et Sturm avaient sauté à l'eau. Le jeune Solamnique avait ramené à la surface un Caramon à moitié noyé, pendant que le kender rendait le même service à Flint. Toussant et crachant, le nain avait juré qu'il ne remettrait plus les pieds sur un bateau pour le restant de ses jours.

— Flint a été héroïque de plonger, car il nage comme un fer à repasser, fit remarquer Tanis.

— Héroïque ou idiot, grommela Raistlin, non sans une certaine douceur.

Il se glissa dans son sac de couchage.

— Ces deux mots vont souvent bien ensemble, gloussa Tanis.

Le demi-elfe leva la tête vers le ciel, admirant la beauté des étoiles.

— Flint a mentionné l'incident plusieurs fois, reprit-il. Il restera à jamais gravé dans sa mémoire. Le pire pour lui, c'est d'avoir été sauvé par Tasslehoff. Flint lui doit la vie, et rembourser cette dette est sans doute la seule raison qui lui fera traverser la Mer de Sang.

Tanis marqua une pause. Le visage de Kitiara surgit dans son esprit, accompagné par une vague d'émotions confuses. Jamais encore le demi-elfe n'avait parlé de sa maîtresse avec Raistlin. Le moment était peut-être bien choisi.

— Dis-moi, Raist, commença-t-il.

Il se tourna vers le jeune mage et vit que celui-ci s'était endormi.

*
* *

Le lendemain, après avoir suivi un chemin aussi étroit qu'escarpé, les compagnons atteignirent l'endroit décrit par l'ogresse.

Debout au fond d'un ravin, Flint désigna une série de promontoires rocheux qui s'élevaient vers le ciel telle une forteresse de grès. Au sommet, on distinguait une corniche de pierre qui avançait vers une impressionnante chaîne de montagnes.

Le nain prit la tête du petit groupe et escalada la falaise en s'aidant de la maigre végétation qui poussait dans les anfractuosités. Tanis venait ensuite, puis Raistlin. Tous trois étaient encordés.

La paroi qui les dominait devait faire plus de trois cents pieds de haut. Flint progressait méthodiquement : il enfonçait au-dessus de sa tête des pitons métalliques longs comme le bras et s'y attachait avant de chercher une nouvelle prise. Raistlin avait été bien inspiré de lui faire emporter ce matériel.

Grâce au nain qui leur ouvrait la voie, Tanis et le mage avaient moins de mal à grimper. Pourtant, l'escalade restait ardue, les bonnes prises se révélaient peu nombreuses. En approchant du sommet, la température se rafraîchit considérablement ; des rafales cinglèrent les compagnons, rendant l'ascension encore plus difficile.

Flint dut admettre que Raistlin avait du courage. Le jeune mage serrait les dents sans se plaindre. Une seule fois, son pied glissa. Tanis eut le réflexe de tendre la corde et il put se rétablir. D'un geste de la main, il fit signe à Flint de continuer.

Deux heures plus tard, les compagnons arrivèrent au sommet. Ils se laissèrent tomber sur le sol, à bout de souffle, avant d'évaluer du regard ce qui les attendait. La corniche était juste assez large pour les laisser passer. Elle surplombait une gorge déchiquetée, dont le fond disparaissait sous un nuage de brume.

Flint se releva sur ses jambes tremblantes. Il réalisa que les rafales provenaient de deux directions à la fois, et que la corniche se trouvait au milieu d'un maelström de forces physiques. Les vents déséquilibraient le nain. Il fit signe aux autres de l'attendre et rampa jusqu'à l'extrémité de la corniche, où il fixa un piton. Puis il y attacha sa corde et regarda en bas.

— Est-ce là que le portail est censé se trouver ? demanda-t-il, sceptique.

Il dut répéter sa question plus fort : le vent avait empêché Raistlin de l'entendre.

— Oui, répondit le jeune mage d'une voix rauque.

Tanis ne dit rien. Ça ne lui plaisait pas, mais ils n'avaient pas le choix. Le demi-elfe ramassa un caillou et le laissa tomber au fond du précipice. Ses amis tendirent l'oreille. Une minute après, Flint crut entendre un léger bruit en contrebas.

— Pas de portail, constata-t-il, dégoûté.

— C'est normal, hurla Raistlin. Il n'accepte pas d'objet inanimé s'il n'est pas porté par une créature vivante. De toute façon, il ne s'ouvrira pas tant que je n'aurai pas lancé le bon sort.

Un silence. Tanis demanda :

— Et comment saurons-nous si ça a fonctionné ou pas ?

Raistlin ne répondit pas. Le vent s'engouffrant dans leurs cheveux, les trois hommes contemplèrent les profondeurs insondables qui s'ouvraient à leurs pieds. La corde de Flint les empêchait de tomber, mais même ainsi, ils devaient lutter pour conserver leur équilibre.

— On ne peut pas savoir ! cria enfin Flint.

— C'est vrai ? interrogea Tanis en se tournant vers Raistlin.

— Oui.

Le nain et le demi-elfe se regardèrent. Flint leva les yeux au ciel. Tanis dégaina son couteau.

— Dans ce cas, lance ton sort.

Raistlin ferma les yeux pour se concentrer. Il murmura quelques paroles anciennes, incompréhensibles pour ses amis. Puis, en commun, il hurla :

— Portail, ouvre-toi !

Tanis trancha la corde qui les retenait au piton. Il rangea son couteau. Comme un seul homme, les trois compagnons sautèrent dans le vide en se tenant par les épaules. Un cri irrépressible s'échappa de leurs lèvres.

Tête la première, ils plongèrent en direction des rochers déchiquetés... Vers une mort certaine.

CHAPITRE VI

Sturm et Caramon dérivèrent pendant des jours. N'ayant aucune idée de l'endroit où ils se trouvaient, ils n'essayèrent pas de nager dans une direction particulière. De toute façon, les cordes qui les ligotaient au mât avaient rétréci dans l'eau salée. Ils arrivaient tout juste à garder le menton hors de l'eau et à agiter les jambes pour ne pas couler.

Au-dessus d'eux, le ciel restait gris et plombé ; le brouillard couvrait l'océan à perte de vue tel un impénétrable linceul. Malgré tout, il faisait plus chaud qu'en plein été à Solace. La chaleur étouffait les deux hommes comme une couverture mouillée, brûlant sans relâche leur peau et leurs yeux.

La tombée de la nuit n'améliorait guère la situation. La température baissait, mais Sturm et Caramon se retrouvaient dans les ténèbres. Ils arrivaient à peine à se distinguer : même les lunes restaient invisibles dans le ciel monolithique et oppressant.

L'eau boueuse et tiède dans laquelle baignaient les deux hommes répandait une odeur saumâtre. Malgré l'absence de vent, de fortes vagues, sans doute créées par un courant sous-marin, agitaient la surface.

Sturm et Caramon ne virent aucun signe de vie. Pas de bateau à l'horizon, ni d'oiseaux de mer ou de poissons.

Pendant deux jours, ils n'eurent rien à boire ni à manger et ne purent prendre le moindre repos.

Alors ils battirent des pieds pour se maintenir à flot, accrochés au tronçon de mât, perdant peu à peu leurs forces et leur courage.

« — Ça pourrait être pire », avait dit Caramon le premier jour.

« — Comment ? » avait répondu Sturm.

« — Ça pourrait être Flint au lieu de moi, avait grimacé son ami. C'est à ma connaissance la seule personne au monde qui nage plus mal. »

Sturm avait hoché la tête en souriant, pour ne pas penser au sort qui les attendait. Vingt-quatre heures plus tard, la faim et la douleur le tenaillaient sans relâche.

— Je me demande..., commença-t-il.

— Quoi ? s'enquit Caramon.

— Où sommes-nous ?

Le troisième jour, le brouillard s'épaissit encore. Vers midi, les deux jeunes gens y voyaient à peine à dix pieds alentour. Des craquements et des grognements se firent entendre. Des cris aigus déchirèrent l'air moite.

Des poutres brisées et des morceaux de bastingage gorgés d'eau heurtèrent Caramon et Sturm. Ce dernier se pencha : avec les dents, il arracha au bois pourri une touffe d'algues qu'il commença mâcher.

— Que fais-tu ? s'enquit Caramon, éberlué.

— Bah, ça a l'air comestible, répondit Sturm, la voix rauque. Qui sait d'où viendra notre prochain repas ?

Les algues avaient une texture caoutchouteuse et un goût amer, mais les jeunes gens n'étaient pas en position de faire les difficiles. Caramon réfléchit quelques instants avant d'imiter son compagnon. Il déchiqueta une poignée d'algues à coups de dents rageurs, s'efforçant de ne pas penser à ce qu'il faisait. Hélas, la nausée fut plus forte. Il recracha tout. Sturm lui jeta un regard sévère.

Les grognements et les cris s'intensifièrent, suivis par un grand choc. On eût dit qu'un navire venait de s'écraser sur des brisants invisibles et que sa coque s'y déchirait avec des gémissements sinistres.

Des gouttes de pluie se mêlèrent au brouillard et coulèrent sur le visage de Sturm et de Caramon. Les vagues se calmèrent, la mer devint un désert gris et fantomatique.

— Que vois-tu ? demanda Caramon, un tremblement dans la voix.

— Rien, répondit Sturm. Et toi ?

— Non plus.

Soudain, une énorme masse jaillit du brouillard. Caramon paniqua, croyant qu'il s'agissait de quelque monstre marin. Puis la vision du jeune homme s'éclaircit : malgré son épuisement, il réalisa qu'il s'agissait d'épaves à la dérive.

Les coques d'un blanc malsain, comme le ventre de poissons morts, étaient criblées de trous béants, leurs poutres étant tachées de sang, de rouille et d'une matière gluante verdâtre. D'étranges coquillages y étaient accrochés. Des lambeaux de voiles pendaient aux mâts. Il semblait impossible que l'ensemble flotte encore.

— Regarde ! cria Caramon.

Une forme sombre glissait vers les deux hommes : le plus gros navire de la flotte fantôme. Sur son pont, trois squelettes se balançaient à un poteau. Une silhouette solitaire, enveloppée d'une cape, se tenait à la proue. Elle se tourna vers Sturm et Caramon, baissa la tête et tendit un doigt vers eux. Tandis que le bateau se rapprochait, Caramon distingua les yeux de la créature : des braises rougeoyantes dans des orbites creuses.

Le navire s'approcha. Les deux amis auraient pu le toucher si leurs mains avaient été libres. Des planches pourrissantes jaillissaient des flancs du navire… Caramon dut rentrer la tête dans les épaules pour ne pas se faire assommer.

Sur son passage, le navire fantôme sema des bouts de bois qui s'écrasèrent dans l'eau autour de Caramon et de Sturm. La silhouette noire ne bougea pas, mais suivit les deux amis des yeux. Sturm se sentit frémir sous son terrible regard.

Aussi soudainement qu'elle était apparue, la flotte fut de nouveau engloutie par le brouillard. L'eau saumâtre s'agita dans son sillage, le vent se leva et souffla en gémissant. Un fort courant ballotta les deux hommes. Des vagues s'écrasèrent sur eux, emplissant leur nez et leur bouche.

Avec ses dernières forces, Caramon battit des jambes pour garder sa tête à la surface. Haletant, il vit que son ami était en mauvais posture. Ses poumons semblaient sur le point d'exploser et il avait du mal à lutter contre le courant.

Sturm ne paniqua pas. Il regrettait de mourir si tôt, mais la mer s'était montrée un adversaire valeureux. Le trépas lui offrirait un repos bienvenu. Il sentit les vagues se refermer sur sa tête pour ce qu'il crut être la dernière fois, lorsque les turbulences se calmèrent soudain. La mer redevint d'huile…

Sturm et Caramon refirent surface, crachant et toussant, et s'accrochèrent au mât qui les emprisonnait mais leur sauvait la vie. Sturm était à demi noyé, au bord de l'évanouissement. Son compagnon, épuisé, luttait contre l'envie de s'endormir.

Pourtant, ils n'abandonnèrent pas. Le matin du cinquième jour, ils étaient toujours conscients, et sérieusement mal en point. Leurs lèvres étaient parcheminées, leur visage brûlé par le soleil. Ils baignaient dans l'eau, mais leur gorge était aussi sèche que du bois.

Ils continuèrent à dériver, ballottés par les vagues brunes. La mer impitoyable s'étendait à perte de vue dans toutes les directions… Caramon avait d'horribles crampes dans les jambes. Sturm avait les yeux si gonflés qu'ils s'étaient réduits à de simples fentes. Leurs efforts incessants pour garder la tête hors de l'eau avaient troublé leur esprit.

— Si... si seulement je pouvais défaire ces liens, balbutia Caramon. Tu aurais une meilleure chance de t'en sortir sans moi.

— Tu plaisantes ! s'exclama Sturm, choqué. Je ne t'abandonnerai jamais ! Ce serait déshonorant !

— De toute façon, soupira son ami, la question ne se pose pas.

Quelques secondes d'un silence résigné suivirent.

— C'est à cause de ce mât, grommela enfin Sturm. Il nous maintient à flot, mais juste assez pour nous torturer. J'aimerais mieux me noyer pour de bon, et qu'on n'en parle plus ! (Le jeune homme regarda autour de lui.) Tiens, les revoilà.

Depuis quelques heures, deux prédateurs aquatiques décrivaient des cercles autour des compagnons. Leurs yeux noirs et ronds émergeaient par intermittence lorsqu'ils faisaient surface pour respirer.

Caramon et Sturm distinguaient leur peau épaisse et noueuse, leurs pattes palmées, leurs puissantes mâchoires garnies de plusieurs rangées de dents triangulaires. Les créatures mesuraient au moins dix pieds de long, mais elles maintenaient une distance respectable entre elles et leurs proies.

— Des vodyanois, cousins des ombres des roches, commenta Caramon. Ils vivent dans les hauts-fonds. Pourquoi n'attaquent-ils pas ?

— Parce qu'ils sont malins mais couards, répondit Sturm. S'ils étaient plus nombreux, ils nous auraient déjà taillés en pièces. Ils savent que nous nous fatiguons : il est plus simple d'attendre…

Le jeune homme ne pensait pas que son ami et lui verraient le coucher du soleil. Il avait l'estomac vide, ses jambes n'étaient plus que des poids morts. Quant à Caramon, il somnolait, le menton posé sur le mât. Sturm voulut le mettre en garde, lui dire de ne pas s'endormir, mais ses lèvres desséchées refusèrent de prononcer un mot.

Une ombre dansa sur la mer. Levant la tête, le Solamnique crut voir un point noir décrire des cercles dans le ciel. De quoi pouvait-il s'agir ? Un autre prédateur ? Un oiseau géant, peut-être ?

Quelque chose tomba dans l'eau juste devant Sturm : un objet rectangulaire de plusieurs pouces d'épaisseur. Le jeune homme tendit le cou et l'attrapa avec les dents. C'était presque aussi dur que du bois, mais il reconnut le goût du pain. Calant la miche contre l'épaule de Caramon, il en arracha avidement plusieurs bouchées.

Son ami s'agita et ouvrit les yeux. Sturm le laissa prendre le pain et se nourrir son tour. Ça ne valait pas les patates épicées d'Otik, mais dans les circonstances présentes, ça leur parut presque aussi bon. Caramon dévora sa part à belles dents.

Un croassement s'éleva au-dessus des deux hommes. Ils levèrent la tête et virent la tache sombre disparaître à l'horizon. La tiédeur de l'eau les engourdissait, la monotonie des vagues endormait leurs sens. Ils recommencèrent à dériver en silence.

Sturm s'assoupit et rêva de son père, Angriff de Lumlane. Il s'était juré de le retrouver, mais il ne possédait que de maigres indices, telles des pierres affleurant à la surface d'une mare. Chaque fois qu'il posait le pied sur l'une, elle se transformait en nénuphar, et le jeune homme s'enfonçait dans l'eau.

Caramon rêva d'une auberge douillette et d'une servante peu avare de ses charmes. Aucun des deux hommes ne remarqua que le brouillard se dissipait et que l'eau perdait sa couleur boueuse.

*
* *

Tasslehoff Racle-Pieds faisait les cent pas dans sa cellule, située dans une annexe souterraine du palais. Il semblait être le seul prisonnier dans cette partie du bâtiment. Dogz lui avait dit qu'il jouissait d'un traitement spécial. Le kender en était très fier, même si le traitement en question se composait surtout de tortures variées.

Une fois par jour, Dogz apportait à Tass une assiette de gruau. Malgré son esprit ouvert, le kender trouvait ça infect. Le reste du temps, l'inquisition faisait son office.

Cleef-Eth voulait savoir pourquoi Tass avait acheté de la jalopine à l'herboriste minotaure Argotz. Il avait récupéré la bourse contenant les herbes, ainsi que les autres possessions du kender, mais c'étaient les *raisons* de l'acquisition qui l'intéressaient par-dessus tout.

Tass ne pouvait ni ne voulait leur répondre. Primo, seul Raistlin savait pourquoi il avait besoin de jalopine. Secundo, Argotz avait été assassiné, et c'étaient sans doute les responsables de sa disparition qui avaient provoqué la (très intéressante) tempête magique.

Aussi avait-il décidé de ne pas coopérer.

Cela faisait maintenant plusieurs jours que les minotaures le torturaient. Pauvres gros bœufs stupides ! Ils avaient besoin de méthode, ne sachant pas comment lui faire assez mal pour qu'il parle sans pour autant le tuer... Et ils ne voulaient pas le mutiler de façon permanente, car ça aurait déplu à un quidam appelé le Maître de la Nuit. Autrement dit, ils ne pouvaient pas menacer de lui couper la langue. Dommage pour eux, songeait Tass, car ç'aurait un moyen de pression très efficace.

Le bourreau avait passé deux jours à bourrer le kender de coups, sans obtenir d'autre résultat que de magnifiques ecchymoses.

Au bout d'un moment, Tass résolut de l'aider.

— Pourquoi ne pas me pendre par ma queue-de-cheval ? suggéra-t-il aimablement.

Cleef-Eth trouva l'idée bonne. Le kender passa vingt-quatre heures suspendu à un crochet, au plafond de la cellule. Son visage prit la couleur d'une betterave, et il dut admettre que ça faisait vraiment mal. Il félicita le bourreau, mais ne parla pas pour autant.

— Coupez ma queue-de-cheval pour me faire honte, improvisa-t-il ensuite. Un kender aux cheveux courts est une sorte de lépreux social, un peu comme une vache sans cornes.

Les minotaures rasèrent la tête de Tass, qui en fut mortifié pendant cinq minutes, jusqu'à ce qu'il réalise que seules de grosses vaches putrides le verraient dans cet état. Toujours poli, il complimenta le bourreau sur la virtuosité de sa tonte.

Cleef-Eth et son exécuteur des basses œuvres avaient quelques idées bien à eux en matière de torture, et certaines n'étaient pas dénuées d'intérêt. Ils tentèrent d'affamer le kender, qui se passa sans problème de l'infâme gruau mais regretta les visites de Dogz.

Ils lui cassèrent les doigts un à un, certains à coups de marteau, d'autres en les pliant en arrière. Ça, ça faisait mal. Les doigts longs et souples d'un kender étaient comme les os d'un bébé humain : ils guérissaient vite. Le sachant, Tass faisait de son mieux pour endurer honorablement la torture, comme l'aurait sans doute réussi son ami Sturm.

En parlant du Solamnique... Où étaient-ils, lui et Caramon ? Morts ? Pendant que le bourreau le torturait, Tass se concentra sur ses compagnons. Il s'inquiétait pour eux : sans doute avaient-ils besoin qu'il vole à leur rescousse. Dès qu'il serait sorti d'affaire, il partirait à leur recherche.

Les minotaures immergèrent Tass dans de l'eau glacée. Ils durent s'y mettre à trois pour le maintenir au fond d'une énorme baignoire. Le kender se débattit comme un beau diable et retint sa respiration le plus longtemps possible, jusqu'à ce qu'il ouvre la bouche malgré lui. Il dut admettre qu'il avait presque failli se noyer.

Pourtant, il continua à se taire.

Cleef-Eth répétait toujours la même question :

— Es-tu un mage ? Pourquoi recherchais-tu ce composant ? Si tu n'es pas un mage, pour qui travailles-tu ?

Tass ne pouvait répondre. Il ne voulait pas attirer d'ennuis à Raistlin. Le jeune mage n'était pas très marrant, mais Tass l'aimait bien, et il avait le sentiment que Raistlin aurait mal supporté la torture.

Puis le kender fut abandonné à lui-même pendant plusieurs jours. Dogz reprit ses visites. La première fois qu'il apporta une écuelle pleine, il la posa devant les barreaux de la cellule et, se relevant, la poussa à l'intérieur du bout du pied.

L'œil droit de Tass était si gonflé qu'il ne pouvait plus l'ouvrir, le gauche était couvert par une croûte de sang séché. Il manquait singulièrement d'appétit, aussi ne se précipita-t-il pas pour manger. Il ne prit même pas la peine de lever la tête vers Dogz.

Quelques heures plus tard, quand il se décida enfin à ramasser l'écuelle, il vit que celle-ci contenait du porridge au lieu de l'habituel gruau… Un vrai festin !

Pendant plusieurs jours, Dogz apporta des repas chauds et Tass se remit lentement. Ses plaies commencèrent à se fermer, ses cheveux à repousser. Un étrange dialogue s'instaura à nouveau.

— Pourquoi ont-ils arrêté de me torturer ? demanda le kender.

Dogz jeta un coup d'œil nerveux par-dessus son épaule.

— Je ne sais pas si je devrais te le dire, marmonna-t-il.

— Pourquoi pas ? répondit Tass innocemment. Tu me racontes tout le reste. Tu m'as déjà parlé de ton frère, qui s'est fait tuer au cours d'une rixe de taverne, de ton oncle, qui appartenait au Cercle Suprême avant de mourir dans l'arène, de la femme de ton cousin, qui s'est disputée avec un forgeron et a reçu un coup de... Hé, as-tu déjà pensé que ta famille était peut-être sous le coup d'une malédiction ? On dirait que personne ne vit très vieux.

Tass s'interrompit pour lécher sa cuillère. Il savait par expérience que Dogz ne lui couperait pas la parole.

— Alors, répéta-t-il, pourquoi ont-ils arrêté de me torturer ?

— Parce que le Maître de la Nuit envoie un haut émissaire pour t'interroger, expliqua Dogz.

— Un quoi ?

— Un des chefs de son culte.

— Oh. C'est une bonne ou une mauvaise nouvelle ?

Le minotaure fronça les sourcils.

— Je n'en sais rien, dit-il, sincère, mais c'est un grand honneur pour Lacynos de le recevoir. Il est rare que le Maître de la Nuit dépêche un des Très-Hauts. Je ne me souviens même plus de la dernière fois que c'est arrivé.

— Pourquoi ne se déplace-t-il pas en personne ? s'enquit Tass.

Dogz rit, découvrant ses grandes dents jaunies.

— Le Maître de la Nuit quitte rarement Karthay. C'est son domaine.

— L'as-tu déjà vu ?

— Bien sûr que non.

— Alors, comment sais-tu qu'il existe ?

Dogz se renfrogna.

— Ce n'est pas drôle, ami Tass. Le Maître de la Nuit est le plus grand prêtre de notre religion, notre lien direct avec le dieu Sargonnas.

— Sargonnas, consort de Takhisis, réfléchit le kender à voix haute.

Il repoussa son bol.

— C'est ça, approuva Dogz, enthousiaste. Fidèle serviteur de la Reine des Ténèbres. Je ne te savais pas aussi calé sur les dieux de Krynn.

— Oh, je touche un peu à tout, avoua Tass. Je ramasse des informations partout où je passe. Dis-moi, que peut bien faire le Maître de la Nuit à Karthay ? Ça doit être passionnant, pour qu'il n'en sorte jamais. Je m'ennuierais à mourir si je devais toujours rester au même endroit...

Dogz hésita, puis secoua la tête. Un cri retentit en haut de l'escalier conduisant aux cellules. Tass reconnut la voix de Sarkis, qui ne se trouvait jamais loin, surtout quand il avait une chance de harceler son cousin.

Embarrassé, Dogz ramassa l'écuelle et la cuillère de Tass. Sans un mot, il battit en retraite.

*
* *

Un jour, peu de temps après, Dogz recommença à apporter du gruau. Tass le prit comme un signe que l'émissaire tant attendu venait d'arriver.

Il ne se trompait pas. Un groupe de minotaures descendit bientôt les marches et vint se planter devant sa cellule pour l'observer. Il y avait là, entre autres, le bourreau, Sarkis, Cleef-Eth… et un nouveau venu qui ressemblait à un chamane.

Jeune et musclé, il était vêtu de fourrures et portait une coiffe de plumes. Ses cornes immenses effleuraient le plafond.

Il s'avança vers Tasslehoff.

— Tâche de bien te tenir, kender, gronda Sarkis. Tu as un visiteur important.

Irrité, le chamane fronça les sourcils. Cleef-Eth jeta un regard furieux à Sarkis.

Toujours heureux de recevoir des visites, Tass fit de son mieux pour avoir l'air amusant. Il était couvert de plaies et de bosses… Avec ses vêtements en lambeaux et ses pieds nus criblés d'ampoules, il savait qu'il semblait pitoyable. Pourtant, il planta son regard dans celui du chamane.

— Nous avons tout essayé sur cette petite vermine, Fesz, geignit Cleef-Eth. Il refuse de coopérer. Je pense qu'il vaudrait mieux s'en débarrasser une fois pour toutes.

— On ne te paye pas pour penser, répliqua sèchement le chamane. Sinon, crois-moi, tu crèverais de faim.

Cleef-Eth écarquilla les yeux, indigné, mais ne répondit pas.

Fesz s'accroupit pour se mettre à la hauteur du kender. Tass sentit son haleine putride, ses aisselles nauséabondes et l'odeur méphitique de ses fourrures non tannées... Mais il était trop bien élevé pour en faire la remarque.

— Tu es si vif et si mignon, ronronna le chamane en tendant une grande main vers la joue de Tass.

Sa voix eut un effet apaisant sur le kender.

— Tu n'es pas notre ennemi mais notre ami, poursuivit le minotaure. Je le vois. Je suis désolé que l'on t'ait si mal traité.

Il secoua la tête d'un air désolé.

— Ces rustres emploient vraiment des méthodes préhistoriques. Mon cœur se serre à l'idée de tout ce qu'ils t'ont fait endurer... C'est le Maître de la Nuit en personne qui m'envoie : je suis venu dès que j'ai eu vent de ton triste sort.

Tass écoutait de toutes ses oreilles. Les mots de Fesz le berçaient. Au fond de ses yeux gros comme des poings, il croyait entrevoir une lueur de bonté qui lui redonnait de l'espoir.

— Je t'ai apporté un fortifiant, Tasslehoff Racle-Pieds, reprit le chamane. Il agira plus efficacement que n'importe quelle torture. Il fera de toi mon ami, de mes amis tes amis, de mes ennemis tes ennemis. Tu aimes œuvrer pour le Bien. Cela te mettra de mon côté, celui du Mal.

La grande main de Fesz se referma autour de la gorge de Tass, qu'elle maintint fermement sans l'empêcher de respirer. Le kender tenta en vain de résister. Le minotaure l'attira vers lui.

Hypnotisé par son regard, Tass ne le vit pas faire signe à un de ses serviteurs. Celui-ci apporta un gobelet dont Fesz se saisit en ouvrant la bouche du kender.

Tass sentit un liquide vert doré lui glisser dans la gorge. *Pas mauvais,* songea-t-il.

Devenir maléfique ? L'idée l'intéressait. Ce fut sa dernière pensée consciente. Alors que la potion faisait effet, son menton tomba sur sa poitrine, et Fesz le laissa s'effondrer sur le sol. Le minotaure se releva et toisa le kender d'un air satisfait.

— Mettez-le dans la chambre d'ami de ma suite, ordonna-t-il. Je m'en occuperai personnellement. A partir de cet instant, il est l'un d'entre nous.

Cleef-Eth se tourna pour donner ses instructions, mais Fesz le saisit par l'épaule et lui flanqua un coup de poing. Le minotaure tituba en arrière, se tenant la mâchoire, sans oser riposter. Mieux, il s'inclina légèrement, pendant que Sarkis et les autres réprimaient une grimace sardonique.

— Ce kender n'est pas un mage ! gronda Fesz, furieux. N'importe quel imbécile s'en serait aperçu.

*

* *

Depuis des siècles, on disait l'île de Karthay abandonnée. Peu de voyageurs s'y arrêtaient, craignant de subir les assauts d'insectes géants, de nuées de sauterelles ou d'ombres des roches… Moins encore survivaient aux vents hurlants, aux tempêtes de sable, à la chaleur impitoyable le jour et au froid pénétrant la nuit.

Des siècles plus tôt, une cité légendaire se dressait sur cette île. Elle abritait des bâtiments somptueux, des rues propres et bien ordonnées, une civilisation florissante. On vantait partout sur Krynn son université et son immense bibliothèque.

Puis le Cataclysme avait ravagé la ville. A présent, la cité gisait sous une falaise effondrée. Çà et là, des ruines encore reconnaissables jaillissaient du sol. De nombreux tunnels formaient un réseau souterrain infesté de gaz empoisonnés et de sables mouvants.

Le climat inhospitalier de l'endroit en faisait une résidence idéale pour le Maître de la Nuit. Malgré quelques contretemps, son plan pour invoquer Sargonnas, le ramener sur Krynn et forger des alliances avec les autres races maléfiques progressait à vue d'œil.

Le grand prêtre des minotaures avait installé son sanctuaire dans une zone déblayée, là où se dressait autrefois la bibliothèque de Karthay. De cet antre millénaire du savoir, il ne restait que quelques colonnes et une poignée de parchemins balayés par le vent. Le Maître de la Nuit avait fait allumer des feux tout autour.

Non loin de lui, satisfaisant le moindre de ses caprices, buvant chacune de ses paroles, se tenaient deux des Très-Hauts. Autour du périmètre du camp, à une distance respectueuse, attendaient un groupe de disciples et une petite armée de fidèles qui restaient à Karthay pour protéger le Maître...

Cette nuit-là, le grand prêtre recevait un étrange visiteur, porteur d'informations vitales. Une créature à la peau écailleuse s'assit sur un muret en ruine pour avaler une chope d'eau-de-vie. Seuls le Maître de la Nuit et les Très-Hauts connaissaient sa véritable apparence, les autres minotaures ne distinguaient qu'une silhouette enveloppée d'une cape.

— Je me suis déguisé, dit le nouveau venu d'une voix nasale. J'ai interrogé tous les habitants de ce trou : personne ne savait où ils étaient allés, ni ce qu'ils avaient été faire.

Une odeur de soufre émanait de la créature. Portée par le vent, elle vint chatouiller les narines des minotaures qui, bien que maître ès effluves corporels, levèrent le nez en reniflant.

Le Maître de la Nuit écoutait son visiteur en se balançant doucement d'un pied sur l'autre. Il avait posé une lourde cape de fourrure sur ses épaules ; de petites clochettes tintaient à chacun de ses gestes.

Le vent soufflait dans les ruines, projetant du sable et de la poussière. La chaleur insupportable de la journée avait laissé place à un froid mordant. Le Maître de la Nuit soupira.

— Grâce à mes contacts, siffla la créature, j'ai découvert que l'un d'eux avait envoyé un message à une femelle... Sa sœur, apparemment. Elle est en route pour votre île !

— Vraiment ?

La créature jeta un coup d'œil prudent par-dessus son épaule. Elle se pencha vers son interlocuteur pour chuchoter que la nommée Kitiara avait bien reçu le message, et qu'elle était partie sur-le-champ. Elle atteindrait Karthay dans quelques jours.

La créature cligna de l'œil et rassura le Maître de la Nuit : ses sources étaient fiables, il pouvait lui faire confiance. Gonflé de fierté, l'étrange visiteur se resservit une chope. Son interlocuteur le dévisagea, impassible.

— Vous croyez, marmonna-t-il, que celui que je recherche est le jeune mage de Solace, pas le prisonnier de Lacynos ?

— Oui, et il vient justement de disparaître, confirma la créature. Deux de ses amis et lui ont quitté Solace il y a quelques jours. Il se peut qu'ils entendent vous rendre visite.

Le Maître de la Nuit leva la tête vers les cieux comme pour lire un présage dans les étoiles. Il avait confiance. Si quelque chose se préparait, ce n'était rien de sérieux.

Ces gens constituaient des obstacles temporaires. Fesz allait s'occuper du prisonnier de Lacynos, et lui-même se chargerait de la femelle. Quant aux autres, on les retrouverait bien un jour. De toute façon, quelle menace pouvaient-ils représenter pour Sargonnas ?

— Je suis content de vous, grogna le Maître de la Nuit.

La créature avala une nouvelle rasade d'eau-de-vie. Elle partirait avant l'aube. Nul ne pourrait dire qu'il l'avait vue…

Personne ne saurait qui servait le Maître de la Nuit.

CHAPITRE VII

Patatras !

Raistlin, Flint et Tanis atterrirent sur le sol d'une petite pièce rectangulaire aux murs blanchis à la chaux. Quelques secondes s'étaient écoulées depuis qu'ils avaient sauté de la corniche, mais le temps leur avait paru s'arrêter durant la chute.

Ils eurent du mal à reprendre leurs esprits. Flint fut le premier à se relever, suivi par le demi-elfe et le jeune mage.

A l'exception d'une épaisse porte de chêne, aucune ouverture ne rompait la monotonie des murs et du plafond. Tanis y colla son oreille, mais n'entendit rien de l'autre côté.

Au centre de la pièce, sur un piédestal de bois incliné, se dressait un énorme morceau de verre ovale et brillant. L'objet évoquait un miroir sans en être un. En son point le plus large, il décrivait une courbe brisée par une fente fine comme le chas d'une aiguille.

Brandissant la gemme noire donnée par l'ogresse, Raistlin s'approcha et murmura une incantation.

— Portail, referme-toi, acheva-t-il en commun.

La surface du portail sembla onduler et la fente disparut. Raistlin enveloppa l'amulette d'un mouchoir et la rangea dans sa poche.

— Je ne voudrais pas me montrer ingrat, déclara Flint, mais où diable avons-nous atterri ?

Tanis secoua la poignée de la porte en chêne.

— Elle est fermée, annonça-t-il.

— Je m'y attendais, approuva Raistlin.

Le demi-elfe se baissa et colla un œil contre le trou de la serrure.

— Je ne vois pas grand-chose. Juste un couloir sombre et d'autres portes.

— De l'intérieur ou de l'extérieur ? s'enquit Flint en approchant.

— Pardon ? De quoi veux-tu parler ? s'étonna Tanis.

— De la porte, bougre d'âne ! s'emporta le nain. Est-elle fermée de l'intérieur ou de l'extérieur ?

— Euh... De l'extérieur, je suppose. Ce serait le plus logique.

— N'en sois pas si sûr, intervint Raistlin en rejoignant ses amis.

Il s'adossa contre le mur et secoua la tête, sous le regard inquiet de Flint et Tanis.

— J'ai un peu le tournis, avoua-t-il. Mais ça va passer.

Le nain se pencha à son tour pour examiner la serrure.

— Elle est fermée de l'intérieur, dit-il en jetant un regard triomphant à Tanis.

— C'est impossible ! protesta le demi-elfe.

Mais déjà Flint ne faisait plus attention à lui. Il sortit un de ses longs couteaux et fourragea allègrement dans la serrure. Plusieurs minutes s'écoulèrent.

— Dommage que Tass ne soit pas là, commenta Tanis avec un sourire. Il l'aurait ouverte depuis longtemps.

Flint se redressa de toute sa modeste hauteur.

— Cette andouille de kender aurait d'abord passé une heure à te raconter comment son oncle Chausse-Trappes s'était tiré d'une situation similaire !

Il se remit au travail et poussa un grognement de satisfaction quand la serrure cliqueta. Sur un léger coup de coude, la porte s'entrebâilla.

— Sans compter que c'est la faute de Tass si nous nous sommes fourrés dans ce pétrin, grommela-t-il.

Raistlin se releva.

— Suivez-moi, dit-il en se glissant dans le couloir.

Ses deux compagnons lui emboîtèrent le pas.

Le passage était plongé dans une obscurité presque totale. Au fond, on distinguait à peine un carré de lumière blanche. Raistlin s'avança pour l'examiner.

— Sois prudent, lui conseilla Flint.

La lumière provenait d'une petite fenêtre qui donnait sur un océan aux eaux noires et démontées. A certains endroits, les vagues venaient mourir sur une plage de sable gris, à d'autres, elles s'écrasaient sur des brisants et de hautes falaises déchiquetées.

Les trois compagnons étaient dans la plus haute tour d'une forteresse perchée sur une colline en pente raide. Un chemin poussiéreux gagnait la plaine en serpentant entre les rochers… Il était bordé de maigres buissons et de cadavres empalés sur des piques.

A l'aplomb de la tour, une herse gardait une extrémité du pont qui enjambait les douves asséchées. Tanis aperçut des ours géants dans le ravin.

Des gardes étaient postés à l'entrée : ils n'avaient rien d'humain. Grands, musclés, ils avaient le nez retroussé, des oreilles pointues et de petits yeux rouges en boutons de bottine. Leurs longs cheveux sales pendouillaient sur leurs épaules ; ils portaient des cimeterres ou des épieux.

Des ogres, se dit Tanis.

L'un d'eux leva la tête vers les trois compagnons, qui reculèrent dans l'embrasure.

— L'Oracle avait raison, souffla Raistlin. Nous sommes sur le rivage de la Mer de Sang, au cœur d'Ogrelien. Il faut sortir d'ici… De préférence en évitant les hordes d'ogres et d'esprits maléfiques.

— Génial, marmonna Flint.

— Je prends la tête, annonça Tanis en faisant volte-face. Venez. Cherchons un moyen de descendre.

Raistlin prit le temps de refermer la porte de la pièce où ils étaient apparus, puis tourna la poignée. Elle était de nouveau verrouillée.

Les trois compagnons ne tardèrent pas à découvrir un escalier. Une main sur sa dague, l'autre sur le mur humide, Tanis descendit avec prudence. Raistlin lui posa une main sur l'épaule, Flint suivit.

Quelques minutes plus tard, ils atteignirent une vaste plate-forme d'où partaient trois couloirs déserts éclairés par la lumière du jour. Des voix et des bruits leur parvenaient dans le lointain.

Flint poussa une porte, révélant une pièce austère meublée d'un lit, d'une table, d'un coffre et d'un placard. Quelqu'un y avait dormi la nuit précédente, mais le lieu était vide. A en juger par le silence environnant, ce devait aussi être le cas des pièces voisines.

— A mon avis, dit Raistlin en ressortant dans le couloir, ce sont les quartiers des visiteurs. Nous sommes en fin d'après-midi : il nous reste un peu de temps libre avant que les occupants reviennent.

— Très bien, ricana Flint. Tu suggères d'attendre la nuit pour choisir l'ogre avec lequel partager un lit ?

— Ou contre qui nous battre..., corrigea Tanis.

Un bruit étouffé s'éleva au bout du couloir. Les trois compagnons virent une silhouette sortir d'une pièce et poser quelque chose par terre. Ils battirent en retraite dans la première chambre.

— Chut ! intima Tanis à Flint, qui le bousculait.

Raistlin referma la porte.

— Et maintenant ? chuchota le nain.

Le jeune mage se dirigea vers la fenêtre en prenant garde à ne pas se faire repérer. A l'ouest, s'étendait une plaine ravagée couverte d'herbes anémiques et de buissons desséchés. Au loin se dressaient de hautes collines.

La forteresse était bâtie sur le flanc abrupt d'une montagne rocheuse. Des ogres montaient la garde le long des remparts.

— Cette personne dans le couloir… Ce n'était que la femme de ménage, dit Tanis en jetant un regard de reproche à Flint.

Il se massa le pied que le nain avait écrasé dans sa hâte.

— Qu'en sais-tu ? aboya Flint en s'asseyant sur le lit.

Tanis eut un sourire en coin et toucha de l'index le coin de sa paupière.

— Ma vision elfique.

Le nain lâcha un chapelet de jurons. Avant qu'il puisse en terminer, la porte s'ouvrit. Une silhouette trapue se découpa sur le seuil de la chambre, éclairée par la lumière du couloir.

Sans réfléchir, Tanis plongea… et fut cueilli au menton par l'extrémité d'un manche à balai. Flint enroula les bras autour de la tête de l'intruse. Celle-ci le mordit à la main et le repoussa sans effort. S'écartant de la fenêtre, Raistlin avança vers le milieu de la pièce.

La furie pénétra dans la chambre en agitant une serpillière. Tanis et Flint reculèrent. Frappé par l'absurdité de la situation, Raistlin rit. L'intruse était bien une femme de ménage… Mais malgré ses muscles noueux, son groin et ses cheveux filasse, elle avait une voix intelligente :

— Dites-moi qui vous êtes et ce que vous faites ici… Et tâchez d'être convaincants si vous ne voulez pas que vos têtes aillent orner la pointe d'une pique !

Tanis posa la main sur la garde de son épée. Flint se frotta le menton. Tous deux étaient surpris par l'apparence de la femme. Jamais encore ils n'avaient rencontré de femelle demi-ogre.

Malgré sa férocité apparente, elle avait quelque chose de résolument joyeux dans le regard. Bien que bestiale selon leurs standards, elle portait des vêtements propres et semblait rompue à l'usage du savon.

Tanis jeta un coup d'œil à Raistlin par-dessus son épaule.

Apercevant Flint, la demi-ogresse poussa un petit cri de joie et se précipita vers lui. Elle approcha son visage du sien tandis qu'il reculait, méfiant.

— Un nain ! s'exclama la femme de ménage. Ventrebleu ! Je n'en avais encore jamais vu... Enfin, pas vivant. Il traîne des tas de squelettes par ici, mais ce n'est pas la même chose.

Elle tendit ses petites mains potelées et empoigna la barbe de Flint.

— Regardez-moi ça ! Qu'il est joli ! s'extasia-t-elle.

Flint leva les yeux au ciel. La demi-ogresse se tourna vers ses compagnons et posa un doigt boudiné sur ses lèvres épaisses.

— Je ne peux pas en parler au chef, marmonna-t-elle. Il tuerait le nain et me demanderait de laver la pièce dix ou vingt fois pour chasser l'odeur.

Elle adressa un signe de tête à Flint en guise d'excuse.

— Je ne veux pas vous offenser, mais c'est la vérité. Puis il mangerait votre cœur pour le déjeuner. Je suppose qu'il donnerait quand même vos entrailles aux autres... Bien sûr, votre tête occuperait une place de choix au bout d'une pique.

Elle secoua la tête et lâcha un petit rire ravi. Flint blêmit.

— Mais vous êtes si joli, soupira la demi-ogresse en battant des cils. Vous me plaisez bien.

Son visage s'assombrit ; elle jeta un regard de conspirateur à Tanis et Raistlin.

— Nous devons nous assurer que personne ne le verra, sinon...

Flint ouvrit la bouche pour parler... Raistlin fut plus rapide. Il s'avança vers la femme de ménage et lui passa un bras autour des épaules.

— Pouvez-vous nous aider à sortir d'Ogrelien ? demanda-t-il.

Son interlocutrice plissa les yeux.

— Je suppose que oui. Je le peux... et je le veux. Voyez-vous, je n'aime pas beaucoup ces ogres. Je suis leur esclave depuis qu'ils ont tué mon pauvre papa, m'épargnant pour m'asservir… Et laissez-moi vous dire que pour des gens aussi crasseux, ils sont très exigeants sur le ménage. Heureusement que je n'appartiens pas à leur race. Je m'appelle Kirsig. Et vous ?

Raistlin fit les présentations. La demi-ogresse sembla plus particulièrement intéressée par le nain.

— Flint Forgefeu, répéta-t-elle, les yeux brillants.

Pour la première fois de sa vie ou presque, Flint se sentait impuissant. Du regard, il appela Tanis à l'aide ; le demi-elfe haussa les épaules en réprimant un sourire.

— Pourriez-vous nous aider à trouver un bateau ? Nous voulons traverser la Mer de Sang, reprit Raistlin.

Kirsig battit des mains comme une petite fille.

— La Mer de Sang ! Ventrebleu ! Je vous trouve bien téméraires ! Pourquoi voulez-vous faire une chose pareille ? C'est un voyage très risqué. Il faut un excellent navigateur pour contourner le Maelström, et les excellents navigateurs coûtent cher.

— Nous paierons cher, dit Tanis d'un air las. Connaissez-vous un capitaine qui accepterait de nous emmener ?

— C'est possible, chuchota Kirsig avec une grimace séductrice. Mais je ne peux pas quitter la forteresse avant minuit, quand j'aurai fini mes corvées. Jusque-là, restez si ça vous chante, mais soyez prudents. Le chef, sa bande, les légions qui gardent Ogrelien..., n'importe qui peut pénétrer ici à tout moment.

La demi-ogresse cligna de l'œil.

— Ils ont un sens de l'orientation lamentable, expliqua-t-elle. Ils errent parfois des heures dans les couloirs, à la recherche de leurs armes ou de leurs chaussures.

« Ce soir, le chef reçoit une délégation tribale de Val-Vipère. Les émissaires logeront juste au-dessus de nous, au dernier étage. Ne faites pas le moindre bruit jusqu'à ce qu'ils dorment. Quand nous serons sortis, vous vous cacherez en attendant que je trouve le capitaine et que je conclue le marché avec lui.

— Etes-vous certaine... ? demanda Raistlin, hésitant.

Kirsig éclata de rire.

— Ne vous inquiétez pas, il fera l'affaire.

— Comment... comment allons-nous fuir la forteresse ? balbutia Flint.

Il répugnait à attirer sur lui l'attention de Kirsig, mais il voulait savoir. La demi-ogresse se tourna vers lui et lui caressa la barbe, pleine de convoitise.

— C'est le problème, admit-elle, mais nous le résoudrons ensemble. Nous allons donner une bonne leçon à ces ogres.

Elle baissa la voix, faisant signe d'approcher à Tanis et Raistlin.

— Il n'existe que deux moyens de quitter Ogrelien. Le premier et le plus sûr, c'est d'être mort. L'autre...

Kirsig hésita.

Elle est encore plus pénible que Tasslehoff, songea Flint.

— Oui ? insista Tanis.

— L'autre est pire, chuchota la demi-ogresse.

*

* *

Ils durent se décider rapidement. Le temps pressait et Kirsig ne pouvait s'absenter longtemps sans qu'on remarque son absence.

Raistlin exposa leur quête à la demi-ogresse. Il raconta la disparition de son frère, de Sturm et de Tasslehoff, et parla même du portail qui les avait amenés à Ogrelien.

Kirsig écarquilla les yeux à l'évocation des îles minotaures. Elle n'avait jamais traversé la Mer de Sang... Comme tout le monde, elle connaissait les nombreuses légendes qui circulaient à son sujet. En outre, expliqua-t-elle au jeune mage, des hommes-taureaux étaient récemment venus à la forteresse pour discuter avec son chef.

— Discuter de quoi ? s'enquit Raistlin, intrigué.

Kirsig secoua la tête.

— Comment pourrais-je le savoir ? Les ogres ne me font pas de confidences. Tout ce que je peux vous dire, c'est que les minotaures sentent encore plus mauvais que mes maîtres, et qu'ils mettent leurs chambres dans un état épouvantable.

Elle cracha par terre aux pieds de Tanis, qui recula avec prudence.

Selon la demi-ogresse, le seul moyen de quitter la forteresse sans combattre les occupants était d'emprunter les égouts. Avec un peu de chance, expliqua-t-elle, leur visite passerait inaperçue.

— Et... ? pressa Raistlin, sentant que Kirsig ne leur disait pas tout.

— C'est dans les égouts que je vide les poubelles et le reste, si vous voyez ce que je veux dire. Je sais où les conduits débouchent : près de la baie, dans un endroit où les gardes ne pourront pas vous voir. Mais...

La demi-ogresse hésita.

— Mais quoi ?

— Les égouts sont hantés par les esprits des morts : des fantômes et des goules. Enfin, c'est ce qu'on dit. Les traverser sera dangereux ; vous pourriez y laisser votre vie.

— Nous prendrons le risque, répondit vivement Raistlin.

— Dans ce cas, restez ici et ne vous montrez pas, ordonna Kirsig. Je reviendrai après minuit. A cette heure, la plupart des ogres sont soûls ou endormis. Vous serez en sécurité dans cette chambre, à condition de ne pas faire de bruit.

La demi-ogresse jeta un dernier regard langoureux à Flint et caressa comme à regret sa barbe poivre et sel. Le nain se tendit.

— Ah, vous êtes si joli, soupira Kirsig en ramassant son seau et son balai.

Elle entrouvrit la porte, jeta un coup d'œil dehors et se glissa dans le couloir. Les trois compagnons l'entendirent s'éloigner.

Tanis se tourna vers Raistlin.

— Crois-tu que nous puissions lui faire confiance ? chuchota-t-il.

Le jeune mage se laissa tomber dans une chaise et hocha la tête. Tanis eut l'air satisfait.

— Mais..., protesta Flint.

Ses deux amis lui jetèrent un regard amusé.

— Jamais elle ne trahirait un aussi joli nain, dit Tanis.

Flint s'empourpra et n'ajouta rien.

*

* *

Au crépuscule, les trois compagnons entendirent des éclats de voix provenant des étages inférieurs. Des convives riaient, criaient, se lançaient des injures ou entonnaient des chansons ogres :

« Pieu d'acier, pic à glace, pince à feu
Perce les cœurs amis ou ennemis
Fais gicler le sang
Ogre maintenant et pour toujours. »

Le vacarme se poursuivit bien après que les deux lunes furent apparues dans le ciel, et Tanis craignit qu'il dure toute la nuit. Enfin, des bruits de pas résonnèrent dans les couloirs, suivis par des grognements et le fracas métallique d'armures jetées sur le sol. Un silence relatif s'abattit sur la forteresse, rompu par quelques ronflements sonores.

De la fenêtre, Tanis assista à la relève de la garde. Peu de temps après, la porte s'ouvrit, et Kirsig entra dans la chambre.

— Suivez-moi, souffla la demi-ogresse.

Rasant les murs, les trois compagnons descendirent les escaliers à sa suite. Par les portes entrouvertes des quartiers d'habitation s'échappait la respiration lourde des ogres endormis. Tanis distinguait de gros pieds dépassant des couvertures, et parfois l'éclat métallique d'un plastron. Mais personne ne vint troubler la progression du petit groupe… Ça n'empêcha pas Tanis et Flint de garder une main sur la poignée de leur arme, au cas où.

Trois étages plus bas, les fugitifs traversèrent une immense pièce haute de plafond, où on voyait les restes d'un banquet. Des os d'animaux gisaient sur une table de chêne, près de gobelets renversés. Des tapisseries représentant des batailles sanglantes couvraient les murs. Le feu mourait dans la cheminée ; déjà, il n'en restait plus que des braises.

A une extrémité de la table, perché sur une estrade, un ogre gigantesque était affalé dans son trône. Il avait la peau jaunâtre, couverte de taches brunes, de bosses et d'ecchymoses. Les pieds posés sur un accoudoir, il ronflait, la bouche ouverte. Un épais diadème d'argent décoré de joyaux verts ornait son front bas.

— C'est Arrast, leur chef, souffla Kirsig en désignant l'ogre. Ne vous inquiétez pas. Il a bu tant de grogs qu'il ne se réveillera pas avant demain matin.

Comme s'il avait entendu la femme de ménage, Arrast s'agita dans son sommeil et se retourna, le visage tourné vers le dossier de son trône. Enfin, poussant un profond soupir, il se remit à ronfler.

Pas très rassuré, Flint se hâta de traverser la salle. A l'autre bout, une grille carrée défendait une fosse sombre. Le nain plissa les yeux, mais ne put en distinguer le fond. Des bruits de succion et des grattements montaient vers lui, accompagnés d'une odeur fétide qui le fit tituber.

— La fosse aux jeux, dit Kirsig en prenant le nain par le coude.

— Et aux saules noirs, grimaça Raistlin.

Tanis hocha la tête.

— C'est ça, approuva Flint, qui n'avait pas la moindre idée de ce que le jeune mage avait voulu dire.

Sa priorité était de mettre le plus de distance possible entre lui et cet endroit sinistre.

Les quatre compagnons franchirent une petite arche et descendirent un escalier de pierre. Une odeur de pourriture régnait dans le sous-sol de la forteresse. Le plancher était jonché d'ossements, de morceaux d'armes brisées et de paille moisie. Les torches fixées aux murs ne fournissaient qu'une maigre lumière.

A la suite de Kirsig, les trois amis pénétrèrent dans une grande salle d'où partaient deux couloirs abritant des cellules. En proie à d'atroces cauchemars, les occupants gémissaient dans le noir.

— Je voudrais faire quelque chose pour eux, pauvres diables, murmura Tanis.

— Aidons-nous d'abord nous-mêmes, répliqua Raistlin.

— Là ! dit Kirsig en désignant une bouche d'aération dans un coin de la pièce.

Les trois compagnons se hâtèrent de rejoindre la demi-ogresse. Tanis et Flint n'eurent guère de mal à soulever la grille, mais la traîner sur le côté fut une autre histoire. Kirsig et Raistlin durent leur prêter main-forte. Enfin, le passage fut dégagé.

Se relevant, Kirsig se trouva nez-à-nez avec un énorme garde à la peau orangée. La créature ouvrit la bouche et aboya quelque chose qu'aucun des trois amis ne comprit, mais qui semblait hostile.

Tanis dégaina son épée et se jeta sur l'ogre. Celui-ci faisait deux fois sa taille. Malgré les apparences, il n'était pas maladroit. Il para l'attaque du demi-elfe et le repoussa avec violence, l'envoyant s'écraser contre le mur.

Flint voulut jouer du couteau. Hélas, le garde avait une bien meilleure allonge que la sienne ; il utilisait une massue cloutée à laquelle il fit décrire un arc pour l'abattre sur la tête du nain. Flint parvint à esquiver, mais il reçut le coup sur l'épaule et s'effondra.

Raistlin incanta, fouillant ses bourses à la recherche du composant nécessaire. L'ogre le vit faire et marcha sur lui, ses petits yeux jaunes brillant d'une lueur malsaine. Il tendit ses mains crochues vers le jeune mage…

Soudain, ses yeux roulèrent dans leurs orbites et il bascula en avant. Raistlin eut à peine le temps de bondir sur le côté pour ne pas être écrasé. Du dos de l'ogre jaillissait le manche d'une dague couverte de sang noir.

Raistlin hocha la tête. Flint et Tanis se relevèrent, à demi-assommés et dévisagèrent l'imprévisible Kirsig.

— J'en garde toujours une sous la main, expliqua timidement la femme de ménage.

Posant un pied sur le dos de l'ogre, elle saisit sa dague à deux mains, la dégagea, puis l'essuya sur sa jupe de cuir avant de la ranger.

— Vous en feriez autant si vous travailliez ici, dit-elle, sur la défensive.

Tanis la félicita de son courage. Kirsig rosit de plaisir.

— Ce n'est rien. Dépêchons-nous, maintenant.

Un par un, Tanis, Flint et Raistlin se glissèrent dans la bouche d'aération. La demi-ogresse utilisa la lance du garde comme un levier pour remettre la grille en place.

— Bonne chance ! dit-elle en agitant la main.

Restée seule, elle traîna le cadavre dans un coin de la pièce et le recouvrit de paille pour le dissimuler aux regards.

*

* *

Le liquide nauséabond brillait dans le noir, des traînées argent et pourpre irradiant une faible lumière. Le courant charriait de l'écume mousseuse, des algues grises et toutes sortes de corps flottants non identifiés qui expliquaient sans doute l'odeur de pourriture et de mort régnant dans le tunnel.

Des poissons charognards se faufilaient entre les déchets, effleurant les jambes des trois amis. Un serpent géant flottait le ventre en l'air, deux protubérances de la taille d'un homme distendant son estomac jaune pâle.

Au loin résonnaient d'étranges cris. Des squelettes blanchis par les ans s'empilaient le long des murs. Tanis entendait sans les voir les rats qui se pressaient dans le tunnel. Il saisit le poignet de Raistlin.

— Ça va ? demanda-t-il, plein de sollicitude.

De l'autre côté du jeune mage, Flint s'enfonçait jusqu'au menton dans le liquide huileux. Il devait parfois donner des coups de pied pour garder la tête hors de l'eau.

— Ça va. Ne t'inquiète pas pour moi, répondit sèchement Raistlin.

Flint poussa un grognement.

— Moi, ça ne va pas du tout, ronchonna-t-il. Personne ne m'avait dit que je risquerais de me noyer avant d'atteindre la Mer de Sang !

Avec une force surprenante, le flot de déchets poussait les trois amis vers l'est… D'après Kirsig, ça correspondait à la direction du rivage. Ils n'avaient qu'à s'accrocher et se laisser porter.

— Tiens-toi bien, dit Tanis à Raistlin. Je suppose que le tunnel est en pente. Nous n'allons pas tarder à prendre de la vitesse.

Le demi-elfe avait vu juste. Flint agrippa l'épaule de Raistlin et sentit la panique l'envahir en même temps que la nausée. Les trois compagnons filaient dans les égouts au milieu des déchets et des choses mortes que le courant emportait avec eux.

Les cris étranges gagnèrent en intensité, puis se firent assourdissants. Soudain, le tunnel plongea, décrivant une courbe. Flint fut projeté contre un mur. Il poussa un cri de douleur et se saisit la jambe. Par chance, Raistlin réussit à le prendre par le col avant qu'il se noie.

Les trois compagnons passèrent devant une créature horriblement défigurée. Jadis, elle avait peut-être été humaine, aujourd'hui, elle appartenait aux légions des morts-vivants. Sa langue se darda entre ses canines aiguisées. Les ongles de ses mains s'étaient changés en griffes acérées. Elle s'accrochait d'une main à la corniche du tunnel… De l'autre, elle fit un geste à la fois menaçant et pathétique.

Tanis leva le bras et parvint à la repousser. La créature ouvrit grand la gueule et poussa des cris de protestation stridents jusqu'à ce que les compagnons aient disparu au loin.

A demi étouffés par la puanteur et l'immonde liquide qui s'infiltrait dans leur gorge, Tanis, Flint et Raistlin filèrent dans le tunnel, emportés par le courant. Enfin, après ce qui leur sembla une éternité, ils débouchèrent dans une crique peu profonde, entourée de rochers et baignée par le clair de lune.

Tanis aida Raistlin à se relever et le conduisit au sec, à l'abri du torrent de débris que continuaient à déverser les égouts d'Ogrelien. Flint ne se trouvait nulle part en vue.

Tanis commença à s'inquiéter pour son vieil ami. Il rebroussa chemin et découvrit le nain assis sur une pierre, trempé jusqu'aux os, le visage tordu par une grimace de douleur.

— Que t'arrive-t-il ?

— Ma jambe, hoqueta Flint. Je ne peux plus m'appuyer dessus. Je crois qu'elle est cassée.

Tanis s'agenouilla pour l'examiner. La jambe droite du nain était fracturée. Elle avait presque doublé de volume et virait lentement au violet. Le demi-elfe chargea son ami sur ses épaules et le porta jusqu'à l'endroit où les attendait Raistlin.

Bien que le jeune mage fût épuisé, le visage couvert d'ecchymoses et de coupures, il se mit en quête d'une branche morte, déchira des bandes de tissu au bas de sa tunique et fit de son mieux pour confectionner une attelle à Flint.

— C'est bien ma veine, se lamenta le nain tandis que Raistlin faisait un nœud au bandage improvisé.

— C'est vrai. Nous aurions dû t'abandonner au lacédon, dit le mage, ironique.

— Le quoi ? demanda Flint.

— La goule, dans le tunnel, expliqua Tanis en se laissant tomber sur le sable. Kirsig avait raison à propos des créatures mortes-vivantes qui peuplent les égouts d'Ogrelien.

— Evidemment, elle t'aurait préféré mort, poursuivit Raistlin en ajustant l'attelle.

Sans cérémonie, le jeune mage se roula en boule au pied d'un rocher et s'endormit presque aussitôt. Flint grommela quelque chose d'inintelligible.

La petite crique était abritée par un piton rocheux. Devant eux s'étendait la Mer de Sang, Lunitari et Solinari jetant des reflets argentés sur ses eaux noires. On n'entendait que le bruit des vagues venant mourir sur la grève.

Pendant des heures, Tanis et Flint attendirent Kirsig en frissonnant. Comme le nain avait cessé de vitupérer depuis plusieurs minutes, Tanis se pencha vers lui et réalisa qu'il dormait assis, sa jambe droite tendue devant lui. Le demi-elfe poussa un soupir et se prépara à monter la garde.

*
* *

Une heure avant l'aube, Tanis aperçut une petite embarcation qui se dirigeait vers la crique. Kirsig était assise sur le siège avant, mais quelqu'un d'autre maniait les rames. Le demi-elfe réveilla ses compagnons.

Alors que le bateau approchait du rivage, Kirsig sauta dans l'eau, suivie par un grand homme à la peau noire, aussi chauve qu'un œuf. Il était torse nu, vêtu d'un pantalon coupé aux genoux et de hautes sandales. Un collier de petits os pendait à son cou musclé, et un couteau au manche orné de joyaux se balançait sur sa hanche.

— Désolée d'avoir mis si longtemps, s'excusa Kirsig. J'ai d'abord dû faire mes bagages, puis aller en ville pour chercher Nugetre... (Ses yeux s'agrandirent de stupeur.) Ventrebleu ! Qu'est-il arrivé au joli nain ?

Elle se précipita vers Flint et s'agenouilla pour examiner sa blessure. Le nain poussa un grognement mécontent.

Les mains posées sur ses hanches, Nugetre examina Tanis et Raistlin.

— Kirsig..., commença le demi-elfe.

— Que voulais-tu dire par « faire les bagages » ? compléta le jeune mage.

La demi-ogresse se tourna vers lui.

— J'ai tué un des gardes, répliqua-t-elle froidement. Je ne peux pas rester là-bas. Alors, je vous accompagne.

— Mais... mais..., balbutia Raistlin.

— Nous ne pouvons pas emmener une femme, protesta Tanis.

— Si vous voulez mon avis..., intervint Flint.

Nugetre éclata d'un rire énorme. Les trois compagnons lui jetèrent un regard interloqué.

— Qu'y a-t-il de si drôle ? demanda Tanis, vexé.

— La moitié de mon équipage est composé de femmes, dit l'homme noir en riant. Elles font le boulot aussi bien, sinon mieux que les hommes.

— Je connais Nugetre depuis des années, expliqua Kirsig. Quand j'étais petite, il achetait des vivres à mon pauvre papa avant de partir en expédition. C'est un des meilleurs marins de la région… Et il accepte de nous faire traverser la Mer de Sang.

— Pour un bon prix, rappela Nugetre en agitant un index sous le nez de la demi-ogresse.

— Et puis, ajouta Kirsig, enthousiaste, Flint aura besoin d'aide médicale. Je m'y connais un peu… Pas de quoi soigner les épidémies, mais assez pour soulager sa douleur et accélérer le processus de guérison.

Flint jeta un regard désespéré à Tanis et à Raistlin. Les deux jeunes gens se consultèrent du regard.

— Très bien, soupira le demi-elfe.

Les compagnons embarquèrent avec Kirsig et Nugetre, qui rama vigoureusement.

Quelques minutes plus tard, ils s'étaient éloignés de plusieurs centaines d'encablures du rivage. La silhouette noire d'Ogrelien se fondait dans la nuit.

CHAPITRE VIII

Quelqu'un saisit Sturm à bras-le-corps. Le jeune homme leva faiblement les yeux, mais sa vision était brouillée. Il sentit qu'on le soulevait et qu'on le déposait au fond d'un petit bateau, à côté de Caramon.

Malgré son épuisement, Sturm regarda son ami. Ce qui restait des vêtements de Caramon révélait une peau brûlée par le soleil, des membres couverts de croûtes et d'ecchymoses. Le jeune homme avait les yeux fermés, mais sa respiration semblait régulière. Soulagé, Sturm se laissa aller et sombra à son tour dans l'inconscience.

Un vieux pêcheur rabougri nommé Lazaril avait repéré les deux hommes perdus en mer et coupé leurs liens avant de les hisser dans sa barque.

Le matin, il était sorti en espérant attraper des anguilles qu'il vendrait au marché d'Atossa, sur la côte nord de Mithas. Il se caressa le menton, dubitatif. Si tout se passait bien, ces deux humains lui rapporteraient davantage que tous les poissons de la Mer de Sang.

A supposer qu'ils s'en tirent. Ils étaient dans un état pitoyable. Lazaril ôta sa veste de cuir et la posa sur le plus mince, puis il s'efforça de laver les visages des naufragés et de rincer leurs nombreuses blessures. Sans doute leur bateau avait-il coulé … A moins qu'ils ne se soient fait attaquer par des pirates. Pas de chance pour eux ; le vieux pêcheur, lui, se frottait les mains.

Les deux compagnons s'éveillèrent brièvement quand Lazaril leur versa de l'eau douce dans la gorge, puis quand il les força à avaler un peu de poisson séché. Toussant, ils tentèrent de repousser le pêcheur.

Le plus imposant des deux leva vers Lazaril des yeux inquiets, puis mâcha avidement avant de s'évanouir à nouveau. Encore plus mal en point, l'autre arrivait tout juste à déglutir.

Lazaril enduisit les deux hommes d'un baume de sa confection pour calmer les brûlures du soleil.

— Tu as raté ta vocation, mon vieux, se dit-il en contemplant son œuvre d'un air satisfait. Tu aurais dû être guérisseur.

Il saisit les rames et, luttant contre un léger vent du sud, se dirigea vers le port d'Atossa qu'il atteignit une heure plus tard. Les deux rescapés n'avaient toujours pas repris connaissance. Lazaril les recouvrit d'une bâche pour qu'aucun de ses concurrents ne repère sa cargaison très spéciale.

Atossa regorgeait d'activité. Pirates et mercenaires humains y côtoyaient les maîtres cornus de l'île. De pitoyables esclaves de toutes races déchargeaient les navires, surveillés par des minotaures qui n'hésitaient pas à faire usage de leurs fouets.

Une fois à quai, Lazaril repéra un gamin et lui offrit une pièce de cuivre pour qu'il aille chercher le capitaine du port, un minotaure au regard vicieux et aux cornes proéminentes, répondant au nom de Vigila. Jusqu'ici, le pêcheur avait fait de son mieux pour l'éviter.

Vigila ne tarda pas à apparaître, l'enfant sur les talons. Lazaril lui donna la pièce promise, puis le congédia d'un signe pendant que le capitaine du port croisait les bras sur sa poitrine musclée.

Vigila était connu pour sa brutalité. C'était lui qui rendait la justice sur les quais, qui collectait les taxes et s'occupait des esclaves. Autrement dit, c'était avec lui que Lazaril devait traiter.

D'un geste théâtral, le pêcheur ôta la bâche qui couvrait les deux naufragés. Il leva un regard plein d'espoir sur Vigila.

— Et alors ? demanda le minotaure avec un rictus méprisant. Que veux-tu que je fasse d'eux ? Ils sont plus morts que vifs.

Lazaril déglutit et esquissa une grimace édentée.

— Votre Excellence, commença-t-il, hésitant, leurs blessures sont superficielles. Ils ont l'air très forts, et il suffirait de quelques soins pour en faire de parfaits esclaves. Un peu d'eau et de nourriture, et il n'y paraîtra plus. Ils sont capables de travailler dur… jusqu'à ce qu'ils en crèvent. Ça devrait vous intéresser, non ?

Vigila ricana.

— Rejette-les à l'eau, vieillard, et tiens-t'en à tes prises habituelles.

Lazaril rassembla tout son courage pour revenir à la charge.

— Celui-ci, dit-il en tapotant l'épaule de Caramon, pourrait faire un excellent gladiateur : il en a la carrure. Songez comme le roi serait content si vous lui rameniez cette curiosité : un guerrier sorti des flots ! Ce serait une étape importante de votre carrière.

Vigila prit l'air songeur. Visiblement, l'idée lui plaisait.

— Les humains ne font jamais long feu dans l'arène, protesta-t-il.

— Mais ils sont très divertissants à regarder, insista Lazaril, même quand ils perdent.

Au fond de la barque, Caramon et Sturm s'agitèrent. Ouvrant les yeux, ils se demandèrent où ils se trouvaient. Après des jours passés à la dérive, ni l'un ni l'autre ne comprenait la scène qui se déroulait devant eux.

Un vieux pêcheur aux cheveux couleur carotte parlait à voix basse avec un énorme minotaure qui le dominait de toute sa taille. La créature cornue portait un pagne de cuir et un assortiment de ceintures. Elle brandissait un gros bâton…, sans doute la marque de son autorité.

On eût dit que le minotaure marchandait avec le vieillard. Caramon et Sturm avaient l'esprit si embrumé qu'ils ne saisirent pas le sens de la discussion.

Vigila jeta un coup d'œil aux deux compagnons et les vit lever pitoyablement la tête avant de la laisser tomber à nouveau.

— Tiens, pêcheur, grommela-t-il. (Plongeant la main dans sa poche, il jeta à Lazaril une poignée de pièces.) Je vais te débarrasser de ces déchets humains. Peut-être arriverai-je à les retaper, peut-être pas.

Il se détourna et fit signe à deux esclaves, qui approchèrent en tirant une lourde carriole de bois. Pendant que Lazaril se baissait pour ramasser les pièces (dont certaines avaient sombré dans les eaux troubles du port), il se pencha vers ses nouvelles acquisitions.

Caramon et Sturm se sentirent soulevés une deuxième fois ; ils étaient trop faibles pour se débattre ou même protester. Vigila les laissa tomber dans la carriole. Un fouet claqua. Les esclaves humains se mirent en mouvement, et le véhicule s'éloigna de la jetée.

— Hé ! Elles sont en cuivre ! se plaignit Lazaril en comptant ses pièces. C'est le prix des esclaves, pas des gladiateurs !

Il avança vers le capitaine du port. Ce fut sa seconde erreur, la première ayant été de hausser la voix. Vigila fit volte-face, les yeux étincelant de fureur. Lazaril se figea.

— Mais ce n'est... pas très grave, balbutia-t-il. Pas grave du tout.

Il n'avait plus qu'une envie : fuir Atossa au plus vite. Reprendre la mer et pêcher son lot quotidien d'anguilles…

Vigila ne lui en laissa pas le temps. Baissant la tête, le minotaure chargea et l'embrocha sur ses cornes. Puis il se redressa, poussant un cri de rage et tourna sur lui-même avant de projeter le cadavre du pêcheur dans la baie.

Le petit messager avait observé toute la scène, se précipita pour ramasser les pièces tombées de la main de Lazaril. Il n'eut pas une pensée pour le vieillard : ce genre d'incident se produisait tous les jours à Atossa. Tout le monde connaissait le mauvais caractère du capitaine du port et savait qu'on le contrariait à ses risques et périls.

*

* *

Alors que Tasslehoff Racle-Pieds subissait les assauts de ses bourreaux maladroits, Sturm de Lumlane et Caramon Majere étaient jetés dans un donjon, à une quarantaine de lieues d'Atossa.

Soulagés d'avoir échappé à la noyade, ils n'opposèrent aucune résistance. Ils n'en avaient de toute façon plus la force. Roulés en boule sur le sol, ils dormirent pendant le reste de la journée et toute la nuit suivante.

Quand ils s'éveillèrent, des gardes faisaient le tour de la prison, munis de deux seaux, un d'eau, un de ragoût. Malgré l'arôme peu appétissant de la nourriture, Caramon et Sturm ne se plaignirent pas. Jamais de leur vie ils n'avaient été aussi affamés.

La deuxième nuit, ils furent capables de s'asseoir et de parler. Jeunes et résistants, ils se remettaient rapidement.

— D'après ce que j'ai entendu, nous sommes sur l'île de Mithas, expliqua Sturm à voix basse. Nous avons été transportés sur des milliers de lieues, du Détroit de Schallmer jusqu'au rivage de la Mer de Sang.

« Pour une raison qui m'échappe, l'auteur de cet incroyable forfait a capturé Tass et a voulu se débarrasser de nous. Nous avons de la chance d'être encore en vie, même si le sort qui nous attend ne s'annonce guère brillant. D'habitude, la Mer de Sang ne rend pas ses proies. »

— A ton avis, demanda Caramon, qu'est-il advenu de Tass ?

Sturm secoua tristement la tête.

Le matin du troisième jour, deux minotaures rendirent visite aux prisonniers. Le premier, qui portait un insigne officiel, écouta le second — un garde — pousser des grognements en désignant Sturm et Caramon.

— Veillez à ce qu'ils retrouvent leurs forces le plus vite possible, déclara-t-il enfin. Ils ont l'air d'être de bons guerriers, et feront certainement des gladiateurs amusants. Dans le cas contraire, nous pourrons toujours les jeter dans une fosse à esclaves.

Caramon écoutait sans réagir. Epuisé, il se moquait du sort qui l'attendait. Sturm se leva d'un bond et vint coller son visage contre les barreaux de leur cellule.

— Je me battrai contre n'importe lequel de vous deux, si vous me laissez sortir d'ici ! s'exclama-t-il, furieux. Mais je ne serai jamais un esclave, et moins encore un gladiateur !

Il cracha aux pieds des minotaures. Celui qui portait l'insigne le saisit à la gorge et lui décocha un terrible coup de poing. Sturm parvint à se dégager et recula, lèvres en sang, sans quitter ses geôliers du regard.

— Celui-ci semble impulsif, mais nous saurons le mater, gronda le minotaure en se frottant le menton.

Il se tourna vers son séide.

— Nourrissez-les correctement pendant quelques semaines, puis nous aviserons. (Il désigna Caramon.) Laissez-le participer aux corvées de la prison. Ce sera sa récompense pour s'être tenu tranquille. Ça lui fera de l'entraînement : quand le temps viendra de montrer de quoi il est capable, ça lui sauvera peut-être la vie.

*

* *

Le lendemain matin, les compagnons furent réveillés sans douceur par les gardes. Un minotaure pointa son épée sur la gorge de Sturm pendant qu'un autre invitait

Caramon à sortir de la cellule. Tendant les deux seaux, il lui ordonna de servir les prisonniers.

Pliant sous le poids de son fardeau, Caramon réalisa combien la semaine passée à dériver dans la Mer de Sang l'avait affaibli. Les gardes ricanèrent en le voyant tituber d'une cellule à l'autre. L'un d'eux retourna à son poste pendant que le second emboîtait le pas au jeune homme, brandissant son épée pour lui interdire le moindre écart.

Pendant trois heures, Caramon ravitailla les malheureux qui partageaient son sort et celui de Sturm. La moitié étaient des minotaures ; malgré leur situation, ils jetèrent au guerrier un regard chargé de mépris. La captivité ne leur avait pas fait changer d'avis : pour eux, les humains restaient des créatures inférieures, qu'elles leur apportent à manger ou non.

La plupart des prisonniers étaient des renégats, des pirates ou pire encore. Certains, blessés, malades ou trop fatigués, ne réagissaient plus à l'arrivée de leur déjeuner. L'un d'eux, recroquevillé dans un coin et couvert d'insectes, devait être mort depuis plusieurs jours. Caramon en avisa le garde, qui haussa les épaules sans s'émouvoir.

Au bout d'un des couloirs se trouvait une cellule isolée. A l'intérieur, une silhouette était enchaînée au mur, dans l'impossibilité de s'asseoir ou de s'allonger. La tête du prisonnier dodelinait sur sa poitrine, son corps semblait brisé. Il leva avec difficulté les yeux vers Caramon en l'entendant approcher.

Il faisait sombre dans la cellule, mais le jeune homme distingua une tête ovale sur laquelle brillaient deux points noirs. Deux longues plaies suintantes, couvertes de sang séché, zébraient ses épaules et son dos, comme si on lui avait arraché un organe vital. Malgré son état pitoyable, il esquissa une grimace en découvrant Caramon.

Le jeune homme se demanda comment le prisonnier allait pouvoir manger et boire. Posant ses seaux, il hésita.

— Vas-y, grommela le garde en lui donnant une bourrade. On le fait manger un peu de temps en temps. Sinon, il peut toujours sentir l'odeur..., ça fait partie de ses privilèges.

Caramon s'agenouilla et prit son temps pour remplir les deux écuelles. Alors que le garde, lassé d'attendre, faisait les cent pas dans le couloir, il chuchota :

— Pourquoi êtes-vous enchaîné ?

— Pour ne pas me suicider, répondit le prisonnier avec un rictus amer. Je préférerais la mort à la captivité.

— Que faites-vous ici ?

— On m'interroge.

— Qu'avez-vous fait ?

— Je ne suis pas l'un d'eux. C'est assez.

Caramon se détourna.

— Attendez ! chuchota l'homme. Etes-vous un des humains que l'on a repêchés en mer ?

Caramon sursauta. Il jeta un coup d'œil vers le garde, qui grattait le sol avec la pointe de son épée.

— Oui, dit-il très vite. Comment le savez-vous ?

— Pas maintenant. Une autre fois, chuchota le prisonnier en voyant le garde porter son attention sur eux.

— Toi là-bas ! s'écria le minotaure en fronçant les sourcils. Arrête de lambiner !

— J'arrive, répondit Caramon.

A contrecœur, il ramassa les seaux et s'éloigna.

*
* *

Bien que personne ne les surveillât, les deux amis attendirent la nuit pour converser, et encore ne le firent-ils qu'à voix basse. Caramon parla à Sturm de l'étrange prisonnier qui était au courant de leur présence à Mithas. Sturm eut beau réfléchir, il ne vit pas comment la nouvelle avait pu lui parvenir. Peut-être les confondait-il avec d'autres, hasarda le jeune Solamnique.

Les compagnons évoquèrent aussi Solace, leurs amis Tanis et Flint, Raistlin. Ils se demandaient ce qu'était devenu Tasslehoff... et pourquoi les minotaures avaient voulu prendre le kender vivant.

— Sans doute pas pour en faire un gladiateur, avança Sturm.

— Qui sait ? souffla Caramon. S'ils le laissaient improviser avec son bâton, il aurait une chance de s'en tirer.

Sturm ne put retenir un sourire à l'idée de Tass brandissant son arme favorite sous le nez d'un énorme minotaure.

— A ton avis, dit-il en changeant de sujet, combien de temps s'est écoulé depuis le naufrage du *Vénora* ?

Caramon fit un rapide calcul.

— Dix ou douze jours.

— Tu as sans doute raison. Crois-tu que Raistlin et les autres s'inquiètent ? J'ai peur que nous ne sortions jamais d'ici.

Caramon posa une main sur l'épaule de son ami.

— Fais confiance aux dieux, dit-il, optimiste.

— Oui, soupira Sturm. Je vais essayer.

Les deux jeunes gens s'endormirent peu de temps après, dos à dos pour partager leur chaleur corporelle.

Quatre jours s'écoulèrent avec une lenteur exaspérante. Parfois, ils entendaient hurler d'autres prisonniers, ou voyaient les gardes sortir des cadavres de leur cellule.

Le minotaure à l'insigne leur rendit une seconde visite. Il était accompagné d'un esclave humain décharné, vêtu de haillons et chaussé de sandales. Il ne dit rien, se contentant d'observer les deux amis d'un air impassible pendant que l'esclave se frottait à ses jambes tel un chiot avide d'affection. Après quelques minutes, il tourna les talons et repartit.

Tous les matins, Caramon sortait de la cellule pour s'acquitter de ses corvées. Ainsi, il put faire travailler ses muscles endoloris : les seaux de nourriture lui semblèrent plus légers chaque jour.

C'était toujours la même chose : deux gardes venaient le chercher, puis l'un regagnait son poste tandis que l'autre l'accompagnait. Une douzaine de minotaures surveillaient la prison à toute heure, rendant une évasion impossible.

L'état du prisonnier enchaîné se dégradait peu à peu. Les gardes devaient le torturer la nuit : au matin, il avait invariablement le dos et les épaules en sang. Caramon essaya de lui parler de nouveau, mais l'homme semblait toujours inconscient.

Le quatrième jour, il leva les yeux vers son visiteur, et un flot de paroles incompréhensibles jaillirent de sa bouche. Il ne s'exprimait pas en commun, mais dans une langue inconnue de Caramon. On eût dit qu'il délirait. Sa tête ne tarda pas à retomber mollement sur sa poitrine.

La plupart des prisonniers étaient des brigands qui n'eussent pas déparé dans un donjon de Krynn. Mais celui-ci éveillait la curiosité et la sympathie de Caramon. Hélas, il ne pouvait rien faire.

Le cinquième jour, il sembla que l'homme étrange avait repris des forces. Il fit signe à Caramon d'approcher. Comme le garde s'était adossé au mur un peu plus loin, le guerrier s'exécuta.

— Tout est arrangé, chuchota le prisonnier.

— Pardon ? s'étonna Caramon en continuant à verser du ragoût dans l'écuelle pour donner le change au minotaure.

Il s'approcha des barreaux de la cellule.

— Que savez-vous à notre sujet ? Et de quoi parlez-vous ?

— J'ai consulté mes frères. Nous pouvons vous faire sortir.

— Pourquoi moi ? s'enquit Caramon, le cœur battant. Pourquoi pas vous ?

— Parce que je suis coincé. Ils n'ouvrent jamais ma cellule, sauf pour me torturer. Mes amis ont entendu parler de vous et de votre ami. Ils vous aideront.

— Pourquoi moi ? répéta Caramon.

— Parce que vous n'êtes pas un minotaure. Parce qu'on vous a envoyé. Et surtout, expliqua l'homme avec un faible sourire, parce que c'est possible.

Caramon jeta un coup d'œil par-dessus son épaule. Le garde somnolait assis dans le couloir.

— Comment communiquez-vous avec les vôtres ? demanda le guerrier d'une voix pressante.

Malgré la sympathie qu'il ressentait pour le prisonnier, il devait se montrer prudent. Avec difficulté, l'homme point un index vers son crâne.

— Par télépathie.

Caramon écarquilla les yeux.

— Et mon compagnon ? demanda-t-il.

Il y eut un long silence.

— Vous devrez l'abandonner, répondit enfin le prisonnier.

— Je ne peux pas faire ça ! protesta Caramon.

— Il le faut.

— Quand vos amis me feront-ils sortir ?

— Demain.

Un bruit de pas apprit au jeune homme que le garde s'était relevé et se dirigeait vers eux.

— De quoi parlez-vous ? grogna la voix maintenant familière.

Caramon empoigna les seaux et fit volte-face.

— Oh, c'est toujours la même chose, dit-il en soupirant. Il se plaint de la nourriture.

Le minotaure jeta au guerrier un regard soupçonneux, puis il haussa les épaules.

— Ça tombe bien, parce qu'on n'avait pas l'intention de le nourrir aujourd'hui, ricana-t-il.

*

* *

Plus tard dans la nuit, Caramon rapporta à Sturm sa conversation. Le jeune Solamnique ne comprit pas plus que lui.

— De toute façon, insista Caramon, je ne partirai pas sans toi.

— Il le faut, répondit Sturm, solennel. Si l'un de nous est libre, il pourra peut-être délivrer l'autre. Il ne sert à rien que nous moisissions ici tous deux. A ta place, je partirais.

— Vraiment ? demanda Caramon, sceptique.

— Vraiment, mentit Sturm.

Caramon réfléchit.

— Très bien, dit-il enfin. Si par miracle je parviens à m'échapper, je jure de revenir te chercher.

Son ami lui serra chaleureusement la main.

*

* *

Le lendemain, les gardes firent sortir Caramon à l'heure du déjeuner. Saisissant les deux récipients de nourriture, le jeune homme entama sa tournée quotidienne.

Il s'efforça de dissimuler son anxiété pour ne pas que les minotaures se doutent de quelque chose. Pourtant, il gardait les sens en alerte, prêts à déceler le plus petit changement dans sa routine quotidienne.

Au bout de deux heures, le garde qui l'accompagnait commença à traîner les pieds et à se laisser distancer dans le couloir. Il ne se méfiait guère du jeune homme, qui n'était pas armé et ne pouvait causer grand tort dans l'enceinte du donjon.

Lorsque Caramon atteignit la cellule de l'homme enchaîné, le minotaure flânait loin derrière, embrochant des rats sur la lame de sa dague. Le prisonnier était dans un état pitoyable. Des ecchymoses pourpres couvraient son visage, ses blessures saignaient, comme si on avait lacéré toute la chair de son dos.

Caramon lâcha ses deux seaux, dont le contenu se répandit à terre, et se précipita vers la grille de la cellule. L'homme enchaîné leva le menton, mais ses paupières étaient si gonflées qu'il ne put les ouvrir.

— Que... ? balbutia Caramon, horrifié.

— Toujours la même chose, mon ami, souffla le prisonnier d'une voix rauque.

— Pourquoi vous torturent-ils ainsi ?

— Je ne suis pas l'un d'eux. Ça suffit.

Rempli de pitié et de honte, Caramon baissa la tête. Ce faisant, il aperçut pour la première fois les pieds de l'homme, ou plutôt, ses pattes semblables à celles d'un oiseau. Bouche bée, il écarquilla les yeux.

— Je n'ai pas le temps de vous expliquer, croassa le prisonnier. Dépêchez-vous. Posez les seaux l'un sur l'autre à droite de la porte. Là ! Qu'ils soient bien en équilibre. Maintenant, grimpez dessus.

Caramon lui jeta un regard sceptique.

— Vite !

Sans savoir pourquoi, le guerrier obéit. Il escalada les deux seaux sans oser regarder où en était le minotaure derrière lui.

— Et vous ? demanda-t-il, hésitant.

— Si j'ai de la chance, ils me laisseront mourir.

Alors, Caramon vit une dalle du plafond glisser sur le côté.

— Levez les bras !

Il s'exécuta en jetant un dernier coup d'œil à son sauveur. Le visage de l'homme s'éclaira d'un bref sourire, puis sa tête retomba sur sa poitrine.

Des mains vigoureuses saisirent Caramon et le soulevèrent.

*
* *

La dalle se remit lentement en place. Caramon ne voyait qu'une silhouette se mouvant dans les ténèbres. Il avançait à quatre pattes dans un tunnel très bas.

Tous les dix ou douze pas, la silhouette tournait la tête et lui criait quelque chose dans un langage inhumain. Mais sa voix aiguë avait des accents pressants que Caramon pouvait interpréter.

Des cailloux pointus écorchaient les genoux et les mains du jeune homme ; des racines et des toiles d'araignée lui effleuraient le visage. Son dos commençait à lui faire mal.

— Hé, chuchota-t-il. Qui êtes-vous ? Où allons-nous ?

La silhouette s'immobilisa, poussa un cri et se remit à avancer. Caramon grogna et accéléra pour ne pas la perdre de vue. Il y avait de nombreux embranchements. Livré à lui-même, il n'aurait su lesquels prendre.

Au bout d'une heure, le passage commença à monter. S'aidant des racines et des pierres, l'inconnu escalada une pente assez raide. Caramon, qui n'avait guère pris d'exercice au cours des dernières semaines, était à bout de souffle. Il aurait aimé se reposer un peu, mais son guide ne lui en laissa pas le loisir.

Le jeune homme se hissa tant bien que mal jusqu'à une ouverture inondée de soleil. Il vivait dans le noir depuis si longtemps qu'il fut aveuglé. Avant que ses yeux s'habituent à la lumière, quelqu'un jeta sur lui un grand sac de toile. Caramon trébucha et tomba ; il sentit qu'on lui attachait les pieds.

Puis il fut soulevé et emporté dans les airs.

*
* *

Le garde qui avait laissé s'enfuir Caramon fut exécuté le lendemain. Le minotaure à l'insigne revint dans la prison, flanqué de son esclave humain, pour reconstituer l'évasion du guerrier. Il arpenta les couloirs en réfléchissant et s'arrêta devant la cellule de l'homme enchaîné, auquel il ne restait qu'un souffle de vie.

C'était un minotaure très intelligent, pourtant, il ne comprenait pas ce qui avait pu se passer. Cela le mit dans une telle rage qu'il passa sa colère sur le compagnon de l'évadé. Ses assistants battirent Sturm comme plâtre, sans résultat aucun puisque le jeune homme ignorait tout des moyens employés par son ami.

Enfin, l'officier minotaure décida qu'il perdait son temps. Il ordonna qu'on panse les blessures de Sturm et qu'on le remette sur pied pour en faire un gladiateur potable. Puis il dicta un message à son esclave.

Aussi déplaisant que ce fût, il fallait apprendre à son roi que quelqu'un s'était échappé de la prison d'Atossa.

CHAPITRE IX

Le capitaine Nugetre gagnait sa vie en convoyant des passagers et des marchandises dans les Mers Orientales. Son équipage, qui avait déjà tout vu, ne s'étonna guère de la présence à bord de Tanis, de Flint, de Raistlin et de Kirsig.

Le demi-elfe avait le sentiment que le voyage ne serait pas paisible. Aussi décida-t-il de tenir un journal de bord sur un parchemin fourni par le capitaine.

Premier jour

Dès que nous nous sommes éloignés du rivage, l'eau est devenue boueuse ; un vent annonciateur de tempête s'est levé, comme pour nous mettre en garde contre les dangers à venir.

Le capitaine Nugetre nous a rassemblés dans sa cabine : Flint, Raistlin, la demi-ogresse Kirsig et moi..., ainsi que son second, une grande femme blonde large d'épaules qui répond au nom de Yuril et dont la stature me rappelle fortement Caramon. Nous avons étudié les cartes et discuté de la route à prendre.

Bien que Nugetre soit très arrogant, son équipage se comporte envers lui avec affection et respect. Kirsig dit le plus grand bien du capitaine, sans doute parce qu'il était ami avec son père. Sa cabine contient un bureau, un placard rempli de cartes et un hamac.

Nugetre nous a prévenu que nous n'avions aucune garantie d'arriver sains et saufs à notre destination, les îles minotaures.

— J'ai souvent traversé la Mer de Sang, mais je sais que chaque fois pourrait être la dernière, a-t-il déclaré. J'espère que vous avez de bonnes raisons pour risquer nos vies à tous.

Flint a voulu dire quelque chose, mais Raistlin l'a interrompu. Bien que Kirsig ait soigné sa blessure, Flint a le teint verdâtre depuis qu'il est monté à bord du Castor. *Il déteste vraiment les voyages maritimes.*

Raistlin a rassuré le capitaine et lui a dit que nous ne renoncerions pas. Pour étayer ses propos, il a posé sur la table un petit sac rempli de gemmes et de pièces : il y en avait pour une fortune. Flint a écarquillé les yeux, son mal de mer oublié.

— Je double la somme si nous effectuons la traversée en moins de dix jours, a annoncé Raistlin.

Kirsig avait déjà dit à Nugetre que nous étions pressés par le temps, et le capitaine nous a exposé son plan pour tenir les délais.

D'ordinaire, les marins évitent la Couronne Extérieure du Maelström, au centre de la Mer de Sang. Les navires qui s'y aventurent sont entraînés dans les anneaux du tourbillon, puis dans les eaux rouge-brun où se dressait autrefois la cité légendaire d'Istar.

Nugetre a proposé de foncer vers la Couronne Extérieure et d'utiliser ses courants sous-marins sans nous laisser happer par le vortex. Dès que nous serions assez près des îles minotaures, à trois cents lieues environ, le Castor *se dégagerait de l'étreinte mortelle.*

— C'est la seule façon de couvrir une telle distance en moins de dix jours, a conclu le capitaine. Sinon, à cause des courants et des vents contraires, le voyage durera plusieurs semaines. Il sera plus sûr, mais aussi plus long.

— Avez-vous déjà tenté cette manœuvre ? s'est enquis Raistlin.

— Non, a répondu simplement Nugetre.

Un lourd silence s'est abattu sur la cabine.

— Moi, oui, a soudain dit Yuril. A l'époque, je travaillais pour un autre capitaine. La traversée fut terrible. Nous dûmes non seulement lutter contre le courant, mais aussi essuyer les tempêtes perpétuelles qui règnent au cœur du Maelström.

« La mort nous guettait à chaque instant. Nous perdîmes plusieurs hommes... Pourtant, le capitaine ne céda pas. Il dégagea le navire au moment où il le fallait, et nous en fûmes quittes pour quelques dégâts matériels. »

Curieux, je demandai ce qu'il était advenu de ce capitaine. Pourquoi Yuril naviguait-elle maintenant avec Nugetre ?

— Peuh, cracha-t-elle. Mon ancien capitaine a perdu la vie sur terre, à Gardesang. C'était un génie en matière de navigation, mais un fieffé imbécile pour le reste. Imaginez : vaincre le Maelström pour périr dans une rixe de taverne ! (Elle a haussé les épaules.) Ça fait deux ans que j'ai embarqué sur le Castor. *Le capitaine Nugetre possède le courage et le talent nécessaires.*

Du doigt, elle a désigné l'endroit où nous devrions pénétrer dans la Couronne Extérieure, ajoutant que si le vent se maintenait, nous l'atteindrions en trois jours.

— Combien de temps resterons-nous à l'intérieur de ce... Maelström ? a demandé Kirsig d'une voix plaintive.

— Deux jours et deux nuits, a répondu Yuril, si tout se passe bien.

Raistlin étudiait la carte avec attention. Flint s'est penché vers moi pour chuchoter :

— Ne penses-tu pas que la méthode lente serait préférable ? Nous n'avons aucune preuve que Sturm, Tass et Caramon courent un réel danger.

Raistlin lui a jeté un regard plein de reproche. Flint a baissé les yeux en tirant sur sa barbe. Je savais qu'il s'inquiétait autant que nous pour nos amis.

— Comme ça, tu retrouveras la terre ferme plus tôt que prévu, ai-je dit pour le rassurer.

Pour ma part, j'approuvais le plan de Nugetre. Raistlin a hoché la tête, et Kirsig m'as surpris en me serrant dans ses bras. Je n'ai pas osé baisser les yeux vers Flint.

A la tombée de la nuit, de fortes bourrasques agitaient les voiles du Castor. *Les eaux étaient noires et insondables, l'air froid et piquant. Aucune étoile ne brillait dans le ciel. Nous sommes encore à trois jours de voyage du Maelström. C'est sans doute mon imagination qui me joue des tours, mais je jurerais sentir déjà son attraction fatale…*

Deuxième et troisième jours

Etranges périodes de calme brusquement interrompues par des bourrasques, des averses et des chutes de grêle. Nous n'avons encore croisé aucun navire. Même en l'absence de vent, le courant nous pousse vers le nord.

Ai-je décrit le Castor *? C'est un navire à deux mâts, muni de rames qu'on utilise rarement. Son équipage se compose de vingt-quatre marins, dont au moins la moitié sont des femmes. Tous humains, ils regardent Flint et Kirsig avec émerveillement, bien qu'ils aient déjà rencontré des ogres au cours de leurs voyages.*

Certains ont la peau noire. Ils viennent de lointaines îles septentrionales, et je les considère avec le même étonnement. Surtout les femmes, car elles sont magnifiques, à la fois fines et musclées. Elles portent des vêtements de cuir et des sandales, et grimpent aux mâts avec une agilité étonnante.

Les marins parlent un argot qui leur est propre, mais beaucoup s'expriment également en commun. Ils ne portent pas d'armes : jusqu'ici ils n'en ont pas eu besoin. Il y a une petite armurerie près de la poupe, où on garde des épées, des arbalètes, des carreaux, de l'huile, quelques armures et une réserve de rhum.

Yuril possède une grande autorité sur l'équipage. Elle a supervisé la construction de quatre gouvernails en forme de nageoires qui ont été placés sur les flancs de la coque, au-dessous du niveau de la mer. Quand nous pénétrerons dans le périmètre de la Mer de Sang, ils stabiliseront le Castor *et, nous l'espérons, l'aideront à résister aux secousses.*

Ces gouvernails additionnels s'accompagnent d'un système complexe de cordes et de leviers, attachés à des bloc de bois cloués au pont. Deux marins se sont portés volontaires pour se suspendre la tête dans l'eau afin de fixer le tout à la coque. Ils ont reçu une double ration de nourriture et les applaudissements de tous leurs camarades.

Le capitaine Nugetre préside à tout. Son port de tête est fier, mais il ne parle pas beaucoup ; on dirait parfois que c'est Yuril qui commande. Pourtant, il se moque d'elle quand il la trouve trop lente, et éclate de rire quand elle l'insulte en retour.

Nous transportons de la nourriture, des pièces de rechange et les armes mentionnées ci-dessus. Près de la cale se trouve une petite cellule vide ainsi que la cabine du second où Yuril dort, si ça lui arrive, ce dont je n'ai guère l'impression.

Raistlin, Flint, Kirsig et moi avons une cabine chacun, sommairement meublée d'un hamac, d'un banc, d'un coffre et d'une petite table. Raistlin passe presque tout son temps enfermé dans la sienne. Je suppose qu'il prend des forces pour l'épreuve qui nous attend. Les rares fois où je l'ai vu sur le pont, il semblait préoccupé. Sans doute s'inquiète-t-il pour Caramon.

Flint ne sort guère non plus, mais pas par choix : sa fracture à la jambe lui laisse une liberté de mouvement relative. Et puis, il préfère ne pas contempler le spectacle de l'océan…

Kirsig s'occupe bien de lui. Sa jambe n'est plus enflée ; elle a repris une couleur normale. La demi-ogresse n'a pas menti : elle possède quelques talents de guérisseuse. Flint devrait marcher à nouveau quand nous toucherons la terre ferme.

Kirsig refuse de quitter son chevet ; elle le gâte comme un enfant, lui caresse la barbe et lui donne toute sorte de petits noms ridicules, en dépit de ses protestations. Il a essayé de la repousser, mais sans résultat.

Tout le monde ne se montre pas aussi dur envers la demi-ogresse. Ce matin, un marin s'est blessé en tombant. La plaie était vilaine, mais Kirsig l'a recousue très proprement. L'indifférence amusée de Yuril à son égard s'est changée en respect.

Quatrième jour

L'eau est devenue aussi sinistre que les cieux. Ici, dans la Couronne Extérieure du Maelström, elle a la couleur du sang. Les vagues s'écrasent sur le pont en projetant leur écume.

Raistlin m'a expliqué que la couleur de l'océan est celle des sols fertiles qui entouraient autrefois Istar. Depuis que la ville a été détruite par le Cataclysme, le Maelström attaque les ruines, rappelant à tous le destin funeste de cette cité légendaire. Le capitaine Nugetre dit que le rouge est celui du sang des milliers de victimes noyées lorsque les dieux déchaînèrent leur colère sur Istar.

Flint s'est levé pour la première fois aujourd'hui. Il venait de nous rejoindre sur le pont quand un vieux marin a provoqué une vive émotion parmi le reste de l'équipage, affirmant que des dragons avaient été repérés dans les parages.

Interrogé, il a admis qu'il n'en avait jamais vu, mais qu'on lui en avait parlé dans une taverne. Les autres se sont moqués de lui... Pourtant, j'ai bien vu que Raistlin avait l'air songeur.

— Des dragons ! a ricané Flint. Et pourquoi pas un génie dans une lampe !

Nous avons été pris par un fort courant qui nous entraîne vers le nord-ouest. Le capitaine Nugetre a fait baisser les voiles : pour l'instant, nous nous laissons porter. Le ciel est tellement sombre qu'on ne distingue plus la nuit du jour. Depuis une heure, des éclairs déchirent les nuages ; une pluie torrentielle inonde le pont.

Le capitaine Nugetre a pris la barre. Il veille à ce que nous ne soyons pas aspirés dans la Couronne Intérieure, au-delà de laquelle s'étendent la Mer de Cauchemar et le Cœur des Ténèbres, l'endroit où la cité d'Istar dort au fond des flots. Personne n'en est jamais revenu.

Kirsig aide Yuril à calmer les marins. Flint s'est proposé pour ramer en cas de besoin. Malgré sa terreur, il est remarquablement calme. Raistlin s'accroche au mât principal, fouetté par les vents mais déterminé à ne rien manquer des événements à venir.

Cinquième jour

La nuit dernière a été épouvantable. De véritables lames de fond balayaient le pont du Castor *; elles ont emporté un marin et glacé les autres jusqu'à la mœlle. Le pont craquait, le vent rugissait autour de nous.*

Yuril et Nugetre ont dû s'y mettre à deux pour empêcher la barre de tourner follement. Personne n'a pu prendre ni repos ni nourriture pendant près de douze heures. Les marins devaient hurler pour se faire entendre.

Ce matin, le temps s'est un peu calmé, et nous avons pu dormir quelques heures.

Sixième jour

La situation empire à chaque minute. J'ai cru que nous allions sombrer corps et biens la nuit dernière. Le ciel et la mer se déchaînaient de concert, le tonnerre nous assourdissait, les embruns nous aveuglaient.

Nous avons dû nous attacher pour ne pas être emportés par les vagues. Un éclair a abattu le mât secondaire qui s'est écrasé sur le pont, brisant le cou d'un marin.

J'ignore depuis combien de temps Yuril et Nugetre n'ont pas dormi. Nous craignons presque les brefs répits que nous accorde le Maelström, car ils sont suivis de reprises meurtrières. La dernière a emporté deux hommes.

Raistlin a passé le plus clair de la journée dans sa cabine. A la grande fierté de Kirsig, Flint n'a pas quitté le pont. Trempé jusqu'aux os, le visage blême mais résolu, il s'accrochait aux cordes des gouvernails.

Vers midi, le Castor *a commencé à tourner sur lui-même à une vitesse plus effrayante que tout ce que nous avions affronté jusque-là. Les marins gémissaient et s'arrachaient les cheveux en désignant le bouillonnement des flots.*

Personnellement, je n'ai rien vu, mais je les ai entendu hurler que des horreurs grimaçantes, pourvues de griffes et de cornes, prenaient plaisir à nous tourmenter. Yuril leur a crié de retourner à leur poste. Le capitaine Nugetre semblait terrifié, mais pas à cause d'un péril imaginaire.

— Nous sommes allés trop loin ! s'est-il écrié. Nous avons pénétré dans la Couronne Intérieure, et nous approchons de la Mer de Cauchemar. Tout le monde aux rames ! Jetez l'ancre ! Préparez-vous à...

Sa voix fut presque noyée par les hurlements de l'équipage. Un brouillard rouge montait des flots déchaînés et envahissait le pont, prenant la forme de minuscules démons aux ailes de chauve-souris, à la queue fourchue, aux cornes aiguës et aux dents d'un blanc étincelant.

Les créatures ont grimpé dans la mâture qu'elles ont commencé à saccager. Un vent de panique a soufflé sur le navire.

— Imbéciles, ce ne sont que des illusions ! cria Nugetre.

Peut-être avait-il raison... Mais l'instant d'après, j'en vis deux saisir un marin et le projeter par-dessus bord.

Debout sur les marches du petit escalier conduisant à nos cabines, Raistlin a baissé la tête et tracé des symboles dans les airs. J'ai vu ses lèvres remuer : il préparait une incantation.

A ma grande surprise, les démons ont disparu brusquement, mais pas le brouillard. Raistlin est rentré dans sa cabine ; personne ou presque n'a remarqué son intervention.

La tempête faisait toujours rage. Flint s'est frayé un chemin jusqu'à moi ; je ne l'avais encore jamais vu aussi effrayé.

— Qu'allons-nous faire ? a-t-il demandé.

J'ai secoué la tête en signe d'ignorance. Alors j'ai vu Yuril et deux autres marins lutter pour détacher l'ancre du Castor, *une tâche rendue difficile par la fureur des éléments. Flint et moi nous sommes précipités pour prêter main-forte.*

— Maintenant ! a crié le capitaine Nugetre.

Malgré le pont qui glissait et tanguait follement sous nos pieds, nous sommes parvenus à jeter l'ancre à la mer. L'épaisse corde s'est déroulée si vite qu'un marin a du jeter un seau d'eau dessus pour qu'elle ne brûle pas.

Pendant plusieurs minutes, l'ancre s'est enfoncée dans les eaux sanglantes. Elle était presque arrivée au bout de la corde lorsqu'elle a touché le fond. Yuril a poussé un cri.

— Jamais encore je n'avais rencontré une telle profondeur !

Comme l'avait prévu Nugetre, l'ancre a stabilisé le vaisseau. Mais ballotté par les vagues, le Castor *menaçait de rompre ses amarres à tout moment.*

Sur l'ordre du capitaine, Flint a abattu sa hache sur la corde. Sa tension était telle que le navire emporté par son élan s'est arraché au Maelström. Je l'ai senti bondir en avant.

Pendant ce temps, Yuril et moi nous sommes dirigés vers la poupe où une poignée de marins manœuvraient les gouvernails secondaires. Alors que le Castor *retombait, avant que le courant s'empare à nouveau de lui, nous détachâmes les gouvernails. Je me penchai par-dessus le bastingage et les vis disparaître dans l'eau, formant comme des nageoires à l'arrière du navire.*

— Maintenant ! cria encore le capitaine Nugetre.

Les rameurs joignirent leurs forces pour propulser le Castor en direction du nord. Tous les hommes et femmes valides allèrent se joindre à eux. Au moment où j'écris ces mots, chaque seconde qui passe nous éloigne un peu plus du cœur mortel de la Mer de Sang.

Septième et huitième jours

Le pire est passé. Nous traversons maintenant Eaudefeu en direction de Mithas et de Karthay.

Les marins ont célébré leur victoire sur le Maelström. Ils faisaient un étrange tableau avec leurs cheveux emmêlés par le vent, leurs lèvres craquelées, leurs vêtements raidis par le sel et leur expression hagarde d'hommes qui ne parviennent pas à croire à leur chance. En guise de récompense, le capitaine Nugetre a fait distribuer du rhum à tout le monde.

Malgré les conditions épouvantables auxquelles il a été exposé, le Castor *a finalement subi peu de dommages. Le vent a brisé son mât secondaire, la mer quelques-unes de ses rames. Des débris projetés par la tempête ont déchiré les voiles en maints endroits, et Kirsig s'est proposée pour les repriser. Les marins lui ont offert leurs chemises pour boucher les trous.*

Cela mis à part, les dégâts ont été réparés en quelques heures. Flint a entrepris de fabriquer une nouvelle ancre, qui servira jusqu'à ce que nous touchions terre. Il a fait le tour du navire, rassemblant tous les morceaux de plomb et de métaux mous qu'il a pu trouver, puis il a fait fondre le tout dans un énorme chaudron avant de forger une ancre rudimentaire que Yuril a jugé satisfaisante.

Les vagues sont encore très hautes, l'eau s'est un peu éclaircie, mais elle garde son étrange couleur de rouille. Nous devons travailler dur pour maintenir le Castor *sur la route. Le soleil se fait plus brûlant chaque jour, et une étrange brume s'est formée dans le ciel.*

Huitième jour, tard dans la soirée

Raistlin est resté dans sa cabine toute la journée, ne sortant sur le pont qu'après le tombée de la nuit. Flint et moi avions deviné qu'il ne nous avait pas tout dit. Quelque chose le préoccupait.

Nous l'avons rejoint sur le pont avant, perdu dans la contemplation d'un ciel sans étoiles. Il n'a même pas tourné la tête à notre approche, et j'ai toussoté pour interrompre sa rêverie.

— Tu dois beaucoup t'inquiéter pour Caramon, ai-je commencé avec prudence.

A ma grande surprise, Raistlin a haussé un sourcil, comme si le salut de son frère était bien son dernier souci.

— Caramon est un grand garçon, a-t-il dit, peu amène. S'il n'est pas mort dans le Détroit de Schallmer, je suis certain que nous le retrouverons. Il y a même plus de chance pour que ce soit lui qui vole à notre secours que l'inverse.

— Mais, ai-je protesté, je croyais que nous avions fait tout ce chemin pour le délivrer des minotaures.

— Oui... en partie, a admis Raistlin.

Il allait ajouter quelque chose mais il se ravisa pour rassembler ses pensées.

— De toute façon, a-t-il enfin déclaré, il y a plus important que le sort de mon frère.

— Explique-toi.

— Par exemple, pourquoi il a été enlevé et l'utilisation qu'on peut faire de la jalopine, l'herbe qu'il était parti me chercher.

Raistlin s'exprimait sur un ton très solennel. Dans les ténèbres, je ne pouvais distinguer l'expression de son visage. Je me suis penché vers lui.

— Sois plus clair. Tu veux parler de ce sort que tu as découvert dans le grimoire de Morath, n'est-ce pas ? A quoi sert-il ?

Raistlin s'est humecté les lèvres.

— Ce sort ne peut être lancé que par un haut prêtre minotaure. Il permet d'ouvrir un portail et d'« inviter » dans notre monde Sargonnas, le consort et serviteur de Takhisis.

Je suis resté muet de stupéfaction. Apprenti magicien, Raistlin croyait aux anciens dieux : ceux du Bien, ceux de la Neutralité et ceux du Mal, sur lesquels régnait Takhisis. Moi, je ne savais pas trop. Et j'ignorais presque tout de Sargonnas.

— Ce n'est pas tout, a poursuivi Raistlin. Ce sort ne peut être lancé qu'à la faveur d'une certaine conjonction astrologique. L'effort requis par sa préparation est colossal.

« Autrement dit, les minotaures ne prendront la peine de le lancer que s'ils ont vraiment besoin de l'aide de Sargonnas. D'après Morath, ils doivent songer à conquérir l'Ansalonie. »

— Ils ne peuvent y arriver seuls, ai-je protesté.

— C'est vrai. Mais pourquoi ne s'allieraient-ils pas avec d'autres races maléfiques, les ogres, par exemple ?

— Ils sont trop arrogants pour ça.

— Pas forcément, a dit Kirsig en sortant de l'ombre.

Elle avait une façon énervante d'épier les gens... Mais pour une raison que j'ignore, Raistlin l'aimait bien et n'a pas semblé perturbé par son apparition.

— Ça expliquerait une chose très curieuse, poursuivit la demi-ogresse.

— Laquelle ? s'enquit Raistlin, sa curiosité piquée.

— A Ogrelien depuis plusieurs mois, des délégations de minotaures arrivent en galion pour parlemen-

ter avec les tribus ogres. C'est assez inhabituel pour qu'on le remarque. D'habitude, les deux races sont plutôt ennemies.

— Tu vois ce que je veux dire ? grogna Raistlin en se tournant vers moi. Le sort de Caramon est le dernier de mes soucis !

Neuvième jour

Tôt dans la matinée, un des marins a cru voir quelque chose bouger sous l'eau, contre le flanc du navire. Tout le monde a redoublé de vigilance.

A midi, nous avons repéré de nouveau la créature : une forme grise et massive qui semblait suivre le Castor. *Ses mouvements étaient sinueux, et elle restait si loin de la surface que nous ne pouvions distinguer vraiment sa silhouette.*

En fin d'après-midi, vu son manque de réaction, nous avons relâché notre attention. Quelques-uns des marins étaient descendus se reposer, d'autres somnolaient à leur poste quand la créature s'est cambrée pour passer à l'attaque.

Je me trouvais sur le pont quand j'ai vu son long corps mou fondre sur le navire, dont elle avait à peu près la taille. Je l'ai identifiée aussitôt : c'était une nudibranche ou limace aquatique géante, très rare dans cette partie du monde.

J'ai eu à peine le temps de m'abriter derrière un canot, avant que la mâchoire gigantesque de la créature projette vers la proue un flot de salive corrosive.

Le Castor *a fait un bond en avant. Les marins qui dormaient se sont éveillés en sursaut. Touché à la jambe, l'un d'eux s'est écroulé sur le pont en poussant des hurlements. Un autre a été dévoré par la nudibranche.*

Le capitaine Nugetre est arrivé en courant et a commencé à crier des ordres. Les marins qui n'étaient pas de quart ont émergé de leur cabine, porteurs d'armes ridicules comparées à la masse de leur adversaire.

Yuril, qui tenait la barre au moment de l'attaque, s'était accroupie près de moi. Sous nos yeux fascinés et horrifiés, la limace géante a levé la tête si haut que nous avons aperçu son ventre blanc, puis elle s'est laissée tomber sur le pont tel un gigantesque bélier.

Des éclats de bois ont volé dans toutes les directions. La nudibranche reposait moitié dans l'eau, moitié sur le navire, qui tanguait dangereusement. Pendant quelques minutes, sa tête a disparu dans les profondeurs du Castor. *On n'entendait que d'immondes bruits de succion et les hurlements des marins pris au piège.*

— Flint ! ai-je crié.

— Chut ! a soufflé mon ami. Je suis derrière toi.

Raistlin et Kirsig s'y trouvaient également. Une femme à la peau noire et aux cheveux ras s'est jetée sur le dos de la limace en brandissant un sabre. Mais la créature avait la peau épaisse et caoutchouteuse ; la lame courbe ne lui a fait qu'une égratignure.

Avec une agilité surprenante, la nudibranche a réussi à tourner sa tête massive, à saisir la femme dans sa gueule et à la couper en deux d'un coup de dents. Puis elle a rejeté son cadavre sanglant dans les flots.

Sans réfléchir, Flint, Kirsig, Yuril et moi nous sommes précipités sur la limace, suivis par une poignée d'autres marins. Nous avons réussi à lui porter quelques coups, sans grand résultat. La nudibranche a assommé plusieurs hommes, ou les a couverts de salive grésillante.

Du coin de l'œil, j'ai vu que Raistlin préparait quelque chose à l'autre bout du navire. Il a appelé Flint et, ensemble, ils ont traîné un objet jusqu'à nous. Deux marins sont venus leur prêter main-forte. Raistlin a abandonné à Flint le contrôle des opérations et il s'est précipité vers le capitaine pour conférer avec lui. Nugetre a paru approuver sa suggestion.

Sur un signal de Flint, pendant que Kirsig, Yuril et moi distrayions la nudibranche, les marins ont soulevé l'ancre et lui ont jetée à la tête. Comme Raistlin l'avait prévu, la créature a ouvert la bouche pour avaler ce qu'on lui lançait.

Une expression presque surprise s'est peinte sur son visage rudimentaire quand le capitaine Nugetre a donné un brusque tour de gouvernail. Le mouvement a fait glisser la limace en arrière, et l'ancre de Flint l'a entraînée rapidement au fond de l'océan couleur de rouille.

L'attaque a laissé le Castor *dans un état pitoyable. Nous avons perdu trois marins, et Flint s'efforce de fabriquer une troisième ancre.*

Dixième jour

Selon Nugetre, malgré l'allure d'escargot à laquelle nous avançons maintenant, nous ne sommes plus qu'à une demi-journée de la côte de Karthay.

Le Castor *est gravement mutilé. L'équipage, réduit de moitié, doit écoper en permanence pour ne pas que nous coulions. Flint, Raistlin, Kirsig et moi aidons de notre mieux.*

Nous avons tenu nos délais, mais Nugetre dit qu'à ce prix, ça n'en valait pas la peine.

— Je ne prendrai pas le risque d'entrer dans Karthay, a-t-il annoncé. Je vous donnerai une chaloupe pour rejoindre le rivage, c'est tout ce que je peux faire.

Malgré les cajoleries de Kirsig, il n'est pas revenu sur sa décision. Raistlin lui a payé la somme promise sans insister. Mieux, il l'a remercié d'avoir si bien rempli sa part du contrat.

Kirsig veut nous accompagner. Flint a tenté de l'en dissuader, mais elle refuse d'abandonner son « si joli nain ».

La plus grande surprise vient de Yuril. Elle aussi souhaite continuer le voyage avec nous. Elle dit que nous lui avons sauvé la vie au moins deux fois, et qu'elle se doit de nous aider.

En l'apprenant, le capitaine Nugetre s'est mis dans une colère folle. Sans succès. Sa rage ne parvenait pas à masquer sa tristesse.

A mon avis, ses rapports avec Yuril n'étaient pas seulement ceux d'un officier en second et de son commandant.

Quatre membres de l'équipage, toutes des femmes, plus dévouées à Yuril qu'à Nugetre, se sont également portées volontaires. Nous sommes neuf, et ce n'est pas d'une mais de deux chaloupes dont nous aurons besoin pour rejoindre la terre.

CHAPITRE X

La potion fonctionna à merveille. Tasslehoff Racle-Pieds fut changé en kender maléfique. Aucun doute, depuis le sommet de son crâne jusqu'au bout de ses orteils, il n'était que méchanceté à l'état pur.

La nouvelle allégeance de Tass lui valait le statut d'invité du roi. On l'avait logé dans des appartements privés, au dernier étage du palais : un sanctuaire garni de fourrures et de velours dominant la cité grouillante de Lacynos.

Fesz, l'envoyé du Maître de la Nuit, résidait juste en face du kender, ce qui lui permettait de le garder à l'œil et de l'interroger le plus souvent possible. Il avait posté des gardes devant la porte de Tass, avec ordre de l'empêcher de leur fausser compagnie tout en satisfaisant le moindre de ses désirs.

Les minotaures n'étaient pas certains d'apprécier le ralliement du kender à leur cause. Maléfique, Tass les embêtait dix fois plus qu'avant. Il éprouvait un malin plaisir à les faire courir en tous sens, à toute heure du jour ou de la nuit.

Par exemple, il avait décidé de prendre trois bains quotidiens à des heures bien précises. Les gardes devaient transporter d'innombrables seaux d'eau bouillante dans les couloirs du palais, et monter plusieurs étages avant qu'elle ne refroidisse trop. Sinon, Tass faisait un scandale, les insultant, les frappant sur la tête avec les seaux vides ou menaçant de leur crever les yeux avec une tringle à rideau.

Les minotaures avaient beaucoup de mal à se contenir. Ils n'avaient pas l'habitude de recevoir les ordres d'un kender, et moins encore des injures ou des coups qu'ils ne pouvaient pas rendre. Mais les consignes étaient les consignes.

Parce qu'il s'ennuyait dans ses appartements, Tass décida que ceux-ci devaient être repeints d'une couleur plus agréable. Le blanc lui semblait trop fade ; il eut bien du mal à choisir la nouvelle teinte.

Un matin, il ordonna à deux des gardes de tout repeindre en bleu indigo avant le coucher du soleil. Alors qu'il examinait le résultat, il faillit s'endormir et en déduisit que l'indigo était une couleur soporifique.

Du coup, le lendemain, il exigea que les mêmes gardes repeignent sa chambre en rouge écarlate. Les malheureux protestèrent d'autant plus que Tass ne cessait de leur taper dessus pendant qu'ils travaillaient.

Hélas, l'écarlate empêcha le kender de dormir la nuit suivante. Il décida que le sol resterait ainsi — à condition qu'on le couvre de tapis —, mais que qu'une couleur plus vive, comme de l'orange, conviendrait mieux aux murs. Le plafond, lui, devait avoir une teinte maléfique, noir d'encre, par exemple.

Les gardes minotaures qui s'en étaient si bien (ou si mal) tirés les jours précédents, eurent le privilège de recommencer le travail.

Ils n'étaient pas les seuls à se plaindre de Tasslehoff. Quiconque pénétrait dans les appartements du kender se voyait criblé de projectiles, attaqué par-derrière ou agoni d'injures.

Dogz, le seul qui échappait à ce traitement, regrettait l'ancien Tasslehoff. Mais Fesz avait déclaré que le kender appartenait maintenant au Maître de la Nuit, et personne n'osait aller contre sa volonté.

Aux yeux du chamane, le comportement agressif de Tass était la preuve qu'il était devenu maléfique. Ainsi, il était facile de lui extorquer des informations au sujet du jeune mage qui l'avait envoyé en Ergoth Méridional chercher de la jalopine.

Tass avait également parlé à Fesz de ses bons amis Flint Forgefeu et Tanis Demi-Elfe, de son oncle Chausse-Trappes et des pauvres Sturm de Lumlane et Caramon Majere, dont les poissons avaient dévoré la carcasse dans la Mer de Sang. Après tout, bon débarras, avait déclaré le kender. Les deux hommes étaient honorables et purs. Ils n'auraient pas eu leur place dans sa nouvelle conception du monde.

Pourtant, Tass aimait à parler de ses amis, ou de ses « ex-amis », comme il les appelait. Parfois, il se mettait à bavarder sur Flint, et Fesz devait le ramener sur Raistlin : un ennemi de la race minotaure, et par là même celui du kender. Cet humain qui étudiait la magie et avait voulu se procurer de la jalopine à cause d'un sort trouvé dans un grimoire moisi…

— Oh, il est très intelligent, pépia Tass. Et plutôt bon, si on considère qu'il n'a pas encore passé l'Epreuve. S'il a deviné où se trouve la jalopine (c'est-à-dire où je me trouve, à Minotaureville), il est sans doute déjà en route.

« Je pense qu'il a dû emmener Tanis et Flint avec lui. Flint va avoir un sacré choc en découvrant que je suis devenu maléfique, mais pas longtemps, parce que je le tuerai.

« Cela dit, tu as raison, Fesz. La véritable menace vient de Raistlin. On ferait bien de chercher un moyen de le capturer, de l'étrangler, de le découper en morceaux et de faire quelque chose de vraiment horrible à son cadavre, comme... Je ne sais pas, moi. Tu as plus d'expérience en la matière. Que suggères-tu ? »

Quand le kender était excité, il faisait les cent pas dans ses appartements, un rictus sinistre tordant son petit visage ridé. Fesz en concevait une grande satisfaction. Il en profitait pour lui faire boire une nouvelle dose de potion, histoire que l'influence de la première ne se dissipe pas.

Cela faisait maintenant une bonne semaine que Tass se montrait si coopératif. Fesz avait couché par écrit les renseignements obtenus sur Raistlin et la jalopine avant de les envoyer au Maître de la Nuit, sur l'île de Karthay.

Malgré sa nouvelle personnalité, le kender était toujours aussi curieux. Il harcela Fesz pour savoir par quel moyen celui-ci communiquait avec son maître. Un jour où il était de bonne humeur, le chamane l'invita dans ses appartements.

— Pourquoi ta chambre est-elle plus grande que la mienne ? s'indigna le kender en regardant autour de lui. Tes tableaux sont plus beaux, et tu as deux fenêtres au lieu d'une !

« J'aime bien les couleurs que tu as choisies : brun et vert foncé. Ça me rappelle la forêt. Ces andouilles de gardes m'ont embrouillé l'esprit avec leur bleu, leur rouge et leur orange. En rentrant, je vais leur dire ce que je pense ! »

Fesz entoura d'un bras les épaules du kender, éprouvant presque un élan paternel envers un être qui lui ressemblait un peu plus chaque jour. Il le conduisit vers le rebord d'une fenêtre où était posé un bocal rempli de grosses abeilles.

— Ces insectes surdoués portent mes messages au Maître de la Nuit, expliqua-t-il en surveillant la réaction de Tass. Ils peuvent parcourir de grandes distances et communiquer télépathiquement. Bien sûr, on peut en faire d'autres usages, plus amusants...

Tass en eut le sifflet coupé. Il n'avait encore jamais entendu parler de tels insectes.

D'un geste théâtral, le minotaure ôta le couvercle du bocal et laissa les abeilles s'en échapper. L'essaim voleta quelques instants sur place, avant de s'élancer en bourdonnant vers le soleil levant.

— Ouah ! s'exclama Tass, retrouvant l'usage de la parole. En rentrant d'Ergoth Méridional, j'ai envoyé un message magique à Raistlin, mais je n'avais qu'une stupide bouteille que j'ai dû jeter dans l'océan. Qui sait où elle se trouve à présent ?

« Si j'avais eu des abeilles comme celles-là... Sauf que je ne vois pas où j'aurais pu les mettre. Dans un sac à dos, le bocal risquerait de se casser... »

Ravi par ce flot d'informations, Fesz s'empressa de mentionner la bouteille magique dans le rapport qu'il était en train de rédiger. En une semaine, il avait réussi à faire une description complète du jeune mage, de ses défauts et de ses faiblesses.

Il avait envoyé des assassins à Solace, au cas où Raistlin s'y trouverait encore. Et si le jeune homme était bien en route pour les îles minotaures, le Maître de la Nuit serait prêt à le recevoir. Ce Raistlin ne pouvait constituer une réelle menace, mais il ne coûtait rien d'être prudent.

Le huitième jour suivant la transformation du kender, Fesz pénétra dans les appartements de Tass, l'air perplexe. Il tenait un parchemin sur lequel figurait un message apporté par les abeilles, qu'il avait lui-même retranscrit.

Heureux de recevoir son nouvel ami, Tass le salua d'une révérence de son invention, puis il lui arracha le message des mains et lut :

Nous avons capturé une femelle sur le rivage. Elle est bien armée, sans doute une guerrière. Elle refuse de me dire son nom ou les raisons de sa présence. Nous la gardons prisonnière en vue d'un sacrifice. Je pense qu'elle est une de ceux que nous attendons. Demande au kender s'il la connaît.

Tass n'eut pas besoin de réfléchir longtemps.

— Je parie que c'est Kitiara ! s'exclama-t-il. Même si je ne vois pas comment elle a pu arriver si vite à Karthay.

— Qui est Kitiara ? demanda Fesz, les sourcils froncés.

— Kitiara Uth Matar, expliqua le kender. Ne t'en ai-je pas déjà parlé ? Je l'oublie tout le temps, parce qu'elle n'est que la demi-sœur de Raistlin. Si elle est venue, c'est sans doute parce que Raist l'a contactée, donc, il ne doit pas être loin derrière...

Fesz se remit à écrire à toute vitesse.

*
* *

Fesz et Tass étaient devenus si bons amis qu'ils prenaient souvent une carriole tirée par des esclaves humains et allaient se promener dans Lacynos. Le grand air rendait le kender plus bavard que d'habitude, ce qui n'était pas peu dire.

Leur véhicule était suivi par un ou deux minotaures, qui gardaient leurs distances… Non à cause du protocole, mais parce qu'ils ne voulaient pas se faire bombarder de cailloux par Tass.

Le kender connaissait maintenant la cité par cœur. Il aimait particulièrement les endroits nauséabonds et maléfiques, comme les fosses à esclaves : de grands trous creusés dans le sol, où vivaient les milliers de malheureux qui effectuaient les corvées à Lacynos.

Les esclaves s'étaient faits capturer par des pirates, avaient été vendus par des professionnels ou condamnés à une période de travaux forcés. On trouvait parmi eux quelques elfes et une poignée de minotaures en disgrâce, mais les humains prédominaient.

Des dizaines de gardes entouraient le périmètre de chaque fosse, derrière les murs « effondrables » prévus pour endiguer un éventuel soulèvement. Une rampe assez large pour y marcher à six ou sept de front constituait le seul accès aux fosses.

Après avoir visité l'une d'elles, Tass, très impressionné, posa de nombreuses questions.

— Quand je rentrerai à Solace..., commença le kender. (Il se reprit :) Non que j'y pense, parce que je m'amuse beaucoup ici... Mais si ça m'arrive un jour, j'aimerais construire une fosse comme celle-là. Ça leur apprendrait.

« Bien sûr, les gens vivent dans les arbres, et techniquement parlant, creuser en l'air risque d'être difficile. Enfin, je trouverai bien quelque chose. »

Debout sur une passerelle, Tass examina les esclaves malades ou blessés qui gisaient sur le sol de la fosse. Une prêtresse agenouillée s'efforçait de les soigner. Un homme vêtu comme un Solamnique se frayait un chemin dans la foule.

Un garde passa trop près du kender, qui lui flanqua un coup de coude. Déséquilibré, le minotaure bascula et alla s'écraser cinquante pieds plus bas, au milieu des esclaves.

— Oups ! Désolé, dit le kender, qui n'en avait pas l'air. Je me demandais juste le bruit qu'il ferait en atterrissant sur la tête.

Fesz eut un sourire indulgent.

Outre les fosses à esclaves, Tass aimait beaucoup l'arène de Lacynos : un bâtiment impressionnant avec ses hauts murs de pierre blanche, ses arches gigantesques et ses confortables galeries. Des milliers d'esclaves étaient morts lors de sa construction, et des milliers d'autres périssaient deux fois par mois au cours des jeux dont les minotaures se régalaient.

Tass et Fesz passèrent un après-midi dans la loge royale, en face de l'entrée des gladiateurs. Le kender regarda deux humains se livrer un combat à mort. Vifs et musclés, ils portaient des vêtements sommaires et des armes redoutables, mais il était presque impossible de les distinguer l'un de l'autre.

Leur duel se poursuivit pendant des heures. Tass ne tarda pas à s'ennuyer ferme malgré l'atmosphère joyeuse qui régnait dans les gradins. De nombreux spectateurs étaient venus en famille, avec femme et enfants. D'une voix forte, ils encourageaient le gladiateur sur lequel ils avaient misé.

— Au fait, dit Tass en réprimant un bâillement, alors que le vainqueur faisait le tour de l'arène en tenant à bout de bras la tête sanglante de son adversaire, ça me rappelle que j'aimerais bien récupérer mon bâton. C'est la seule arme que j'utilise, et il a une valeur sentimentale.

— Où se trouve-t-il ? demanda aimablement Fesz.

— Il était avec mes sacoches, mais on m'a tout confisqué.

— Très bien. Je veillerai à ce qu'on te rende tes affaires.

Le lendemain, les nouveaux amis allèrent se promener sur le port. A voir l'activité qui y régnait, Tass comprit que les minotaures se préparaient à la guerre, ou au moins à une action militaire d'envergure. De gigantesques piles de bois s'alignaient sur les quais, et des centaines d'esclaves munis d'outils s'agitaient en tous sens.

— Ils travaillent même la nuit, expliqua Fesz, à la lueur des torches. Nous devons êtres prêts pour l'heure où Sargonnas entrera dans notre monde.

Tass hocha la tête. Il savait déjà ce que mijotait le Maître de la Nuit. Fesz le lui avait peu à peu révélé, à mesure que le kender le renseignait sur Raistlin Majere.

La jalopine devait permettre de lancer un sort qui ouvrirait un portail pour le dieu des minotaures. Celui-ci permettrait alors à son peuple élu de dominer les races inférieures d'Ansalonie : c'est-à-dire toutes les autres. Le grand prêtre incanterait quand les lunes, le soleil et les étoiles formeraient une configuration spéciale dans le ciel.

« — Très bientôt, avait dit Fesz. »

Etant lui-même maléfique, Tass se sentait très excité par cette perspective. Il espérait faire la connaissance de Sargonnas ; c'était pourquoi il cultivait l'amitié de Fesz.

— Es-tu certain que les minotaures pourront conquérir le monde seuls ? demanda innocemment le kender.

Il regarda autour de lui. Les galions des minotaures étaient impressionnants, mais il y avait sur le continent un grand nombre d'elfes, de nains, d'humains et même de kenders pour les accueillir. Ses nouveaux alliés vivaient en reclus depuis trop longtemps : ils sous-estimaient l'opposition qu'ils allaient rencontrer.

— C'est très malin de poser la question, Tass, dit Fesz jetant un regard soupçonneux par-dessus son épaule. La réponse est non. Bien que nous soyons très puissants, nous aurons besoin d'alliés.

« Nous avons déjà conclu un accord avec les ogres et leurs cousins aquatiques, les orughis. Nous avons envoyé des diplomates discuter avec les trolls, malgré leur manque évident d'organisation, et avec certaines tribus barbares. Nous serons également aidés par certains... hum... éléments dont je ne suis pas libre de discuter avec toi. »

— Oh ! dit Tass, vexé. Et les kenders ?

— J'avoue ne pas y avoir pensé, répondit Fesz, pris au dépourvu. S'ils sont tous comme toi, c'est vrai qu'ils pourraient nous être utiles. Vois-tu, il y a une semaine encore, nous ne savions pas grand-chose sur les tiens.

Tass gonfla la poitrine pour se donner l'air important.

— J'intercéderai en votre faveur auprès de mon peuple, dit-il fièrement. Je suis célèbre à Kenderfoule, ou du moins, je l'étais la dernière fois que j'y suis passé : il y a dix, vingt ou trente ans, avant ma période de vagabondite.

« Mon oncle Chausse-Trappes est encore plus connu, mais je ne suis pas sûr qu'il veuille s'associer à vous, car il est plutôt difficile sur le choix de ses amis. Il n'est pas très amical avec ses ennemis non plus. Avec un peu de chance, il ne sera pas là, et je n'aurai pas besoin de le tuer. »

— Très bien, dit Fesz en bon diplomate. Je vais prévenir le Maître de la Nuit des possibilités offertes par la race kender.

— Précise bien que c'est mon idée, ajouta Tass.

Le minotaure hocha la tête.

Quand ils rentrèrent au palais, Dogz les attendait, porteur d'un message du roi. Il le tendit à Fesz en évitant le regard de Tasslehoff, comme s'il avait honte du kender.

Ce dernier lut par-dessus l'épaule du minotaure.

Nous avons capturé deux humains près d'Atossa. L'un s'est échappé par des moyens inexplicables, sans doute magiques. Pourrait-il être le mage que vous cherchez ? Faites un rapport immédiat au Cercle Suprême.

Fesz jeta un regard interrogateur à Tass.

— Eh bien, dit le kender, je ne sais pas trop. Je ne pense pas que ça puisse être Raistlin… Le message parle de *deux* humains. Or Flint est un nain et Tanis un demi-elfe.

Fesz fronça les sourcils.

— Attends une minute ! s'écria Tass, tout excité. Ce sont peut-être Sturm et Caramon. Bien sûr, ils sont censés être morts, et aucun des deux ne connaît la magie… Mais Raistlin a pu apprendre quelques trucs à Caramon quand ils étaient petits. C'est probablement ça. Je me demande lequel des deux s'est échappé.

— Sturm et Caramon, marmonna Fesz. Ce sont les deux humains qu'on a jetés dans la Mer de Sang, n'est-ce pas ?

— C'est ça.

— A supposer qu'ils soient encore vivants, pourquoi Raistlin aurait-il enseigné des sorts à Caramon ?

— Je ne sais pas. Ils sont jumeaux, alors...

— Jumeaux ! s'écria Fesz, d'une voix si forte que Dogz sursauta. (Le minotaure s'efforça de reprendre son calme.) Tu ne m'as jamais dit que Raistlin avait un frère !

Tass haussa les épaules.

— Tu ne me l'as jamais demandé. Et on croyait tous les deux que Caramon était mort. Ça change quoi ? Je t'ai dit que Raistlin avait une sœur, non ? Une demi-sœur, en fait, mais bon...

— Attends !

Fesz leva la main, poussa un gros soupir et sortit de quoi écrire.

— Avant de continuer, dit-il en faisant un effort visible pour se maîtriser, Raistlin a-t-il d'autres frères et sœurs que tu aurais omis de mentionner ?

— Non, déclara joyeusement le kender, qui ne voyait pas pourquoi son ami se mettait martel en tête. Du moins, aucun dont j'ai entendu parler.

— Juste Kitiara et Caramon.

— Voilà.

Fesz gribouilla quelque chose sur un morceau de parchemin, qu'il fourra ensuite dans sa poche.

— Je me demande si c'était Sturm ou Caramon, murmura Tass.

— Nous devons nous rendre à Atossa pour nous en assurer, annonça Fesz.

Un immense sourire fendit le visage du kender.

— Dès que j'aurai fait mon rapport à la Cour Suprême, ajouta le minotaure.

— Le Cercle Suprême ? Ouah ! s'exclama Tass. Je n'avais encore jamais rencontré des gens suprêmes. J'ai hâte d'y être.

Derrière lui, Dogz posa une grande main sur son épaule.

— Je suis navré, ami Tass, mais je dois y aller seul, dit Fesz. Le Cercle Suprême n'apprécierait pas la présence d'un kender.

*

* *

Autour de la table de chêne ronde, dans la grand-salle du palais, huit minotaures étaient assis en compagnie de leur roi. Celui-ci arrivait tout droit de sa résidence principale, dans la cité de Nethosak, pour assister à la réunion d'urgence.

Si les autres participants semblaient mécontents, les yeux du roi brillaient d'une colère meurtrière qu'il avait du mal à contenir. Il avait des milliers de choses importantes à faire, et il n'appréciait guère qu'on vienne bouleverser son emploi du temps.

Le premier des huit autres membres du Cercle Suprême se nommait Inultus. Il était assis à la gauche du roi et commandait la police et l'armée de terre.

Beaucoup de gens avaient donné à Attacca, le second minotaure, le sobriquet ridicule d'Akz, mais personne ne lui disait jamais en face. Akz était le commandant de la marine. Il détestait Inultus, qui le lui rendait bien. Dans l'intérêt de la nation, tous deux étaient parfois obligés de coopérer, ce qui n'allait pas sans difficultés. Akz portait pour tout vêtement un gilet de cuir orné de joyaux.

Près de lui se tenait le vétéran de l'assemblée : un minotaure au pelage poivre et sel nommé Victri. Il était le représentant des agriculteurs, que les guerriers méprisaient mais dont ils dépendaient pour vivre. Chacun à Lacynos connaissait la sagesse, le sens de l'honneur et la férocité au combat de Victri. Il était vêtu comme un paysan, jusqu'au foulard drapé sur ses larges épaules.

A sa gauche était assis Juvabit, historien et érudit dans une société qui n'avait que faire de l'érudition. Bien qu'il fût un intellectuel selon les standards de sa race, rien ne le distinguait physiquement de ses confrères, à part le gland doré à l'or fin qui pendait à son épaule droite.

Le gland était l'insigne de l'Ordre du Roi, la plus haute distinction minotaure. Juvabit était le seul membre du Cercle à l'avoir gagnée. La décoration lui conférait une assurance démesurée : le minotaure se savait plus malin que ses collègues et il se sentait capable de les battre tous à mains nues en cas de besoin.

Atra Cura venait ensuite. Il supervisait les pirates humains ou minotaures qui sévissaient dans les océans alentour et taxait leur butin au nom du roi. Connu pour ses colères meurtrières, il était craint de tous. Il portait des vêtements aux couleurs flamboyantes, abondamment décorés de gemmes. Des sabres et couteaux se balançaient à sa ceinture.

Le seul membre féminin du Conseil, Kharis-O, était le chef d'une bande d'amazones qui méprisaient les mâles et vivaient à l'extérieur des cités. Son clan comptait des fidèles dans toutes les îles minotaures, mais les amazones se mêlaient rarement aux secteurs organisés de la société.

Pourtant, personne ne mettait sa loyauté en doute. Le roi savait qu'il pouvait compter sur Kharis-O et les siennes en temps de guerre. La minotaure avait un visage particulièrement laid. Rien dans ses vêtements ne la distinguait d'un mâle de sa race.

Les deux derniers participants à la réunion étaient Bartill et Groppis. Bartill dirigeait la guilde des architectes et celle des maçons. Très puissant, personne n'osait le contrarier.

Quant à Groppis, son inévitable allié dans les débats du Cercle, il occupait le poste de Trésorier Royal. Il collectait les taxes, tenait à jour la comptabilité et décidait du montant des dépenses.

Le roi entrait dans sa quatorzième année de règne. Il avait l'arrogance propre aux monarques et une puissance physique impressionnante. Pour garder son trône, il devait chaque année affronter les prétendants en duel. A quatorze reprises, il avait transpercé, étranglé ou décapité les candidats à sa succession. Le mince diadème d'argent et de diamants qu'il portait sur le front reviendrait un jour à son vainqueur.

Le regard fixé sur Fesz, le roi demanda comment progressaient les plans du Maître de la Nuit. L'incident de la prison les remettait-il en cause ?

— Je me rendrai à Atossa dès demain, expliqua le chamane, puis à Karthay pour assister le Maître de la Nuit dans ses derniers préparatifs.

— L'humain qui s'est échappé est-il le mage que vous cherchiez ? Je ne veux pas mobiliser ma flotte sans avoir l'assurance que rien ne viendra troubler l'arrivée de Sargonnas dans notre monde.

— Nous avons investi une grande quantité de ressources dans les plans du Maître de la Nuit, fit remarquer Groppis.

— Quant à moi, intervint Atra Cura, je fais confiance à notre grand prêtre, mais certains membres de ma... fédération... ont l'esprit très indépendant. Il leur faudra plus que ma parole pour s'impliquer dans cette affaire.

Un murmure d'assentiment parcourut l'assemblée. Fesz prit une longue inspiration pour calmer la colère qu'il sentait monter en lui.

— Je suis l'un des trois Très-Hauts choisis par le Maître de la Nuit, gronda-t-il, et je n'ai que faire de vos problèmes. Vos craintes mesquines déshonorent le Cercle Suprême et la race des minotaures.

« Le Maître de la Nuit vous a informés qu'il jettera un sort permettant à Sargonnas, Seigneur de la Vengeance, de pénétrer dans notre monde. Nous aussi, nous avons investi beaucoup de temps et d'efforts pour préparer l'incantation. Nous serons récompensés lors de la conjonction qui se produira dans quatre jours, quand les étoiles seront à leur zénith. »

Les membres du Cercle Suprême poussèrent des hoquets de surprise. Jusque-là, le Maître de la Nuit n'avait pas révélé la date précise de l'incantation. Leurs soucis et leurs questions s'évaporèrent.

— Et le prisonnier en fuite ? demanda le roi.

— Je ne crois pas qu'il s'agisse de l'humain nommé Raistlin, répondit Fesz, mais je m'arrêterai à Atossa pour m'en assurer. De toute façon, où que puisse être le mage, il ne nous posera pas plus de problèmes qu'un moustique au cul d'un mammouth à poils laineux.

Le vieil adage minotaure fit glousser les membres du Cercle. Le roi hocha la tête d'un air satisfait.

— Et le kender ? voulut-il savoir. Est-il toujours sous l'effet de la potion ?

— Oui, et il fait un allié très efficace. Je l'emmènerai avec moi à Karthay. Je pense persuader le Maître de la Nuit qu'il pourrait tenir un rôle dans le rituel.

Le roi fit une grimace sceptique.

— Ne craignez rien, le rassura le chamane. Avant de partir, je doublerai sa dose de potion.

CHAPITRE XI

Sa position était très inconfortable.

Les efforts de Caramon pour faire un trou dans le sac s'étaient révélés vains… Pourtant, il n'avait pas l'impression de courir un danger immédiat.

Il supposa que son sauveur l'emmenait loin de la prison minotaure, mais ça ne répondait pas à ses questions. Et Caramon regrettait d'avoir laissé Sturm en arrière. N'avait-il pas seulement échangé une captivité contre une autre ?

Au cours des heures suivantes, le malaise du jeune homme ne fit qu'amplifier. Ne sentant aucune surface solide, il craignait d'être transporté par voie aérienne. Les seuls bruits qui parvenaient à ses oreilles étaient des battements d'ailes et des cris d'oiseaux géants.

Enfin, il eut l'impression de piquer vers le sol et toucha terre brutalement. Quelques secondes plus tard, une main ouvrit le sac de toile. Caramon se dégagea et se releva sur des jambes tremblantes.

Une vision spectaculaire l'attendait. Il se tenait sur une corniche rocheuse, dans un canyon profond dont les murailles de pierre s'étendaient jusqu'à l'horizon. Les parois abritaient des dizaines de cavernes où étaient perchées des créatures de légende.

Un comité d'accueil entourait Caramon. Moitié humaines, moitié faucons, les créatures qui l'entouraient appartenaient à une civilisation millénaire. Les êtres marchaient sur deux jambes terminées par des serres d'oiseau. D'énormes ailes couvertes de plumes jaillissaient de leur dos, attachées à leurs bras et à leurs mains.

Caramon comprit soudain qui était le prisonnier enchaîné. Il réalisa que les minotaures avaient dû lui trancher les ailes.

L'être le plus proche de Caramon était celui qui l'avait tiré des griffes des minotaures. Malgré la minceur de sa silhouette, il dominait le guerrier d'une tête. Ses traits couleur de bronze étaient étrangement séduisants. Il n'avait pas de cheveux, mais sa tête était couverte de plumes dorées. Pour tout vêtement, il portait un pagne de cuir.

— Qui êtes-vous ? demanda Caramon.

— Dans votre langage, répondit fièrement l'homme-oiseau, on me nomme Fend-Nuage.

Caramon chercha la formulation appropriée.

— A quelle race appartenez-vous ?

Fend-Nuage fronça les sourcils et, de son aile droite, désigna un autre membre de son groupe. Tournant la tête, le guerrier vit un ancien qu'il n'avait pas remarqué auparavant, et qui semblait inspirer un grand respect à tous.

Le vieillard s'approcha de Caramon d'une démarche à la fois digne et gracieuse. Les plumes de son crâne, qui descendaient jusque sur sa poitrine, étaient d'un blanc argenté. Des années d'exposition aux éléments avaient bruni et ridé son visage. Ses membres fins semblaient encore souples et musclés. Il inclina la tête; une lueur amicale brillant dans ses yeux jaunes.

— Nous sommes les kyries, expliqua-t-il d'une voix flûtée. Je me nomme Arikara : dans votre langue, Plume-soleil, chef du peuple des cieux.

— Les kyries ? répéta Caramon, étonné.

Le vieillard plissa les paupières.

— Vous n'avez jamais entendu parler de nous ?

Caramon balaya du regard les centaines d'hommes-oiseaux qui le regardaient. Des murmures circulaient. Certains kyries tendaient le doigt vers le jeune guerrier.

Celui-ci secoua la tête. Raistlin lui avait sans doute parlé des kyries, mais Caramon avait du mal à retenir tout ce que lui disait son frère.

— Je m'y attendais, admit Plumesoleil en posant une aile sur l'épaule du jeune homme.

Il le conduisit vers un abri taillé à flanc de canyon.

Un groupe d'hommes-oiseaux franchit un rideau couleur de grès qui se confondait avec la paroi rocheuse. Il y avait là un second ancien au visage couvert de taches brunes, Fend-Nuage et deux femelles aux vêtements de cuir décorés de perles et de plumes.

A l'intérieur, la caverne formait un vaste dôme. Son sol de terre battue était couvert de brindilles et d'herbe séchée. Un feu dispensait une chaleur bienfaisante ; des armes et des ustensiles de cuisine étaient accrochés aux murs. Une pile de fourrures se dressait près de l'entrée.

Plumesoleil prit les deux femmes à part et leur donna des instructions que Caramon ne comprit pas. Il fit signe au jeune homme de s'asseoir près du feu, en face du second ancien qu'il présenta sous le nom de Trois-Yeux. Puis il s'accroupit, saisit un bâton et traça dans la poussière une carte rudimentaire.

— Il y a plusieurs siècles, les kyries étaient un peuple migrateur. Nous ne restions jamais longtemps au même endroit. La Pierre du Nord nous permettait de traverser les océans… Nous prîmes l'habitude de nous reposer sur elle, et perdîmes notre sens instinctif de l'orientation. Hélas, un jour, la pierre tomba entre les mains de nos pires ennemis, les minotaures.

La femelle kyrie la plus âgée distribua aux hommes des chopes remplies d'un liquide clair tacheté d'ambre. Caramon but avidement. Le breuvage tiède ne ressemblait à rien qu'il connût : il était parfumé, rafraîchissant et nourrissant.

Un pli amer au coin de la bouche, Plumesoleil poursuivit son récit :

— Désespérés, nous nous rassemblâmes ici, la plupart sur Mithas, les autres dans les îles voisines. Nous pouvons encore voler sur de longues distances, mais nous ne traversons plus les océans. Sans la Pierre du Nord, nous sommes prisonniers de cette partie du monde. Nous vivons ici du mieux que nous pouvons, dans la paix quand cela est possible.

Les questions brûlaient les lèvres de Caramon.

— Que me voulez-vous ? Pourquoi m'avez-vous tiré du donjon d'Atossa ?

Fend-Nuage répondit à la place de Plumesoleil :

— Je vous ai vu avec votre ami, quand vous avez failli vous noyer dans la Mer de Sang. J'ai fait ce que j'ai pu pour vous aider.

Caramon écarquilla les yeux.

— Ainsi, c'était vous ! s'exclama-t-il. Vous nous avez jeté du pain !

— C'était ma ration, expliqua le kyrie.

Caramon lui prit les mains.

— Vous nous avez sauvé la vie, dit-il avec chaleur. Puis vous avez risqué la vôtre pour me sortir de prison. Je vous dois plus que je ne pourrai jamais vous rendre.

Fend-Nuage accueillit ces effusions avec un peu de gêne, mais Plumesoleil eut un sourire rayonnant.

— C'est mon fils, dit-il, très fier.

Fend-Nuage baissa les yeux, toute trace d'arrogance disparue.

— J'en ai deux, poursuivit Plumesoleil, vibrant d'émotion. Mon aîné... Matinciel... est celui que vous avez rencontré à Atossa.

La voix du vieillard se brisa. Caramon ne sut que répondre. Plumesoleil savait-il que son fils était aux portes de la mort, car les minotaures le torturaient depuis des semaines ? Et que Matinciel avait fait preuve d'un grand courage et méprisait la peur ?

Un silence douloureux s'abattit sur la pièce.

— Je sais comment les minotaures traitent mon fils, dit doucement Plumesoleil, comme s'il avait lu dans les pensées du guerrier. Nous n'avons aucun espoir de le revoir libre parmi nous.

Caramon le regarda avec étonnement ; le chef des kyries pointa un index vers son crâne. Le jeune homme se souvint : Matinciel lui avait dit qu'il était télépathe.

— Pourquoi ne pas avoir libéré votre fils à ma place ? protesta Caramon.

— Parce qu'il est enchaîné, répondit Plumesoleil. Sinon, il se suiciderait. C'est une des rares choses que les minotaures savent de mon peuple. Pour un kyrie, être capturé vivant est la disgrâce suprême.

Caramon vida sa chope. Qu'il soit libre alors que Matinciel pourrissait en prison paraissait si injuste…

— Si nous lancions une attaque sur le donjon, nous pourrions peut-être..., commença le jeune homme.

— Ce serait la mort assurée, intervint Trois-Yeux, prenant la parole pour la première fois. Nous sommes courageux, mais pas stupides.

— Et le tunnel ?

— Il est trop étroit, soupira Fend-Nuage. Il faudrait plusieurs heures à une poignée d'entre nous pour s'introduire dans la prison, ensuite, nous y serions coincés. Nous devrions affronter une douzaine de gardes, et il faudrait scier les barreaux de la cellule de mon frère. Nous avons tout envisagé.

Le kyrie fronça les sourcils ; une ombre passa sur son visage.

— C'est sans espoir. Matinciel est perdu.

Les épaules de Caramon s'affaissèrent.

— Pourquoi le torturent-ils ? demanda le jeune homme d'une voix que le chagrin rendait rauque.

— Faute de pouvoir nous chasser de leurs îles, les minotaures ont juré de nous exterminer, expliqua Plumesoleil. En temps normal, ils ne s'aventurent guère à l'intérieur des terres : ils sont de meilleurs marins qu'alpinistes.

« Pourtant, ces derniers mois, ils se sont montrés plus intrépides. Ils ont localisé cinq de nos aires, massacrant nos guerriers, leurs femmes et leurs enfants. Des créatures écailleuses volantes leur ont montré la route. »

— Des dragons ? grimaça Caramon. Ils n'existent que dans les contes.

Fend-Nuage secoua la tête.

— Pas des dragons, corrigea-t-il. Des créatures d'un type nouveau. Nous n'en avions encore jamais vu de semblables.

Caramon eut l'air sceptique.

— Nous n'avons pas de preuve, intervint Plumesoleil. Il ne reste aucun témoin. Les minotaures ont brûlé les aires et tué tous leurs occupants. Ils font rarement des prisonniers.

— Et Matinciel ?

— Mon fils est l'exception qui confirme la règle, dit le vieillard en s'efforçant de maîtriser son émotion. Il a été capturé dans l'avant-poste qu'il défendait. Comprenant qu'il possédait un haut rang dans notre société, les minotaures ont tenté de lui extorquer des renseignements sur nos coutumes, nos rituels et l'emplacement de nos aires.

Plumesoleil reposa sa chope et fit signe à Fend-Nuage de continuer.

— Mon frère n'a pas parlé, dit fièrement le kyrie. Quel que soit le traitement ignoble auquel ses geôliers le soumettent, il ne dira rien. Il poussera son dernier soupir sans même leur avoir révélé son nom.

Fend-Nuage avait les mêmes yeux noirs et résolus que Matinciel. La plus âgée des femelles kyries s'approcha de Plumesoleil et lui chuchota quelque chose à l'oreille. L'ancien hocha la tête.

— Et vous, ami ? demanda gentiment Trois-Yeux, rompant le silence. Comment vous appelez-vous ? Quelle est votre histoire ?

Caramon raconta tout : le voyage en Ergoth Méridional, la tempête magique, la capture de Tasslehoff. Il expliqua comment Sturm et lui avaient dérivé pendant des jours avant d'être livrés aux minotaures.

Les kyries écoutèrent, très intéressés. Pas plus que le jeune homme, ils ne comprenaient pourquoi leurs ennemis ancestraux se souciaient tant d'un kender.

— La jalopine est commune à Mithas et Karthay, mais très rare dans les autres parties du monde, expliqua Fend-Nuage. Les minotaures la considèrent comme sacrée et lui attribuent des propriétés magiques.

La plus jeune femelle kyrie apporta des assiettes qu'elle disposa devant les quatre hommes. Elle avait des traits délicats et une splendide chevelure rousse aux reflets d'or.

Suivant l'exemple de ses hôtes, Caramon trempa ses mains dans une bassine d'eau claire, puis les essuya sur un torchon. Dans un saladier, il choisit un assortiment de noix, de baies et de légumes, tandis que la femelle la plus âgée posait dans son assiette plusieurs cubes de viande crue.

Pendant quelques minutes, on entendit dans la caverne des bruits de mastication. Puis Fend-Nuage reprit la parole :

— Une sentinelle surveille le tunnel, au cas où un changement interviendrait dans la situation de mon frère. Elle parle parfois avec Matinciel, qui lui répond quand il en est capable. Nous ne craignons pas que les gardes l'entendent : ils ne comprennent pas notre langage, et croient sans doute que mon frère délire.

« C'est ainsi que nous avons pu informer Matinciel de votre arrivée à la prison. Après en avoir débattu avec lui, nous avons décidé de vous libérer. »

— Pourquoi ?

— D'abord, parce que j'ai vu la façon dont vous traitiez mon frère.

— Comment est-ce possible ? s'étonna Caramon.

— Quand c'est mon tour de garder le tunnel, et que je me trouve suffisamment près de Matinciel, j'arrive à voir avec ses yeux, par-delà les murs de pierre. Mon cœur bat au même rythme que le sien. Mon esprit partage ses pensées. J'ai entendu vos paroles et compris que vous étiez doté de compassion.

Caramon ne répondit pas. Il pensait à son propre frère, Raistlin. Le lien qu'ils partageaient ressemblait fort à celui de Fend-Nuage et de Matinciel.

— Nous ne connaissons pas beaucoup les humains, intervint Plumesoleil. En trois cents années d'existence, c'est la première fois que je me trouve face à l'un d'eux.

— Trois cents ans ! s'exclama Caramon.

Le jeune homme savait que les elfes et les nains avaient une espérance de vie supérieure à celle de sa propre race, mais Plumesoleil battait tous les records !

— Oui, admit le kyrie en riant. Je suis vieux ; j'ai déjà fait mon temps. Après mon départ, c'est Fend-Nuage qui...

— Père ! s'exclama le kyrie, furieux.

Les femelles froncèrent les sourcils. Trois-Yeux baissa la tête. Plumesoleil se mordit la lèvre.

— Mon fils a raison, soupira-t-il. Il n'est pas bon de parler de Matinciel comme s'il était déjà mort. Etant le fils aîné, c'est lui qui aurait dû me succéder.

La voix du vieillard se brisa. Trois-Yeux se hâta de changer de sujet :

— La plupart des humains dont nous avons entendu parler sont des brigands ou des esclaves. Pourtant, nos légendes disent qu'ils peuvent être intelligents, sensibles et loyaux. Et ridiculiser les minotaures de la prison valait bien les risques que nous avons pris. La nouvelle de votre évasion amènera le déshonneur sur eux.

— Ne risquent-ils pas de punir Matinciel ? s'inquiéta Caramon.

— Ils n'exécuteront pas mon frère, répondit Fend-Nuage à regret. Ils le garderont en vie aussi longtemps que possible.

Le repas terminé, la femelle kyrie la plus âgée apporta des pipes, du tabac à fumer et priser et un bol rempli de morceaux de racines. Fend-Nuage choisit une pipe à long tuyau et commença à fumer, le regard dans le vague. Trois-Yeux prit une pincée de tabac. Plumesoleil saisit un morceau de gomme.

Caramon l'imita poliment.

Dehors, la nuit était tombée. Les femelles firent le tour de la caverne, touchant une demi-douzaine de sphères fixées au mur qui se mirent à briller d'une lueur bleue.

Caramon mâcha en silence. La journée avait été longue ; ses muscles lui faisaient mal. Le jus sucré coula dans sa gorge et il sentit ses membres se détendre. Sa fatigue et sa tristesse s'envolèrent.

Les pensées du jeune homme revinrent à Raistlin. Il se demandait où était son jumeau, ce qu'il faisait en cet instant. Kitiara lui avait si souvent répété qu'il devait veiller sur lui ! Pourtant, cette fois, c'était Raistlin qui s'inquiétait.

Caramon songea à Tasslehoff. Il craignait que le kender soit déjà mort. Que pouvaient lui vouloir les minotaures ? Tass ne se trouvait pas à Atossa : les kyries l'auraient remarqué. Le kender n'était pas du genre à passer inaperçu.

Caramon regarda les kyries, se demandant s'ils pouvaient lire dans ses pensées. A cet instant, il était presque capable de deviner les leurs. Il sentait la tristesse que leur valait le sort de Matinciel, mais aussi leur vaillance et leur fierté. Il était honoré que Plumesoleil l'ait invité.

Soudain, la honte envahit le jeune homme. Sturm n'aurait pas laissé les kyries le traiter comme un coq en pâte, si lui, Caramon, était resté en prison. Et si les minotaures avaient intérêt à garder Matinciel en vie, rien ne les empêchait de se venger sur le Solamnique.

— Je dois y retourner, déclara brusquement Caramon, rompant l'harmonieux silence qui régnait dans la caverne Je dois délivrer mon ami Sturm.

Autour de lui, les visages se firent désapprobateurs.

— Ce serait très imprudent, dit Plumesoleil.

— Voire suicidaire, renchérit Fend-Nuage.

— Je... je..., balbutia Caramon, regrettant de ne pas posséder l'éloquence de son frère. Je dois y aller. Sturm de Lumlane en ferait autant pour moi. Aucun risque ne le ferait hésiter… Ce serait pour lui une question de devoir et d'honneur.

— Comment pénétrerez-vous dans la prison ? demanda Trois-Yeux, les yeux plein de sympathie. Plus important, comment en ressortirez-vous ?

Caramon se tourna vers Fend-Nuage.

— Vous avez bien dit qu'une sentinelle montait la garde dans le tunnel ?

— C'est exact, approuva le kyrie. Jour et nuit.

— Dans ce cas, j'attendrai que ses rapports m'informent d'une occasion d'agir. Même si rien ne se produit, je devrai y aller.

Personne ne répondit. Caramon sonda le visage de Plumesoleil, mais l'ancien arborait une expression indéchiffrable.

— J'accompagnerai l'humain ! déclara abruptement Fend-Nuage.

Plumesoleil eut l'air choqué.

— Tu ne peux faire une chose pareille, mon fils ! Tu as déjà pris trop de risques. Tu ne dois pas penser qu'à ton avenir, mais aussi à celui de notre peuple.

— Allons, père. Tu sais très bien que tu ferais de même si tu étais encore en état.

Ses mots touchèrent Plumesoleil. Les yeux du vieillard brillaient de fierté.

— J'admire Caramon, reprit Fend-Nuage. Je voudrais aider son ami comme je l'ai aidé.

Le jeune homme serra les mains du kyrie. Trois-Yeux prit la parole :

— Si Fend-Nuage y va, ceux d'entre nous qui souhaitent combattre les minotaures devraient l'accompagner. Je propose que nous conduisions l'humain devant l'Assemblée des Guerriers.

Fend-Nuage parut reconnaissant au vieillard de cette suggestion. Caramon ignorait tout de l'Assemblée des Guerriers, mais il fut surpris par la ferveur qui faisait vibrer la voix de Trois-Yeux.

Une longue minute, Plumesoleil dévisagea son fils sans rien dire.

— Tu dois faire ce que te dicte ton cœur, soupira-t-il enfin. Mais promets-moi de ne pas agir inconsidérément.

Fend-Nuage hocha la tête, la gorge serrée par l'émotion.

*
* *

Les jours suivants, Caramon vécut parmi les kyries dans le village de cavernes. Partout où Fend-Nuage l'emmenait, il était l'objet d'une grande curiosité, mais on l'accueillait toujours avec chaleur.

En le voyant, les femelles chuchotaient entre elles dans leur langue ; les hommes-oiseaux se forçaient à parler le commun en sa présence. Beaucoup connaissaient déjà l'histoire de son évasion et ses liens avec Matinciel.

Caramon s'émerveilla de l'ingéniosité dont ses hôtes avaient fait preuve pour survivre dans cette contrée hostile, où le soleil brûlait dans la journée et où un froid mordant régnait la nuit. Un système de canaux étroits permettait de récupérer l'eau de pluie, en exposant un minimum de surface à l'évaporation ou au gel.

Les chasseurs ramenaient au village des lièvres sauvages, des lapins de garenne et de petits rongeurs. Chaque famille cultivait un jardin irrigué par les canaux, dans lequel poussaient des cactus, des noix, des haricots et du grain. Les kyries ne faisaient qu'un seul repas par jour et ne semblaient pas s'en porter plus mal.

Caramon demanda à Fend-Nuage d'où venaient les orbes bleus qui éclairaient le village la nuit. Le kyrie lui expliqua que son peuple possédait de modestes capacités magiques : entre autres, il savait communiquer avec les animaux. Certains kyries pouvaient même prédire ou altérer le temps. Quant aux orbes, c'était un jeu d'enfant de les fabriquer.

Pendant que les hommes chassaient, les femmes faisaient de la poterie, tannaient le cuir ou fabriquaient les paniers que les kyries s'accrochaient à la ceinture pour transporter leurs affaires. Leur arme traditionnelle était une massue de bois incurvée appelée mordente ; les chasseurs avaient en outre un arc long et un carquois.

Plusieurs fois par jour, éclaireurs et messagers venaient faire leur rapport à Fend-Nuage dans la langue des hommes-oiseaux. Caramon, qui s'inquiétait pour Sturm, pressait son nouvel ami de traduire ce qu'ils disaient. Fend-Nuage, évasif, lui conseillait de se montrer patient.

— Où se trouve Atossa ? demanda le guerrier le matin du quatrième jour.

Il se tenait sur la corniche depuis laquelle il avait découvert le village pour la première fois.

Fend-Nuage désigna le sud.

— Par là, à environ cent lieues.

— Je pourrais y retourner et prendre un tour de garde dans le tunnel, suggéra Caramon, qui bouillait d'impatience.

Le kyrie posa une main sur l'épaule du jeune homme.

— Non, dit-il fermement. Il est trop tôt. Ton ami est toujours vivant, et mon frère aussi. Nous devons attendre…

Cette nuit-là, Caramon venait juste de s'allonger dans sa caverne quand Fend-Nuage l'y rejoignit. Le jeune homme sursauta en apercevant son ami, dont la peau nue était couverte de perles, de coquillages et de peintures de guerre.

Fend-Nuage lui tendit un bandeau que Caramon noua à contrecœur sur les yeux. Il eut la sensation désormais familière d'être soulevé et emporté dans les airs. Cette fois, le voyage fut de courte durée.

Quand une main défit son bandeau, le jeune homme se trouvait dans une vaste caverne, entouré par une douzaine de mâles vêtus comme Fend-Nuage. La plupart lui étaient inconnus.

Les kyries étaient assis en cercle, les jambes croisées. Se levant pour accueillir les nouveaux venus, le premier se présenta sous le nom de Volesprit. Avec des cendres, il traça des symboles sur le visage de Caramon, puis le para de plumes et de bijoux.

Une forte odeur d'encens flottait dans la caverne. Se tenant les mains, les hommes-oiseaux invitèrent Caramon à prendre place parmi eux, puis ils entonnèrent un chant kyrie. Le jeune homme regarda autour de lui et vit que Fend-Nuage avait disparu. Malgré son appréhension, il ne tarda pas à s'immerger dans la solennité du rituel.

Le chant cessa, tirant Caramon de sa transe. Fend-Nuage sortit d'un coin obscur de la caverne, portant un coffre de bois qu'il plaça au milieu du cercle. Tous retinrent leur souffle tandis qu'il soulevait le couvercle, révélant un dragon aquatique.

Caramon sursauta. Le dragon ressemblait à une tortue géante à tête de lézard ; il avait une carapace sombre et épaisse, des pattes palmées et des nageoires massives. C'était une créature réputée pour sa férocité, qui attaquait les navires sans se laisser capturer. Elle respirait aussi bien dans l'air que dans l'eau, mais ne pouvait survivre longtemps hors de son milieu naturel.

Fend-Nuage saisit l'animal et le tendit à Volesprit, qui était assis en face de Caramon. Le dragon aquatique agita la tête et fit claquer ses mâchoires. De longues minutes durant, Volesprit le tint en l'air en fredonnant une mélopée lancinante. La créature essaya de se dégager pour le prendre à la gorge.

Volesprit rendit le dragon à Fend-Nuage, qui le fit passer au kyrie voisin, et ainsi de suite jusqu'à Caramon. Tous les regards se posèrent sur le guerrier, qui hésita. Vue de près, la créature était semblait très dangereuse.

Le jeune homme prit une inspiration et, imitant les kyries, tint l'animal au-dessus de sa tête pendant que les autres chantaient. Quand les muscles de ses bras furent tétanisés, il le rendit à Fend-Nuage.

Le dragon aquatique avait fait le tour du cercle. Fend-Nuage le ramena au centre. Il sortit un long couteau effilé et le plongea à plusieurs reprises dans la carapace de l'animal. Volesprit se précipita avec une jatte pour recueillir son sang et ses fluides corporels.

Le dragon cessa de se débattre. Un kyrie replaça son cadavre dans le coffre et emporta le tout.

De nouveau, Fend-Nuage se tourna vers Volesprit et lui offrit son couteau. L'homme-oiseau s'entailla profondément l'avant-bras et laissa son sang couler dans la jatte. Un à un, les autres kyries firent de même.

Quand vint son tour, Caramon les imita sans hésiter, mais par manque d'expérience, il se coupa trop profondément et dut arrêter le flot avec sa main.

Fend-Nuage fut le dernier à s'exécuter. Un silence grave tomba sur la caverne. Immobiles, les kyries regardèrent le fils de leur chef porter la jatte à ses lèvres et avaler une gorgée de liquide âcre.

Fend-Nuage allait tendre le récipient à Volesprit quand il se ravisa et se tourna vers Caramon. Le jeune homme dissimula un haut-le-cœur, mais il ne pouvait plus reculer. Saisissant la jatte à deux mains, il la porta à ses lèvres.

Relevant les yeux, il croisa le regard approbateur de Fend-Nuage. Les autres kyries hochèrent la tête avec un léger sourire, et la jatte fit le tour du cercle.

Dix minutes plus tard, Caramon dut sortir précipitamment de la caverne pour vomir. Grimaçant, Fend-Nuage lui expliqua que ce n'était pas un déshonneur. En buvant le sang du dragon aquatique, Caramon s'était purifié. Désormais, les kyries le considéraient comme l'un d'eux : il était membre honoraire de l'Assemblée des Guerriers.

CHAPITRE XII

Tôt dans la matinée, avant de quitter Atossa, Tass but une double dose de potion. Il commençait à apprécier le goût laiteux, aussi ne fit-il aucune difficulté.

Parce qu'il connaissait bien le kender, Dogz avait reçu pour mission de les accompagner. Il n'en éprouvait aucune joie : depuis sa transformation, son ami se conduisait de façon répugnante. Le minotaure tenta de se dérober à sa mission, mais Fesz ne l'entendait pas de cette oreille.

— Tass pense que tu l'aimes bien. De toute façon, c'est un ordre, dit-il, catégorique.

Il fallut aux trois compagnons une demi-journée pour atteindre Atossa. Ils voyageaient à bord d'un carrosse royal tiré par deux étalons noirs. Pour la gloriole autant que pour leur protection, une phalange de minotaures armés courait à côté d'eux, soulevant des nuages de poussière sur son passage.

Par la fenêtre du carrosse, Tass découvrit un paysage désolé de roches et de buissons faméliques. Entre la chaleur, le bruit et les cahots de la route, ce n'était pas une excursion très agréable…

Vers midi, ils arrivèrent à la prison où on les accueillit cérémonieusement. Un minotaure porteur d'un insigne voyant fit maintes courbettes à Fesz et l'invita à un banquet donné en son honneur. Le chamane, que le voyage avait mis de mauvaise humeur, insista pour qu'on le conduise sans tarder au prisonnier humain.

— Et que ça saute ! ajouta Tass, féroce.

*
* *

— C'est bien lui, grommela Dogz, l'air vaguement coupable. C'est un des humains que nous avons jetés à la mer. Nous aurions dû le tuer sur-le-champ.

— Ça oui ! aboya Tass. Quand je pense aux ennuis que nous cause ta négligence ! Il ne faut jamais remettre au lendemain ce qu'on peut faire le jour même, surtout en matière d'assassinat. Si tu m'avais demandé mon avis, ce n'est sans doute pas celui que je t'aurais donné à l'époque, mais...

— Comment s'appelle-t-il, déjà ? demanda Fesz en penchant la tête de côté.

Les trois compagnons se tenaient devant la cellule de Sturm de Lumlane. Assis sur une chaise, les mains liées derrière le dos, le Solamnique leur faisait face. Il était couvert d'ecchymoses et de croûtes, mais les gardes avaient fait un effort pour le rendre présentable.

Sturm était perplexe. D'abord agréablement surpris de voir Tasslehoff, il avait vite constaté que quelque chose ne tournait pas rond chez le kender. Celui-ci passait son temps à chuchoter à l'oreille du minotaure qui l'accompagnait (sans doute un haut dignitaire) et refusait de croiser son regard. Que mijotait-il donc ?

— Sturm de Lumlane, dit Tass en réponse à la question du chamane.

Le kender cracha par terre comme il avait vu les minotaures le faire en parlant de leurs ennemis.

— Il se prend pour un Chevalier Solamnique, expliqua-t-il, mais il se fourre le doigt dans l'œil. Encore un type qui n'est pas à la hauteur de ses ambitions. C'est une longue histoire, et je ne suis pas sûr que tu aies envie de l'entendre. Tout a commencé avec son père...

— J'aimerais le voir de plus près, grogna Fesz.

Un garde déverrouilla la cellule. Tass et le chamane entrèrent. Dogz attendit à l'extérieur, l'air suprêmement ennuyé.

Fesz s'approcha de Sturm en fronçant les sourcils, suivi par le kender qui imitait la moindre de ses attitudes. Ayant appris à ses dépens que les réactions impulsives ne payaient pas, le Solamnique décida de garder le silence jusqu'à ce qu'il ait compris le jeu que jouait Tasslehoff.

— Quelle erreur, dit le kender en secouant la tête d'un air navré. Visiblement, ils l'ont torturé, une perte de temps, si tu veux mon avis. Ce type se laisserait crever plutôt que de trahir son code d'honneur.

« C'est la même chose pour Kitiara, mais dans son cas, ça n'a rien à voir avec l'honneur : c'est juste de l'entêtement. En arrivant à Karthay, j'en parlerai au Maître de la Nuit, s'il ne s'en est pas déjà aperçu. Ce qui m'étonnerait, vu ses pouvoirs. »

Sturm tendit l'oreille. De quoi parlait donc Tasslehoff ?

— Torturer Sturm en lui tapant dessus ne sert à rien. Il est imbibé jusqu'à la mœlle d'âneries solamniques, et il ne répond pas aux sévices corporels de la même manière que les autres humains. Si j'étais le bourreau, j'aurais recours à une méthode plus créative.

Fesz fit les cent pas dans la cellule, ses narines frémissant. Il s'efforçait de mémoriser l'odeur du second humain, celui qui s'était enfui, le frère de Raistlin Majere.

Tass fouilla dans ses sacoches et en sortit une petite paire de ciseaux. De sa main libre, il saisit une extrémité de la longue moustache de Sturm.

— Voilà ce que je ferai ! s'écria-t-il, triomphant, en coupant une énorme touffe de poils.

Sturm jeta un regard noir au kender, mais ne dit rien.

— Regarde ! pavoisa Tass en brandissant son trophée sous le nez de Fesz. Ça, c'est ce que j'appelle de la torture ! Les Solamniques sont très fiers de leur moustache.

Il se pencha vers Sturm en grimaçant.

— Ça faisait longtemps que j'en avais envie, ricana-t-il. Très, très longtemps. Tu te crois supérieur parce que tu peux te laisser pousser la moustache, pas vrai ? Eh bien, si je voulais, je pourrais en faire autant. Et la mienne serait aussi longue que ma queue-de-cheval !

Sans prêter attention au babillage du kender, Fesz se tourna vers le garde.

— Montrez-moi la cellule du kyrie et l'endroit où a disparu l'autre prisonnier, ordonna-t-il.

— Oui, Votre Excellence.

Fesz prit Tass par les épaules et l'entraîna dans le couloir. Le kender se tordit le cou et continua à hurler en direction de Sturm :

— Tu crois peut-être que nous avons fait tout ce chemin pour te voir, Triste-Moustache ! Pas du tout : nous sommes seulement en route pour Karthay, où nous avons rendez-vous avec le Maître de la Nuit pour lancer un sort très puissant qui amènera Sargonnas dans notre monde. Kitiara est retenue prisonnière là-bas, alors, tu penses bien que nous avons des tas d'autres gens à torturer...

Tass, Fesz et le garde disparurent à un détour du couloir. Dogz jeta un regard pensif à Sturm avant de leur emboîter le pas.

Resté seul avec sa moustache ruinée, le Solamnique s'efforça en vain de donner un sens à la scène.

*
* *

Tass et les trois minotaures se dirigèrent vers la cellule du kyrie. Celui-ci, expliqua Fesz au kender, appartenait au peuple des hommes-oiseaux, ennemis séculaires des minotaures.

— Ton ex-ami Caramon était chargé de la distribution de nourriture aux autres prisonniers. La dernière fois qu'on l'a vu, il se tenait dans ce couloir. Puis il a disparu comme par magie, ajouta le chamane.

— Si s'était Raistlin, fit remarquer Tass, nous aurions eu l'embarras du choix : sort d'invisibilité, voyage dans le temps, téléportation, métamorphose en insecte... Mais le pauvre Caramon est trop bête pour effectuer ce genre de tours.

— Ce Raistlin semble vraiment très puissant, grommela Fesz, impressionné malgré lui.

— Oh que oui ! mentit Tass. Je n'ose même pas te dire à quel point, parce que le temps que les mots sortent de ma bouche, il aura déjà appris des sorts supplémentaires !

Le kender fut très déçu par le spectacle pitoyable qu'offrait le kyrie. A part ses pattes, il n'avait rien d'un oiseau. Et il bougeait si peu qu'il aurait pu être mort, ce que Tass s'empressa de faire remarquer.

— C'est parce qu'on lui a arraché les ailes, expliqua Dogz. Tu vois les cicatrices dans son dos ?

— Quoi ? s'exclama le kender, se tournant vers le garde et lui flanquant un coup de pied vicieux dans la rotule. Pour une fois que j'ai une chance de voir un kyrie, il faut que vous me le mutiliez !

« Sans ses ailes, on dirait presque un humain ! C'était bien la peine de faire le voyage depuis Lacynos pour voir ça ! Vous auriez au moins pu attendre que... »

Fesz arracha Tass au garde, qui mourait d'envie d'assommer le kender… Mais Dogz lui jeta un regard d'avertissement très explicite.

Le chamane examina les abords de la cellule. S'agenouillant pour tester le sol, il fit courir ses doigts le long des murs.

— Si vous croyez qu'on a pas déjà essayé, marmonna le garde entre ses dents.

Dogz, qui avait l'ouïe fine, le foudroya du regard. Le minotaure baissa la tête et s'absorba dans la contemplation de ses sandales.

Fesz se releva et invita Tass à mener ses propres investigations. Le kender s'appliqua à reproduire les gestes du chamane, mais il ne découvrit rien de nouveau.

— Caramon a-t-il laissé un indice derrière lui ?

— Non, rien, dit le garde à regret. Juste les deux seaux qu'il portait. Ils étaient renversés par terre.

Tass marcha de long en large dans le couloir. Il regarda Fesz, puis le kyrie, puis le plafond qui était encore plus haut que Caramon Majere… d'à peu près deux seaux et une longueur de bras.

— Je pense..., commença le kender.

— Oui ? demanda avidement Fesz.

— Je pense, reprit Tass d'une voix forte, que nous devrions punir Sturm de Lumlane.

— Punir Sturm de Lumlane ? répéta le chamane, perplexe.

— Parfaitement. C'est une question de principe, claironna Tass. Il devait savoir que Caramon s'échapperait, et puisqu'il refuse de coopérer...

— Nous l'avons torturé de notre mieux, protesta le garde.

— De votre mieux ? explosa Tass. Et vous voulez me faire avaler ça ?

Le garde rentra la tête dans les épaules et recula d'un pas. Le kender se tourna vers Fesz.

— Votre peuple pratique-t-il des exécutions rituelles ? demanda-t-il d'un ton solennel.

Le chamane réfléchit. Il était ravi que Tass consacre son imagination à des sujets dignes d'intérêt.

— Eh bien… la Fosse des Enfers me semble appropriée. Avant qu'on m'envoie à Karthay pour servir le Maître de la Nuit, j'aimais beaucoup assister aux combats de prisonniers.

— La Fosse des Enfers ? répéta Tass, alléché.

— Les condamnés se livrent à une danse de la mort autour d'un lac de lave, expliqua Fesz. C'est d'autant plus humiliant que tous les regards des spectateurs sont fixés sur eux.

Tass écarquilla les yeux.

— La Fosse des Enfers ! hurla-t-il. C'est parfait ! Ce sera une punition idéale pour Triste-Moustache.

— Le seul problème, objecta Fesz, c'est que nous devons être à Karthay dans trois jours.

— Trois jours ! répéta Tass à tue-tête. Pourquoi ne pas jeter ce vieux Sturm dans la fosse demain matin ? Ainsi, nous pourrions quitter la ville avant midi.

— D'accord, approuva Fesz, mais il faut nous dépêcher de prendre les dispositions nécessaires.

— Allons-y ! s'écria joyeusement Tass. Je serais ravi de voir ce Solamnique pédant mordre la poussière comme il le mérite. Et puis, je ne sais pas si je te l'ai déjà dit, mais j'adore les fosses, qu'elles contiennent des esclaves ou non.

Fesz s'éloignait déjà vers la sortie. Le kender se hâta de le rattraper, sans oublier, au passage, de décocher un dernier coup de pied au garde.

*

* *

Le lendemain matin, une centaine de minotaures se pressaient dans la galerie semi-circulaire qui garnissait la paroi intérieure de la Fosse des Enfers.

Grognant et tapant des pieds, ils manifestèrent leur impatience jusqu'à l'arrivée des officiels, sans qui le duel ne pouvait commencer. Le combat du jour opposerait le champion local, un certain Tossak, au prisonnier humain Sturm de Lumlane, jusqu'à ce que mort s'en suive.

Une procession d'une douzaine de fonctionnaires escortait Dogz, Tasslehoff et Fesz, qui pénétrèrent dans l'arène et allèrent s'asseoir dans une loge privée. Les spectateurs se tordirent le cou pour apercevoir le kender qui avait le privilège de siéger près d'un Très-Haut. Tass releva le menton et se rengorgea, comme il convenait à une personne dans sa position.

La veille, un garde avait averti Sturm : sur la suggestion du kender maléfique Tasslehoff Racle-Pieds, il livrerait douze heures plus tard un combat à mort. Le jeune homme avait accueilli la nouvelle sans broncher.

Le bon côté des choses, c'était qu'on lui avait apporté le meilleur repas qu'il eût fait depuis longtemps, ainsi qu'une paillasse pour dormir. On avait aussi desserré ses liens, et on lui avait promis qu'il pourrait se battre avec l'arme de son choix.

Après avoir passé en revue les différentes options, Sturm avait opté pour une mince épée à double tranchant munie d'une garde finement ciselée. Quelle que soit l'issue du duel, il entendait donner le meilleur de lui-même et, le cas échéant, mourir honorablement.

Epuisé par la torture et la captivité, le Solamnique ne comprenait rien à ce qui se passait. Pourquoi Tass coopérait-il avec les minotaures ? Se pouvait-il qu'il soit leur allié ? Sturm se creusa la tête la moitié de la nuit sans trouver de réponse à ses questions.

Le lendemain matin, perplexe mais déterminé, il suivit le garde jusqu'à l'entrée d'un étroit passage. Alors qu'il remontait vers l'arène, un souffle d'air chaud le frappa au visage.

La Fosse des Enfers était une gigantesque cuvette remplie de lave, à la surface de laquelle se promenaient des bulles de gaz empoisonné. Des îlots de pierre noire, reliés entre eux par des passerelles, jaillissaient du liquide bouillonnant. Toute chute signifiait une mort immédiate.

Pénétrant dans l'arène, Sturm dut lever un bras pour se protéger contre la lueur aveuglante et la chaleur qui s'en dégageaient. Des cris et des sifflements saluèrent son entrée. Le jeune homme balaya du regard la galerie des spectateurs, mais il ne vit Tass nulle part.

En face de lui, un minotaure se tenait immobile au bord de la fosse. Il mesurait plus de sept pieds, sans compter ses longues cornes effilées et luisantes. Une crinière blond pâle cascadait sur ses épaules. Deux anneaux d'or pendaient à son oreille droite, et des muscles impressionnants roulaient sous la peau de sa poitrine.

Sa main gauche disparaissait dans une mandole : un gantelet de fer garni de pointes aux jointures et d'une lame de dague le long du pouce. Dans sa main droite, il tenait une lourde hache à la lame dentelée.

— Tos-sak ! Tos-sak ! hurla la foule en délire.

Le minotaure rejeta la tête en arrière et poussa un meuglement de défi. Avec une vitesse et une agilité qui prirent son adversaire de court, il chargea, bondissant d'îlot en îlot jusqu'à la passerelle, en face de Sturm.

Puis il brandit sa hache d'un air menaçant.

— Tos-sak ! Tos-sak !

Sturm sentit sa tête tourner. La chaleur étouffante, les cris de la foule, les rugissements du champion le déstabilisaient. A son tour, il surprit les spectateurs... par la vitesse à laquelle il s'éloigna de son adversaire.

Bondissant, Sturm atterrit sur une autre passerelle, d'où il aurait une bonne vue sur Tossak tout en se soustrayant temporairement à ses attaques. Les règles de la chevalerie n'excluaient pas la prudence, et dans le cas présent, celle-ci exigeait que le jeune homme gagne du temps.

Enervé par la retraite de Sturm, Tossak piétina le sol de ses sabots. Il ne semblait pas incommodé par la chaleur qui brûlait les yeux du Solamnique. D'un bond puissant, il revint se placer face à son adversaire et réitéra son défi.

A nouveau, Sturm prit ses jambes à son cou. Il zigzagua d'îlot en îlot pour mettre le plus de distance possible entre Tossak et lui, sans toutefois sortir de l'arène. La chaleur pompait son énergie, la sueur lui dégoulinait dans les yeux. Sous ses pieds, la lave bouillonnait dans la fosse.

— Tos-sak ! Tos-sak ! scandait la foule.

Convaincu d'avoir affaire à un lâche, le minotaure leva les yeux au ciel et fit rouler les muscles de ses épaules, déchaînant les vivats des spectateurs. Cette fois, il prit son temps pour traverser et venir se placer en face de Sturm. Puis il se remit à gesticuler pour impressionner son adversaire.

Profitant de l'opportunité, Sturm chargea, l'épée en avant. Il avait l'impression que ses jambes étaient de plomb et que son arme pesait une tonne. Après plusieurs jours passés à dériver dans la Mer de Sang, sans compter les tortures subies entre les mains de ses geôliers, il n'était pas en état de combattre un champion minotaure.

Pourtant, il avait l'avantage. Distrait par les hurlements de la foule, persuadé que son adversaire tremblait comme un lapin, Tossak ne réagit qu'au dernier moment. Seuls ses réflexes lui permirent de bloquer le coup de Sturm avec sa main gantelée.

Le choc métallique se répercuta dans toute l'arène. Le Solamnique lâcha son épée, qui glissa jusqu'au bord de la passerelle et s'arrêta en équilibre au-dessus de la fosse volcanique. Sturm plongea pour la rattraper ; il s'en empara juste à temps pour pouvoir faire volte-face et frapper le minotaure qui fondait sur lui.

Sa lame entama la cuisse de Tossak, qui poussa un hurlement de rage et fit un pas en arrière. Puis il revint à la charge. De sa main gantelée, il arracha l'épée de Sturm et la projeta dans la fosse, où elle fut aussitôt engloutie par la lave. La foule applaudit à tout rompre.

Tossak essuya le sang, sur sa cuisse, et se lécha les doigts sans quitter Sturm du regard. Il avança vers le Solamnique en brandissant sa lourde hache, tandis que le jeune homme reculait, cherchant désespérément une ouverture.

Tossak voulut porter un coup de taille à son adversaire. Celui-ci plongea, se jeta sous la lame meurtrière et faucha les jambes du minotaure, qui s'étala sur le sol. Avant que Tossak, plus surpris que meurtri, puisse réagir, Sturm flanqua un coup de pied à sa hache et l'envoya rejoindre son épée dans la fosse.

Les spectateurs excités sifflèrent en levant le poing. Furieux et humilié, Tossak se releva et marcha sur Sturm. Un poing s'écrasa sur le visage du Solamnique ; un coup de pied l'envoya rouler à terre.

Le jeune homme tenta de se redresser, mais le minotaure ne lui en laissa pas le temps. Il le saisit par sa cheville droite, le souleva et le tint au-dessus de la lave bouillonnante.

Sturm comprit que sa dernière heure était venue.

*

* *

Tass avait suivi le duel avec fascination. Pourtant, quelque chose le dérangeait, car les chances n'étaient pas égales. Il s'agita dans son siège, espérant que les événements prennent un tour inattendu.

Tossak s'apprêtait à délivrer le coup de grâce. Il leva son gantelet gauche, fit jaillir la dague de son pouce, puis poussa un meuglement de triomphe. Tenant toujours Sturm par la cheville, il arma son bras pour l'éventrer comme un lapin.

A cet instant, une ombre tomba sur l'arène. Une mordente maniée de main de maître s'abattit sur le bras droit de Tossak, pendant qu'une autre, garnie de pointes, écrasait son museau.

Le minotaure hurla. Il porta les mains à son visage et lâcha Sturm, qui vit la lave bouillonnante se précipiter à sa rencontre. Au dernier moment, une silhouette piqua sur lui et le saisit sous les aisselles.

Le Solamnique se sentit emporté dans les airs.

Pour ajouter au chaos ambiant, la foule siffla et tapa des pieds. Fesz secoua la tête. Une seconde évasion, survenant à quelques jours de l'arrivée présumée de Sargonnas, ne pouvait être qu'un mauvais présage.

Tass sautillait sur place, les yeux exorbités.

— Le voilà ! hurla-t-il en désignant un guerrier aux longs cheveux bruns qui venait de faire irruption dans l'arène, porté par un autre kyrie. C'est le type dont je vous parlais, Caramon !

Un garde minotaure se précipita vers les intrus en brandissant un trident. Deux massues cloutées l'atteignirent simultanément. Le garde bascula et, poussant un cri terrifié, disparut dans la fosse au moment où les hommes-oiseaux reprenaient leur envol.

Du sang coulant des blessures qui le laisseraient à jamais défiguré, Tossak brandit son poing gantelé vers le ciel.

*
* *

A Karthay, le Maître de la Nuit s'inquiétait du nombre grandissant de mauvais présages.

Il s'était déjà aperçu que torturer la femelle humaine ne servirait à rien. De toute façon, ça ne l'intéressait pas. Il allait faire d'elle un bien meilleur usage : avec un peu de chance, elle attirerait dans l'île les deux mâles dont la présence avait été signalée à Atossa. Sinon, il serait toujours temps de la sacrifier lors du rituel d'invocation de Sargonnas.

Depuis qu'on l'avait surprise à rôder autour du camp du Maître de la Nuit, dans les ruines volcaniques de l'ancienne cité, la femelle avait fait plus que sa part de dégâts. Bien que deux fois plus petite qu'un minotaure, elle était parvenue à décapiter un de ses adversaires et à trancher la main d'un autre avant sa capture. Depuis, elle n'avait cessé de hurler des injures à ses geôliers, refusant de leur révéler les raisons de sa présence.

Pourtant, grâce à son réseau très développé d'espions et d'assassins, le Maître de la Nuit savait qui elle était : Kitiara Uth Matar, demi-sœur de Raistlin Majere. Si elle se trouvait à Karthay, le jeune mage ne devait pas être loin.

On avait enfermé Kitiara dans une cellule improvisée : une cage de bois ramenée de Lacynos pour garder des animaux. Le Maître de la Nuit avait ordonné qu'on ne la nourrisse pas. Après plusieurs jours de jeûne, la furie commençait à se calmer.

Kitiara Uth Matar n'était pas le principal souci du grand prêtre, car il avait l'étrange sentiment que les choses allaient mal tourner. D'abord, à cause du kender et des deux humains qui avaient acheté la jalopine au renégat Argotz.

Certes, un assassin s'était « occupé » de l'herboriste, et le kender avait été rallié à leur cause. Fesz se portait garant de lui ; il arrivait d'ailleurs à Karthay en sa compagnie.

Mais les deux mâles humains auraient dû se noyer dans la Mer de Sang et ils avaient survécu. Pire encore, l'un d'eux, le frère de Raistlin, s'était échappé de la prison où on l'avait jeté.

Et voilà que le second venait de jouer la fille de l'air ! Apparemment, il avait forgé une alliance avec les kyries, des ennemis ancestraux des minotaures.

Bref, les choses se présentaient mal. D'heure en heure, le Cercle Suprême devenait plus nerveux.

Les orughis répugnaient à confier leurs troupes aux officiers minotaures.

Les tribus ogres avaient déclaré qu'elles ne participeraient pas à l'invasion du monde, tant qu'elles n'auraient pas la preuve formelle de l'existence de Sargonnas. Les alliances s'effilochaient… Le Maître de la Nuit soupira, puis saisit une poignée de cendres qu'il laissa glisser entre ses doigts. Il était entouré par une ville pétrifiée, des escaliers qui ne menaient nulle part et des colonnes qui ne soutenaient rien.

Une table et une chaise se dressaient près d'un feu de camp. Des livres et des bocaux de composants garnissaient les étagères. Faute de murs, de porte et de plafond, son sanctuaire était un simple assemblage…

Le prêtre leva les yeux vers le ciel piqueté d'étoiles. Encore trois jours et deux nuits. Il s'inquiétait, mais gardait foi en Sargonnas. S'enveloppant dans sa cape, il se roula en boule sur le sol pour profiter des dernières heures de fraîcheur.

CHAPITRE XIII

Le *Castor* franchit l'embouchure de la baie et pénétra en haute mer. Tanis le suivit du regard, mettant sur son dos le sac qui contenait les provisions fournies par le capitaine Nugetre.

Près de lui, Flint s'appuyait lourdement sur sa jambe indemne, tandis que Kirsig le couvait des yeux. Yuril et ses quatre compagnes s'affairaient au bord du rivage, tirant au sec leurs deux chaloupes. Un peu à l'écart, tournant le dos à l'océan, Raistlin scrutait le paysage.

L'étroite plage de graviers était bordée de dunes, au-delà desquelles le jeune mage devinait un labyrinthe de ravins et de plateaux. L'île semblait désolée et inhospitalière. Bien qu'on fût à peine au milieu de la matinée, le soleil était déjà brûlant. Un vent sec soulevait des nuages de poussière.

Raistlin se dirigea vers Tanis et lui posa une main sur le bras. Le demi-elfe sursauta. Le jeune mage s'était déplacé si furtivement qu'il ne l'avait pas entendu approcher.

— Il nous faudra environ deux jours pour atteindre les ruines de Karthay, annonça Raistlin. Crois-tu que la jambe de Flint tiendra jusque-là ?

— Le vieux renard va beaucoup mieux, dit Tanis. Je te parie qu'il nous enterrera tous !

Il regarda le nain, auquel Kirsig offrait en vain de faire un cataplasme. Le blessé tempêtait en repoussant la demi-ogresse. Raistlin et Tanis échangèrent une grimace.

— Tout de même, dit le demi-elfe, redevenant sérieux, j'aimerais savoir où nous allons. Tu ne nous a pas dit grand-chose sur le sort qui doit ouvrir un portail pour Sargonnas.

Le scepticisme se mêlait à l'impatience dans la voix du demi-elfe.

— Je n'ai pas plus que toi la preuve que les anciens dieux existent, répondit Raistlin. Mais le sort que j'ai lu semble à la fois très vieux et très puissant. S'il y a la moindre chance pour qu'il amène dans notre monde une force maléfique, nous devons tout faire pour l'en empêcher.

— Et Sturm, Caramon et Tasslehoff ? Se trouvent-ils ici ? N'est-ce pas pour les délivrer que nous sommes venus ?

— Je n'ai pas de baguette magique pour les localiser, rétorqua sèchement Raistlin. Mais tu as entendu comme moi les propos de Kirsig : les minotaures forgent des alliances avec d'autres races. C'est un fait sans précédent dans l'histoire de Krynn.

« Si, comme je le crains, ils en appellent à Sargonnas pour réaliser leurs plans de domination du monde, peu importe où se trouvent Caramon et les autres, ils ne seront nulle part en sécurité. »

Raistlin s'interrompit et prit une profonde inspiration pour se calmer.

— La jalopine n'était qu'un des ingrédients nécessaires au lancement du sort, dit-il. Celui-ci requiert également le sacrifice d'une victime intelligente. A mon avis, c'est pour ça que Tass, Sturm et Caramon ont été enlevés.

« Nous n'avons pas beaucoup de temps. La conjonction propice à l'ouverture du portail ne se produit qu'une ou deux fois par siècle, et la prochaine aura lieu dans trois nuits. A présent, laisse-moi te montrer une carte que j'ai copiée dans un atlas de Morath. »

Flint et Kirsig les avaient rejoints. Le demi-elfe étudia le morceau de parchemin que lui tendait Raistlin. Il était couvert de lignes et de symboles géographiques.

— Je pense que le lancement du sort se fera à proximité des ruines de Karthay, expliqua le jeune mage. Durant le Cataclysme, la cité fut détruite par une éruption volcanique et ensevelie sous des tonnes de cendres. Ses vestiges constituent un site sacré pour les minotaures.

Raistlin désigna une chaîne de montagnes sur la carte.

— Nous devrions y arriver à temps, mais le voyage sera dangereux. Ceux qui ne se sentent pas capables de l'entreprendre peuvent rester ici et attendre notre retour, dit le jeune homme en levant les yeux, non vers Flint, mais vers Yuril et ses compagnes.

Apparemment, les cinq femmes avaient déjà pris leur décision.

— J'ai une dette à rembourser, déclara fièrement Yuril, et mes amies sont des aventurières chevronnées. En notre nom à toutes, je promets que nous vous accompagnerons jusqu'au bout de votre quête.

Comme pour souligner ses paroles, elle posa la main sur la garde de son épée courte, faisant saillir ses biceps bronzés.

Nous avons de la chance de les avoir avec nous, songea Tanis.

— La cité en ruine sera sans doute bien gardée, intervint Flint, et nos amis aussi. Que comptes-tu faire une fois que nous serons sur place ?

— Je n'en sais rien, avoua Raistlin. Il faudra d'abord que j'évalue la situation. A nous tous, nous trouverons bien un plan. (Un silence.) Allons, nous avons assez tardé. Mettons-nous en route.

*

* *

Se fiant à la carte de Raistlin, les compagnons suivirent le lit asséché d'une ancienne rivière qui menait aux ruines de Karthay.

Le paysage semblait dénué de vie végétale ou animale. Sur les plateaux, le vent soufflait, projetant du sable dans les yeux des voyageurs. Les ravins offraient un refuge contre la chaleur étouffante du soleil, mais la progression y était souvent ardue.

En fin d'après-midi, le petit groupe était assoiffé et épuisé. Raistlin et Tanis marchaient en tête, Flint et Yuril à l'arrière.

Puis ils arrivèrent au pied d'une falaise d'une cinquantaine de pieds, trop abrupte pour être escaladée. Ils durent rebrousser chemin, et leur moral très bas en prit encore un coup.

Le temps qu'ils contournent l'obstacle, le soleil se couchait à l'horizon. Déjà, des ténèbres glaciales s'abattaient sur le paysage. Tanis frissonna. Il vit Flint se laisser tomber sur le sol, aussitôt imité par Yuril et ses compagnes. Quelques pas plus loin, Raistlin tournait et retournait la carte dans ses mains.

— Le lit de la rivière ne suit pas le tracé prévu, se plaignit-il.

— Ça ne m'étonne pas, dit Tanis. Ton atlas devait être trop vieux. Qui sait combien de glissements de terrain se sont produits depuis ?

Raistlin fronça les sourcils.

— Je ne crois pas que nous puissions aller plus loin aujourd'hui, reprit le demi-elfe en indiquant Flint et les jeunes femmes, derrière lui.

— Nous devons arriver à Karthay avant deux jours, déclara Raistlin. Tu n'imagines pas les conséquences désastreuses que pourrait avoir un retard !

— Les deux lunes nous fourniront peut-être assez de lumière pour couvrir encore un peu de terrain cette nuit, avança Tanis, diplomate. Mais pour l'instant, nous avons besoin de nous reposer et de manger un morceau. Et puis, j'ai repéré des terriers de fourmilions dans le coin ; je n'aimerais pas trébucher dessus dans le noir.

— Des fourmilions ? s'exclama Flint en relevant la tête. Je suis d'accord avec Tanis. Nous devrions dresser le camp ici.

Raistlin hésita.

— Nous serions mieux abrités contre le froid au fond d'un ravin, ajouta le nain, mais nous y serions plus vulnérables aux attaques de créatures sauvages.

Le jeune mage poussa un soupir et hocha la tête à contrecœur. Une grande fatigue se lisait sur ses traits pâles et tendus. Il ne voulait pas l'avouer, mais lui-même ne se sentait guère capable d'aller plus loin.

La température continua à baisser. Les compagnons s'installèrent pour la nuit derrière un amas de rochers qui les protégeraient un peu contre la morsure du vent. Yuril proposa de chasser pour le souper, mais Tanis déclina son offre.

— Il fait trop sombre, expliqua-t-il. A la limite, je pourrais m'en charger, grâce ma vision elfique, mais si j'attrapais quelque animal, nous ne pourrions pas le faire cuire. Mieux vaut ne pas allumer de feu tant que nous ne serons pas certains de notre position. Sur ce plateau, ça risquerait d'attirer l'attention de visiteurs indésirables.

Tanis fit le tour du petit groupe, distribuant les provisions données par Nugetre : du pain au son, des fruits séchés et une demi-tasse d'eau pour chacun. De la journée, les compagnons n'avaient pas croisé une source, et ils mouraient de soif.

En arrivant près de Flint, Tanis remarqua que Kirsig n'était nulle part en vue.

— Ne t'inquiète pas pour elle, dit le nain. Elle s'est esquivée après ton petit discours au sujet des feux de camp. Je ne sais pas où elle est, mais au moins, j'ai la paix.

Alarmé, Tanis balaya le plateau du regard.

En dépit de ses protestations, Flint s'inquiétait aussi. Les deux hommes allaient partir à la recherche de la demi-ogresse lorsque celle-ci réapparut, portant un sac rebondi sur son dos.

— Bonsoir, mes chéris. Regardez ce que je vous apporte ! s'écria-t-elle en répandant le contenu du sac aux pieds de Flint.

— Qu'est-ce que c'est ? grimaça le nain en saisissant un petit objet vert et humide.

— Des racines de smague, expliqua Kirsig, triomphante. Le trésor du désert, comme disait toujours mon pauvre papa.

— J'en ai entendu parler, intervint Raistlin en rejoignant ses amis. Cette plante a sauvé la vie de nombreux voyageurs égarés dans des régions arides. Mais je suis surpris que tu aies pu en trouver dans le noir.

Kirsig eut un sourire rayonnant.

Tanis prit une racine et en croqua un bout. Sa texture ressemblait à celle d'une pomme de terre crue, mais elle était sucrée et très rafraîchissante. Le petit groupe mâcha avec avidité ; quand les estomacs furent pleins, il restait encore de quoi remplir la moitié du sac.

Après ce dîner frugal mais satisfaisant, les compagnons se préparèrent à dormir sur le sol dur et froid. La nuit était sans étoiles, de gros nuages s'amoncelaient dans le ciel.

— Je vais prendre le premier tour de garde, proposa Tanis.

— Non, laisse-le-moi, intervint Raistlin à la grande surprise du demi-elfe. Je n'ai pas vraiment sommeil, et j'ai besoin de calme pour faire le point.

Tanis haussa les épaules. Il s'allongea et se retourna pendant plusieurs minutes à la recherche d'une position confortable. Faute de la trouver, il se dressa sur un coude. Raistlin était assis contre un rocher, les yeux clos, perdu dans ses pensées.

Deux grondements déchirèrent le silence. Tanis sursauta, puis sourit en réalisant d'où ils venaient. A l'autre bout du camp, Flint et Kirsig ronflaient si fort que le demi-elfe n'entendit pas approcher la menace.

Soudain, un poids s'abattit sur ses épaules, suivi par une sensation d'étouffement. Tanis voulut crier pour avertir ses amis mais il ne réussit qu'à se remplir la bouche de plumes. Il tenta d'attraper le couteau glissé à sa ceinture… Ses bras étaient immobilisés contre ses flancs. Des serres pointues lui pinçaient le cou.

Des sons étouffés lui indiquèrent que les autres membres du groupe avait subi le même sort. Une voix mélodieuse s'éleva dans la nuit :

— Ce ne sont pas des minotaures. On dirait plutôt qu'ils te ressemblent.

Le cocon de plumes s'ouvrit ; quelqu'un brandit une torche devant le visage de Tanis, l'aveuglant. Le demi-elfe se sentit enveloppé dans une étreinte d'ours.

— Tanis ! Je croyais ne jamais te revoir ! Et Raistlin, mon frère !

Le mage fut le second à manquer se faire briser les côtes par Caramon. Il eut un large sourire.

— Nous pensions te trouver prisonnier, pas nous faire capturer par toi ! Mais comme je l'ai dit à Tanis, j'étais certain que tu allais bien.

Les jumeaux se tenaient côte à côte, les bras musclés de Caramon autour des frêles épaules de Raistlin. A la lueur vacillante de la torche, Tanis s'émerveilla une fois de plus à ce spectacle. Comment les frères Majere pouvaient-ils être à la fois si semblables et si différents ?

L'étrangeté était accentuée par l'accoutrement de Caramon : un diadème et une tunique couverte de plumes. Le demi-elfe regarda autour de lui, et vit que les compagnons du guerrier portait les mêmes vêtements. A moins que... Non, c'était impossible. On eût dit qu'ils avaient des ailes à la place des bras !

Flint s'approcha de Caramon.

— Comptes-tu nous présenter à tes amis, ou devons-nous le faire nous-mêmes ? bougonna le nain en jetant un regard nerveux aux nouveaux venus.

Caramon grimaça.

— Excuse-moi.

Il se tourna vers Fend-Nuage.

— Voici mon frère Raistlin, mes amis Tanis Demi-Elfe et Flint Forgefeu de Solace. Je ne connais pas les femmes qui les accompagnent, mais je serai ravi d'y remédier au plus vite.

Il cligna de l'œil en direction de la sculpturale Yuril, qui ne broncha pas.

— Raistlin, Flint, Tanis, voici mes amis les kyries, des êtres nobles, ennemis jurés des minotaures. Ce sont eux qui nous ont tirés de la prison où nous croupissions sur l'île de Mithas.

— Nous ? répéta Flint.

— Sturm et moi, expliqua Caramon.

— Alors où est-il ? s'enquit le nain. Et même si je vais probablement regretter cette question, où se trouve Tasslehoff ?

— Je suis ici, dit une voix rauque, à l'extérieur du cercle de lumière de la torche.

Volesprit s'écarta, révélant un Sturm titubant et mal en point. Moins de quarante-huit heures après son sauvetage dans la Fosse des Enfers, il n'était pas encore bien remis. Il approcha de ses amis en clopinant.

Flint fronça les sourcils.

— Qu'as-tu fait à ta moustache ? demanda-t-il, stupéfait.

— Peu importe. Ne vois-tu pas qu'il se sent mal ? dit Kirsig, en se précipitant vers le jeune Solamnique. Venez, laissez-moi vous aider.

Sturm, trop poli pour manifester son étonnement face à l'apparence grotesque de la demi-ogresse, jeta un regard interrogateur à Flint.

— Tu peux la laisser faire, dit le nain à contrecœur. Kirsig est une amie, et une guérisseuse passable.

— Beaucoup mieux que passable, protesta Raistlin. Qui sait ce que nous serions devenus sans elle ?

Yuril et ses compagnes s'autorisèrent un murmure approbateur. Rose de plaisir, Kirsig prit Sturm par la main et le conduisit jusqu'à son paquetage.

— Que faites-vous là ?

La question avait jailli simultanément des lèvres de Caramon et de Raistlin. Malgré le froid et leur situation peu enviable, les jumeaux sourirent.

— Je crains que vos récits respectifs ne soient très longs. Nous devrions d'abord allumer un feu pour nous réchauffer, suggéra Fend-Nuage.

— C'est que... nous ne voudrions pas révéler notre présence, protesta Tanis.

— Ne craignez rien, le rassura le kyrie. Nos éclaireurs ont survolé l'île. L'ouest est désertique, le nord occupé par une forêt tropicale. Les minotaures campent dans les ruines de Karthay, à deux jours de marche… A quelques heures de vol pour nous.

Les hommes-oiseaux avaient apporté un peu de bois, et la perspective d'un feu ragaillardit considérablement le groupe de Tanis. Kirsig fit chauffer de l'eau et prépara pour Sturm un thé de sa composition.

Pendant que le jeune Solamnique buvait en silence, Caramon raconta leur périple. Quand il arriva à leur séjour dans la prison d'Atossa, l'intérêt de Raistlin redoubla.

— D'abord, j'ai cru que les minotaures voulaient faire de nous des gladiateurs, expliqua Caramon.

— Mais après que les kyries l'eurent délivré, intervint Sturm à voix basse, des officiers sont venus m'interroger. Ils connaissaient ton nom, Raistlin, et aussi celui de Kitiara. Ils ont mentionné un certain Maître de la Nuit. Le plus bizarre, c'est que Tass les accompagnait : il avait même l'air de collaborer avec eux.

— Tass ? répéta Flint, ahuri. Je savais qu'il n'avait pas l'étoffe d'un héros, mais de là à s'allier aux minotaures ! Peut-être l'obligeaient-ils à faire semblant, pour te saper le moral.

— Non, personne ne le forçait, répondit amèrement Sturm. Il leur a donné des conseils pour me torturer… C'est même lui qui a coupé ma moustache, et qui a suggéré qu'on me jette dans la Fosse des Enfers !

« D'après ce que j'ai entendu avant que les kyries viennent à mon secours, les minotaures tiennent Kitiara. C'est pour la délivrer que nous sommes venus : nous ignorions de votre présence. »

Raistlin se leva et arpenta le campement, les mains croisées derrière le dos.

— Le Maître de la Nuit doit soupçonner notre arrivée, déclara-t-il, l'air préoccupé. Ça ne fait pas mon affaire, et l'idée qu'il ait Kit ne m'enchante pas non plus.

Il se tourna vers Sturm et Caramon :

— Vous ne le savez peut-être pas, mais les minotaures se sont rassemblés ici pour ouvrir un portail à une de leurs divinités maléfiques. Leur sort nécessite le sacrifice d'une créature intelligente.

— Qui est le Maître de la Nuit ? voulut savoir Flint.

La même question brûlait les lèvres de Tanis.

— C'est leur grand prêtre, expliqua Raistlin. Celui qui lancera le sort.

Le jeune mage retraça brièvement le voyage qui l'avait conduit, en compagnie de Tanis et de Flint, sur l'île de Karthay.

— Je crains que les minotaures invoquent Sargonnas pour qu'il les aide à conquérir le monde, conclut-il. Nous devons empêcher le Maître de la Nuit de mettre son plan à exécution.

— Sargonnas, siffla Fend-Nuage, les yeux brillants de colère.

— Vous avez entendu parler de lui ? s'enquit Raistlin.

— Selon nos légendes, un condor rouge géant appelé Sargonnas faillit massacrer les kyries il y a plusieurs générations. Il s'allia avec un noble dégénéré qui lui remit notre artefact le plus précieux : la Pierre du Nord, dont notre peuple se servait pour voyager d'un continent à l'autre.

« Depuis, nous sommes confinés sur ces îles, en guerre perpétuelle contre les minotaures. Nous vous aiderons avec joie à mettre des bâtons dans les roues à ce monstre. »

Quelques instants, personne ne dit mot. Tous étaient effarés par l'ampleur de la tâche.

— Pour le moment, nous ne pouvons rien faire, déclara Tanis. Je suggère de nous reposer afin de reprendre des forces pour demain.

*
* *

Le groupe se composait maintenant de huit humains, un nain, une demi-ogresse, un demi-elfe et six kyries. D'autres hommes-oiseaux survolaient l'île en éclaireurs ; l'un rejoignit les compagnons au petit matin.

Raistlin fut ravi d'apprendre que les kyries pouvaient, en deux voyages, les transporter à proximité du campement des minotaures, ce qui leur ferait gagner un temps considérable et leur épargnerait beaucoup de fatigue. La première vague comprendrait les jumeaux, Tanis, Sturm et Yuril.

Flint, qui n'avait guère apprécié la traversée de la Mer de Sang, ne montra aucun enthousiasme à l'idée d'un voyage aérien.

— Je vais d'abord vous regarder partir. Si vous ne tombez pas, que vous ne percutez pas une montagne et que le soleil ne vous carbonise pas, je songerai peut-être à vous imiter.

— Ça m'ennuie de te laisser derrière, protesta Tanis.

— Bah, ne t'inquiète pas. Kirsig veillera sur moi, plaisanta Flint.

Le demi-elfe sourit.

— C'est vrai. Je crois que Lolly Ockenfels a trouvé une concurrente sérieuse.

— C'est la dernière fois que j'essaie d'avoir une conversation civilisée avec toi ! explosa le nain, rouge de colère. Tu ne me témoignes aucun respect !

Il continua à râler jusqu'à ce que Tanis et les autres ne soient plus que de petits points dans le ciel.

*
* *

Les kyries avaient eu le temps de fabriquer des harnais de cuir et de chanvre pour leurs passagers. Etre suspendu les jambes dans le vide n'était pas une façon très gracieuse de voyager, songea Tanis, mais l'efficacité primait.

Un kyrie nommé Cœur de Tonnerre emmena le demi-elfe jusqu'aux ruines de Karthay. Tanis se félicita de l'ombre qu'il lui fournissait, car le soleil avait recommencé à cogner dur.

A l'approche des ruines, Fend-Nuage décrivit un grand demi-cercle et alla se poser sur une plate-forme rocheuse surplombant le volcan éteint appelé Sommet du Monde. Les autres kyries le rejoignirent, le temps de déposer leurs passagers et de partir chercher le reste du groupe.

Quelques milliers de pieds plus bas, la cité en ruine évoquait un paysage lunaire. A cette distance, les compagnons ne pouvaient distinguer ses occupants.

— Yuril, Sturm et toi allez attendre les autres ici, ordonna Raistlin. Pendant ce temps, Caramon, Tanis et moi reconnaîtrons les environs pour nous assurer qu'aucun minotaure n'y rôde. Peut-être trouverons-nous aussi quelque chose à manger pour ce soir.

Yuril hocha la tête. Elle s'assit en tailleur, puis, saisissant une pierre, entreprit d'aiguiser son épée.

Les trois compagnons descendirent vers la vallée en empruntant un étroit chemin couleur de cendres. Ils n'avaient pas parcouru une lieue quand la piste se sépara en deux. Raistlin se frotta le menton.

— De ce côté, dit Caramon en pointant un doigt vers la gauche.

— Non, de celui-là, protesta Tanis en indiquant l'autre.

— Je vais prendre celui de droite, trancha Raistlin. Vous deux, celui de gauche.

La perspective de laisser le jeune mage seul horrifia Caramon et Tanis, mais ni l'un ni l'autre ne trouvèrent les mots pour le dire. Raistlin les dévisagea froidement.

— Alors ? demanda-t-il, une pointe d'impatience dans la voix.

— Ne... ne crois-tu pas que nous devrions rester ensemble ? balbutia Caramon.

Tanis approuva d'un hochement de tête.

— Il vaut mieux vérifier des deux côtés, objecta Raistlin. Tu ne t'inquiètes quand même pas pour moi, j'espère ? Après tout, j'ai traversé la moitié du monde sans ton aide.

— N-non, répondit Caramon, l'air misérable.

— D'accord, intervint Tanis, à condition qu'on se retrouve ici dans deux heures.

— Très bien.

— Et appelle si tu vois quelque chose, ne put s'empêcher d'ajouter Caramon.

— Bien sûr, répondit Raistlin, irrité.

A contrecœur, Caramon et Tanis regardèrent le jeune mage s'éloigner. Ils soupirèrent à l'unisson, puis s'engagèrent sur la piste de gauche.

La chance leur sourit. Caramon tua un gros serpent dont la chair ferait un excellent ragoût, et Tanis découvrit de petits fruits comestibles sur un buisson qui s'accrochait obstinément au sol aride. Nulle part ils ne virent de minotaure.

Ils rebroussèrent chemin et attendirent plus d'une heure à l'endroit convenu, sans succès. Ils revinrent vers Sturm et Yuril, espérant que le mage était rentré avant eux, mais là encore, leurs espoirs furent déçus.

Les kyries arrivèrent avec le reste du groupe : Flint, Kirsig et les compagnes de Yuril.

Le nain était blême de peur et lâchait des chapelets de jurons

La demi-ogresse jurait qu'elle ne s'était jamais autant amusée ; quant aux anciennes du *Castor*, elles avaient l'habitude des voyages mouvementés.

— Auriez-vous aperçu Raistlin ? demanda Caramon, anxieux.

— Non, répondit Fend-Nuage en fronçant les sourcils. Je le croyais en votre compagnie.

— Je le savais ! s'exclama Caramon en flanquant un coup de pied rageur dans un caillou. Je le savais !

Etonné, Flint haussa un sourcil.

— Caramon a raison, soupira Tanis. Nous n'aurions pas dû le laisser seul.

— Que se passe-t-il ? s'enquit Fend-Nuage. Où est-il allé ?

— A mon avis, grommela Caramon, mon cher frère est parti jouer un tour au Maître de la Nuit. J'espère qu'il ne se fera pas tuer.

— En attendant, que fait-on ? demanda Flint, toujours pragmatique. La cérémonie n'aura pas lieu avant demain soir.

— A moins que Raistlin soit revenu d'ici là..., commença Tanis.

— Ce qui m'étonnerait fort, coupa Caramon.

— ... Nous devrions dresser un plan sans tenir compte de lui.

Fend-Nuage approuva le demi-elfe. Il envoya trois de ses guerriers survoler les ruines et prendre contact avec le reste des éclaireurs.

— Soyez de retour demain matin au plus tard, ordonna-t-il. Quoi qu'il arrive, il faudra passer à l'attaque.

S'efforçant d'oublier leur inquiétude pour Raistlin, les compagnons entreprirent de dresser le camp.

CHAPITRE XIV

A plusieurs lieues de la pointe orientale de Karthay, des centaines d'orughis se rassemblaient, leurs épaules grises et musclées émergeant des flots, leurs pieds palmés s'agitant sous la surface.

Leur tête levée vers le ciel révélait un front haut, un nez épaté, des oreilles pointues, de petits yeux ronds et des cheveux blonds filasse. Certains portaient des haches de guerre et des dagues, d'autres le boomerang métallique appelé tonkk.

Les orughis étaient tournés vers l'ouest. Appartenant à une espèce amphibie, ils pouvaient nager pendant plusieurs jours sans ressentir de fatigue. Pour l'heure, ils faisaient du sur place, attendant que Sargonnas se manifeste.

Un peu plus loin, dissimulée par une nappe de brouillard, une flotte de navires de guerre ogres se balançait dans la baie. Elle se composait de quelques dizaines de bâtiments, mais chacun d'eux représentait une tribu différente.

Au signal convenu, leurs capitaines devraient se mobiliser… Pour l'instant, ils maintenaient une certaine distance entre eux et leurs cousins aquatiques, pour qui ils n'éprouvaient que mépris.

Le commandant de la flotte ogre, Oolong du clan Xak, surveillait les orughis à l'aide de sa longue-vue. Il poussa un grognement agacé, gratta son crâne infesté de poux et passa les doigts dans ses longs cheveux emmêlés. Comment les minotaures avaient-ils persuadé son chef de s'allier avec cette race inférieure ?

Oolong Xak n'était pas le seul à éprouver des doutes. A des centaines de lieues de là, dans le palais de Lacynos, les huit membres du Cercle Suprême et leur roi attendaient l'arrivée de Sargonnas avec enthousiasme, impatience ou scepticisme.

Le roi des minotaures voulait conquérir l'Ansalonie pour impressionner ses sujets. Il avait investi beaucoup de troupes et d'argent dans le plan du Maître de la Nuit : une réussite soulignerait la sagesse dont il avait fait preuve.

Son seul soutien inconditionnel venait d'Atra Cura, le représentant des pirates, pour qui toute guerre était bonne à prendre. Les autres membres du Cercle avaient sur la question un avis plus mitigé.

Des dizaines de navires de guerre se tenaient prêts dans le port de Lacynos. Partout autour de Mithas, les charpentiers mettaient la dernière main à des centaines d'autres. Akz avait malmené ses esclaves pour tenir les délais imposés, même si les ambitions du Maître de la Nuit le laissaient indifférent. Il n'était pas très religieux ; au cours de ses nombreuses années de siège au Cercle Suprême, il avait vu quantité de plans échouer de façon inattendue.

Cela dit, personne n'avait encore osé invoquer Sargonnas. Un tel acte requérait du courage et une sacrée dose d'ambition. Et puis, si le sort ne fonctionnait pas, les galères pourraient toujours servir à autre chose. Akz n'avait pas envie d'engager sa flotte et ses troupes dans un conflit de longue haleine..., à moins que les dieux n'approuvent vraiment celui-ci. Par conséquent, il n'agirait que si Sargonnas daignait se montrer.

Bien qu'Inultus et Akz se détestassent, ils s'accordaient sur la plupart des questions militaires. Le commandant des armées minotaures voulait bien participer à la conquête du monde, à condition que Sargonnas lui donne son aval. Dans le cas contraire, il lui semblait hors de question d'honorer un pacte contre nature avec les ogres et les orughis.

Deux autres membres du Cercle Suprême soutenaient le roi malgré leurs réticences personnelles. Victri était toujours prêt à se battre, et l'amitié de Juvabit avec son souverain datait de leur enfance. Pourtant, tous deux désapprouvaient le culte obsessionnel du Maître de la Nuit, et espéraient secrètement que ses plans échoueraient.

Groppis n'avait pas d'opinion sur la question. Il déplorait que les préparatifs de campagne eussent coûté aussi cher, et il défaillait à l'idée du trou que creuserait dans le trésor royal un conflit à grande échelle.

Quant à Bartill et Kharis-O, ils avaient clairement exprimé leur désaccord avec les plans du Maître de la Nuit : le premier parce qu'il était préoccupé par ses projets personnels et avait toujours besoin d'argent, la seconde parce qu'elle représentait un clan séparatiste et qu'elle avait l'esprit de contradiction. Pourtant, elle ne rechignait pas à se battre, et se soumettait loyalement aux décisions du Cercle.

Les huit membres du conseil avaient été convoqués par leur roi pour assister à la venue de Sargonnas. Aujourd'hui, assis à leur place habituelle, certains tambourinaient sur la table de chêne, tandis que d'autres arpentaient la salle.

Encore une nuit et un jour à attendre.

*
* *

Tasslehoff devait reconnaître que le sanctuaire du Maître de la Nuit avait quelque chose de fascinant. Ça manquait un peu de couleur, mais il aimait bien le côté anarchique des ruines et les fissures qui couraient à ses pieds. Se promenant, il ramassa plusieurs débris couverts de cendres, statuettes brisées ou des morceaux de poterie, qu'il fourra joyeusement dans ses sacoches.

— Ce kender n'est-il pas étonnant ? demanda Fesz, debout près du Maître de la Nuit. Je pensais que ce serait une bonne idée de l'amener ici. Tasslehoff s'est montré très coopératif, il m'a fourni de nombreux renseignements au sujet de ses amis. Et il mourait d'envie de venir.

— Es-tu certain qu'il soit maléfique ? demanda le Maître de la Nuit en observant Tass, qui sautillait au milieu des ruines.

— Il boit une double dose de potion chaque jour. Rien, dans son attitude, ne me pousse à douter de sa conversion.

— Et cet étrange bâton, sur son dos ?

— C'est l'arme traditionnelle des kenders. Tasslehoff dit qu'elle le rend invincible ; même si c'est une idée puérile, elle ne peut pas nous causer de tort.

Le Maître de la Nuit lança un regard en coin à son disciple. Fesz lui succéderait un jour. Il était digne de confiance, mais il accordait parfois la sienne un peu trop facilement.

— Et l'évasion de cet humain, Sturm de Lumlane ?

— Un incident regrettable, reconnut Fesz. Mais nous ne pouvons en blâmer Tasslehoff. Il était près de moi dans l'arène au moment où son ami allait perdre le duel, et croyez-moi, il applaudissait avec autant d'enthousiasme que nous tous.

« Aucun minotaure ne fut plus dégoûté que lui par le sauvetage de l'humain. Il a insisté pour que les gardes soient exécutés en guise de punition, et il a même demandé à se charger de l'un d'eux. Nos lois interdisent ce genre de pratique, aussi ai-je dû refuser. »

Le Maître de la Nuit sembla ruminer cette information. Puis, haussant les épaules, il revint vers la pièce sans murs qui lui tenait lieu de sanctuaire. Il se déplaçait avec une grâce animale, faisant tinter les clochettes suspendues à ses cornes.

— Hé, attendez-moi ! s'écria Tasslehoff en lui courant après.

Le Maître de la Nuit ne rendit pas son salut au kender. Il s'assit à sa table de travail, pendant que deux Très-Hauts lui apportaient les grimoires et les composants de sorts. Disposant ces derniers devant lui, il les examina en prenant des notes sur un bout de parchemin.

— Il n'est pas très bavard, hein ? demanda Tass, mécontent.

— L'heure approche, répondit Fesz. Il doit se concentrer sur la tâche qui l'attend. Moi, je dois l'aider.

Le minotaure alla prendre sa place parmi les acolytes du Maître de la Nuit, dont il exécuta les ordres avec célérité.

Livré à lui-même, Tass se dirigea vers la cage où était emprisonnée Kitiara. La jeune femme avait l'air fatiguée, mal nourrie et pas très propre. Il vit que Dogz, allongé sur une couverture, non loin de là, le dévisageait avec attention.

— Alors, Kit, demanda Tass d'un air dégagé, comment es-tu arrivée si vite à Karthay ? Je suis impressionné. Tu as utilisé la magie, n'est-ce pas ?

Kitiara toisa le kender sans rien dire.

— Quand même, reprit Tass, ça m'étonne que tu te sois laissée capturer aussi facilement. Je croyais que Caramon était le seul imbécile de la famille Majere.

— Combien de fois devrais-je te dire que je ne suis pas une Majere ! cracha Kit.

Tass haussa les épaules.

— Une demi-Majere alors. Sans doute la moitié qui s'est fait capturer, gloussa-t-il.

Il se trouvait de plus en plus spirituel.

— Au cas où tu ne l'aurais pas remarqué, répliqua sèchement Kitiara, l'endroit grouille de minotaures. Et je n'étais pas au courant.

— Dans ce cas, tu ne dois pas savoir non plus que tu seras sacrifiée demain soir, pas vrai ? Si tu as un message à transmettre à Raistlin, tu ferais mieux de me le dire tout de suite.

Avec le peu de forces qui lui restaient, Kitiara se jeta contre les barreaux de sa cage. Ceux-ci tremblèrent sous le choc. Le kender recula d'un pas.

— J'ignore quel mauvais coup tu prépares, Tasslehoff Racle-Pieds, grogna la jeune femme en pressant son visage entre deux barreaux. Mais si j'arrive à sortir d'ici, je jure que les vautours festoieront sur ta petite carcasse de traître !

— Tu n'es pas obligée de le prendre sur ce ton, dit Tass, offensé, surtout que nous sommes de vieux amis. A moins que tu ne sois jalouse... Avoue que ça t'aurait plu de devenir maléfique à ma place !

Les yeux de Kitiara lancèrent des éclairs. Grimaçant, Tass se dirigea vers Dogz, qui baissa la tête.

— Que t'arrive-t-il ? demanda le kender en se laissant tomber sur la couverture à côté du minotaure.

— Rien, ami Tass, mentit Dogz en évitant son regard.

— Rien, ami Tass, répéta le kender d'une voix moqueuse.

Autour de lui, une douzaine de gardes armés jusqu'aux dents veillaient sur le sanctuaire du Maître de la Nuit. D'autres arpentaient le reste du camp… Mais ni les Très-Hauts ni le grand prêtre ne portaient de lame. Seul Dogz avait une épée large, un katar et un fléau.

Le minotaure baissa la voix :

— Parfois, je m'interroge à ton sujet, Tass.

— Vraiment ? Pourquoi donc ?

— A voir comment tu traites ces gens, d'abord Sturm, puis cette femelle, on ne dirait pas qu'ils sont tes amis.

Tass flanqua une petite tape sur l'épaule de Dogz.

— Hé, je suis maléfique, tu te souviens ? J'essaie de me comporter comme tel, c'est tout. Sturm et Kitiara étaient mes amis quand j'étais bon. Maintenant, je suis mauvais, et j'essaie de faire mon boulot du mieux possible. Tu devrais être fier de moi.

— Ou-oui, dit Dogz, hésitant.

— Vois les choses de cette façon, suggéra Tass, s'allongeant et croisant les mains derrière sa nuque : je suis devenu un « minotaure honoraire ». Ne m'as-tu pas dit un jour que la raison du plus fort était toujours la meilleure, et que ton peuple était né pour dominer le monde ?

— Si.

— Eh bien, je prouve ma loyauté à la nation minotaure. Si tu avais le choix entre trahir ton peuple ou tes amis, pardon, tes ex-amis, que ferais-tu ?

Le minotaure baissa sa grosse tête cornue. Quand il la releva, ses yeux bovins étaient emplis de tristesse.

— Je ne sais pas. Je trahirais mes amis, je suppose, répondit-il lentement.

— N'es-tu pas impatient que Sargonnas pénètre dans notre monde ? s'enquit Tass.

Dogz jeta un coup d'œil par-dessus son épaule, vers l'endroit où le Maître de la Nuit consultait ses grimoires. Les Très-Hauts se tenaient derrière lui, attentifs à satisfaire le moindre de ses désirs.

— Si, répéta le minotaure sans conviction.

— Tu vois ? Moi, c'est pareil, dit Tass, triomphant.

Il tapota la main de son ami.

— Ne t'inquiète donc pas, ou tu vas avoir des rides sur le museau.

Le kender étouffa un bâillement exagéré.

— Maintenant, si ça ne te fais rien, je vais rattraper mon sommeil en retard.

Il ferma les yeux. Quelques secondes plus tard, il les entrouvrit pour observer la réaction de Dogz.

Le regard dans le vague, le minotaure polissait ses armes. Autrefois, ses amis et ses ennemis étaient clairement définis. Les kenders, par exemple : il les détestait sans même en avoir rencontré. Tass lui était d'abord apparu comme une créature répugnante, une des plus basses sur l'échelle de l'évolution.

Mais il avait passé beaucoup de temps avec lui durant sa captivité, et peu à peu, il en était venu à l'apprécier. Il aimait sa vivacité et son sens de l'humour, admirant le courage dont il avait fait montre face à la torture.

Au cours de leurs conversations, il avait appris à connaître ses amis de Solace (particulièrement le vieux nain bougon, Flint Forgefeu) et il s'y était attaché malgré lui. Dogz avait une grande famille, mais le concept d'amitié lui était étranger jusqu'à ce que Tass entre dans sa vie.

Hélas, après avoir bu la potion de Fesz, le kender était devenu maléfique. Il s'était mis à donner des ordres, à se montrer exigeant et irritable. Peut-être aiderait-il le Maître de la Nuit à invoquer Sargonnas.

Dogz regrettait amèrement l'ancien Tass.

Le minotaure soupira. Il se pencha pour essuyer la poussière qui recouvrait son katar, une longue lame à la poignée en forme de H.

Vingt pas plus loin, Kitiara ruminait dans sa cage, tendant l'oreille pour surprendre des bribes de conversation. Elle n'était pas une grande admiratrice de l'ancien kender, mais sa nouvelle personnalité lui déplaisait plus encore.

Le Maître de la Nuit avait mentionné Sturm : le Solamnique devait donc être toujours vivant. La veille, Kit l'avait entendu parler de Caramon et de Raistlin. On eût dit que tous ses amis se trouvaient dans les parages, et que le prêtre craignait leur irruption.

La pensée amena un sourire sur les lèvres de Kitiara.

*
* *

— J'apporte de mauvaises nouvelles, déclara un officier en se campant devant le Maître de la Nuit. Les intrus qui ont accosté au sud de l'île viennent d'être rejoints par un vol de kyries.

Arraché à ses travaux, le prêtre fronça les sourcils.

— Des kyries, répéta-t-il, mécontent. Combien ?

— Une douzaine, sans doute membres de l'Assemblée des Guerriers. Mais nous pouvons nous occuper d'eux.

L'officier hésita.

— Oui ? demanda impatiemment le Maître de la Nuit.

— Ils marchent vers nous. Ils semblent savoir précisément où aller.

— Comment ça, « ils marchent vers nous » ? Pourquoi les kyries ne les ont-ils pas transportés jusqu'ici ?

— C'est la question que nous nous posons, Excellence. Peut-être sont-ils trop nombreux pour les hommes-oiseaux, à moins que ceux-ci aient besoin de se reposer après leur voyage.

— Peuh ! cracha le Maître de la Nuit. Les kyries peuvent voler longtemps sans ressentir la moindre fatigue. Il doit y avoir une autre raison.

— Dans ce cas, nous ne tarderons pas à la découvrir. Ils devraient être ici demain à midi, annonça l'officier.

— Très bien.

Le Maître de la Nuit congédia le soldat.

Ainsi, les humains avaient formé une alliance avec les kyries. C'était inattendu, mais pas insurmontable. Bizarrement, le prêtre se sentait ragaillardi par cette nouvelle. Les yeux brillants, il se remit au travail.

Derrière lui, Fesz et les deux autres Très-Hauts échangèrent un signe de tête. Ils avaient confiance en leur maître.

Derrière eux, Tass ne dormait que d'un œil.

Et derrière lui, dans sa cage, Kitiara accroupie n'avait pas perdu une miette de la conversation.

*
* *

Tasslehoff s'éveilla en sursaut. Plusieurs heures s'étaient écoulées ; une obscurité glaciale enveloppait le camp.

Autour du kender, le sanctuaire du Maître de la Nuit bourdonnait d'activité. Les Très-Hauts emballaient des objets dans des caisses et des sacs. Une demi-douzaine de gardes s'étaient rapprochés et semblaient attendre des ordres.

Le Maître de la Nuit finissait de débarrasser sa table. Il avait revêtu une robe de cérémonie et jeté une cape écarlate sur ses épaules. De longs chapelets de plumes et de grelots pendaient à ses cornes.

— Que se passe-t-il ? demanda Tass en se dirigeant vers Dogz, qui faisait lui aussi ses bagages.

— Le Maître de la Nuit dit que l'heure approche, répondit solennellement le minotaure. Nous allons profiter des ténèbres pour nous déplacer vers un endroit où les humains et les kyries ne pourront pas nous retrouver.

— Bonne idée, s'enthousiasma Tass.

Fesz s'approcha du kender.

— Mon maître te permet de nous accompagner, déclara-t-il, très excité. C'est un grand privilège pour un non-minotaure.

« D'habitude, les seuls personnes présentes pour le lancement de ce sort sont le Maître de la Nuit, les Très-Hauts et la victime sacrificielle. Mais nous avons pensé qu'un représentant d'une race connue pour sa chance pourrait être agréable à Sargonnas, surtout si ce témoin est aussi maléfique que toi. »

Le regard de Tass se posa sur Kitiara qui se tenait immobile dans sa cage.

— Je suis très flatté, dit-il en gonflant la poitrine. Et même davantage. Je suis... bouleversé. Je vais de ce pas remercier le Maître de la Nuit.

Alors que Tass faisait mine de se diriger vers le prêtre, Fesz le retint par le col de sa tunique.

— Je ne crois pas que le moment soit bien choisi, fit-il remarquer. Mon maître est très occupé.

— Oh. C'est vrai, concéda le kender.

Il regarda deux gardes ouvrir la cage pour en tirer une Kitiara Uth Matar furieuse qui les injuria, les griffa et leur flanqua force coups de pied avant qu'ils ne parviennent à l'enchaîner et à lui lier les mains et les chevilles.

— Si vous croyez que je vais me laisser sacrifier à un stupide dieu des Ténèbres, vous vous fourrez le doigt dans l'œil jusqu'au coude ! s'exclama vertement Kit.

Les gardes la bâillonnèrent pour couper court à ses protestations. Le Maître de la Nuit, qui avait entendu l'éclat de la jeune femme, marcha sur elle les poings serrés. Furieux, il lui cracha au visage.

— Immonde vermine ! gronda-t-il. Comment oses-tu mentionner le nom du Seigneur de la Vengeance ? Tu n'es pas digne d'exister dans le même monde que lui ! Demain, tu mourras, et tu échangeras ta place avec Sargonnas. Tu seras envoyée dans son royaume pendant qu'il pénétrera dans le nôtre pour ne plus le quitter !

Dogz et les Très-Hauts parurent surpris par la véhémence du prêtre. C'était la première fois qu'ils le voyaient se mettre dans un état pareil. Tass allait dire quelque chose quand une voix mélodieuse monta depuis les ténèbres :

— Le sort ne serait-il pas plus efficace si la victime répugnait moins à mourir pour la gloire de Sargonnas ?

Raistlin ! Tass aurait reconnu la voix du jeune mage n'importe où. Kit cessa de se débattre et regarda autour d'elle, mais son demi-frère n'était nulle part en vue.

Dogz et les gardes dégainèrent nerveusement leurs armes. Les Très-Hauts se regroupèrent, prêts à incanter. Le Maître de la Nuit pivota sur les talons, et Tass fut surpris de lire un certain soulagement dans ses yeux exorbités. Comme s'il avait anticipé toute la scène.

— Est-ce toi ? demanda le prêtre. Es-tu celui qu'ils appellent Raistlin, le demi-frère de cette insolente femelle ?

— C'est exact.

— Alors, montre-toi.

Tass entendit un rire léger.

— J'aime mieux pas, répondit le jeune mage.

— Je comprends. Tu t'es rendu invisible pour franchir le périmètre de sécurité, n'est-ce pas ? Je me demandais comment tu allais t'y prendre. Tes compagnons sont-ils avec toi ?

Raistlin hésita.

— Je suis venu seul, déclara-t-il enfin.

— Parfait.

— Laissez partir ma sœur. Je prendrai sa place.

Tass entendit un cri étouffé derrière lui. Kitiara tentait de s'arracher à l'étreinte des gardes, que la voix jaillie de nulle part semblait mettre mal à l'aise.

— Quelle idée géniale ! s'écria le kender. Salut, Raistlin. C'est moi, Tasslehoff ! As-tu bien reçu ma bouteille magique ?

— Oui, dit le Maître de la Nuit en jetant à Tass un regard sévère. C'est une idée « géniale ». Mais comment puis-je savoir si tu n'essaieras pas de me doubler ?

— Comment puis-je savoir si *vous* n'essaierez pas de me doubler ? riposta le mage.

Le Maître de la Nuit réfléchit.

— Voici ce que nous allons faire, déclara-t-il enfin. Mon premier disciple, Fesz, va te lier les mains. Dès que tu te seras rendu à lui, son fidèle Dogz accompagnera la femelle jusqu'à la sortie du camp et la relâchera. Je t'en donne ma parole.

— D'accord, dit Raistlin après quelques instants de réflexion.

L'écho de sa voix résonnait encore aux oreilles de Tass quand sa silhouette se matérialisa près de Fesz. Le chamane empoigna Raistlin sans douceur et lui attacha les mains derrière le dos. Epuisé par la concentration qu'avait réclamé le sort d'invisibilité, le mage tomba à genoux. Tass se précipita vers lui.

Le Maître de la Nuit fit un signe de tête à Dogz, qui se saisit de Kitiara et la chargea sans cérémonie sur son épaule. Il s'éloigna et les ténèbres l'engloutirent.

— Raistlin ! s'écria Tass. Je savais que tu viendrais !

Une main écarta brutalement le kender et le projeta sur le sol. Le Maître de la Nuit se pencha vers le mage, lui soufflant son haleine pestilentielle à la figure.

— Voici donc le puissant Raistlin, gronda-t-il.

Le jeune homme ne répondit pas, mais fixa le minotaure sans ciller.

— Cet humain n'est rien à côté de vous, intervint Fesz, méprisant. Il refuse même de se battre pour sauver sa peau !

— Ne le détache pas ! ordonna le Maître de la Nuit. S'il veut boire ou manger, donne-lui ce qu'il faut. Mais ne le sous-estime pas. Qu'il reste toujours sous bonne garde.

« A présent, il est temps de partir. Je ne veux pas prendre de risque. Il a peut-être menti en disant qu'il n'était pas seul. »

Les minotaures se hâtèrent d'obéir.

Tasslehoff se releva. Ce Maître de la Nuit avait beau être un gros bonnet, il avait besoin qu'on lui enseigne la politesse. Le kender massa son épaule douloureuse, une idée germant peu à peu dans son esprit.

*

* *

Dogz avait à peine parcouru une centaine de pas quand un des gardes le rattrapa près d'un portique en ruine et lui tendit un message.

— De la part du Maître de la Nuit, expliqua-t-il.

Dogz déplia le bout de parchemin.

*Tue la femelle humaine.*C'était marqué de l'écriture inimitable de son maître.

Le minotaure hésita. Il laissa tomber son fardeau sur le sol et, comme Kit se tortillait en lui jetant des regards furieux, il plaqua un sabot dessus pour l'immobiliser.

— Je dois parler avec la prisonnière, dit-il au garde. Tu peux t'en aller.

Le soldat obéit. Dogz traîna Kit jusqu'à une colonne de pierre et l'attacha. Puis il se laissa tomber lourdement sur une pierre plate.

L'ordre du Maître de la Nuit le perturbait : d'abord, parce que la femelle humaine avait été une amie du « bon » Tasslehoff, ensuite, parce que le prêtre avait donné sa parole qu'il la relâcherait.

Dogz réfléchit longuement, puis il se dirigea vers Kit.

— Mon maître veut que je te tue, annonça-t-il. Mais je ne suis pas d'accord avec lui. Je vais te laisser ici jusqu'à notre retour, ensuite, j'aviserai.

Kitiara tira sur ses liens en marmonnant quelque chose. Dogz se mordit les lèvres.

— Si tu cries, je te casse la tête, déclara-t-il fermement.

Il ôta le bâillon de la jeune femme.

— Je... je me moque de ce qui m'arrivera, balbutia Kit. Mais Raistlin... C'est mon frère. Pouvez-vous faire quelque chose pour lui ?

Dogz toisa la jeune femme avec mépris.

— Raistlin aura l'immense honneur d'introduire Sargonnas dans notre monde. Même si je le pouvais, je ne lèverais pas le petit doigt pour le délivrer.

Le minotaure fit mine de replacer le bâillon de Kit.

— Attendez ! s'écria la jeune femme.

Dogz s'immobilisa.

Mille pensées se bousculaient dans la tête de Kit. Elle se souvint de la conversation entre Tass et le minotaure qu'elle avait surprise. Cela lui donna une idée, sans doute la seule qui pourrait sauver Raistlin.

— Vous êtes... vous êtes l'ami de Tasslehoff, n'est-ce pas ? demanda Kit.

— Moui, répondit Dogz, dubitatif.

— Dans ce cas, pourriez-vous lui donner quelque chose de ma part ?

Les yeux du minotaure s'agrandirent quand la jeune femme lui dit de quoi il s'agissait. Il recula et flanqua un coup de pied rageur dans un petit monticule de cendres. Kit l'observa, le cœur battant à tout rompre. Il fallait que ça marche, il le fallait !

Enfin, le minotaure prit une inspiration et hocha la tête. Kitiara lui dit où se trouvait l'objet. Par chance, il était si petit que les gardes ne l'avaient pas découvert durant la fouille corporelle. Dogz s'en empara et le rangea dans sa ceinture, avant de replacer le bâillon de Kit.

Il appela un garde et lui ordonna de veiller sur la jeune femme jusqu'à nouvel ordre. Puis il courut rejoindre le Maître de la Nuit.

CHAPITRE XV

Au crépuscule, Tanis avait perdu le compte du nombre de kyries qui avaient rejoint le camp : plus d'une vingtaine, en tous cas. Les chances des compagnons s'amélioraient, dit-il à Flint.

Le nain ne semblait pas partager son optimisme. Un pli soucieux barrant son front, il attendait avec impatience que Fend-Nuage leur communique les informations des éclaireurs.

Flint, Tanis, Sturm et Caramon se dirigèrent vers le chef des kyries.

— Savons-nous où ils retiennent Kitiara ? Quel est l'état des forces ennemies ? s'enquit anxieusement le nain.

— En survolant les ruines de Karthay, mes éclaireurs ont vu qu'elles étaient occupées par des dizaines de soldats minotaures en armes, répondit Fend-Nuage. Les quartiers du Maître de la Nuit se trouvent à peu près au centre, à l'air libre, mais bien gardés. C'est là qu'ils gardent la femelle humaine dans une cage.

« Le camp connaît une grande agitation : mes éclaireurs n'osent pas s'en approcher de peur de se faire repérer. Un de mes cousins pense avoir aperçu une petite créature, ni humaine ni minotaure, qui traînait dans les parages. »

— Ce maudit kender, marmonna Flint.

— Et mon frère ? demanda Caramon, anxieux.

— Pour l'instant, il n'a pas donné signe de vie.

— Si je comprends bien, dit Tanis, les ruines grouillent de minotaures. Combien sommes-nous à présent..., vingt-cinq, trente ?

Personne ne répondit. Le demi-elfe regarda les visages tendus mais déterminés de ses amis. Tous savaient que leurs adversaires auraient l'avantage du nombre.

Fend-Nuage haussa les épaules.

— Volesprit ne va pas tarder à revenir. Peut-être apportera-t-il de nouvelles informations ou une idée intéressante. C'est un excellent tacticien.

— De toute façon, nous devrons passer à l'attaque demain, déclara Sturm, résolu.

Les compagnons hochèrent la tête. Sans se concerter, tous levèrent les yeux vers le ciel. Le soleil se couchait déjà à l'horizon, un crépuscule ambré annonçant l'arrivée de la nuit.

— Nous avons du pain sur la planche, grommela Flint. Nous ferions mieux de commencer nos préparatifs.

*

* *

Alors qu'il revenait vers le camp, un mouvement attira l'attention de Volesprit. Le kyrie vira sur l'aile et revint en arrière. Un soldat s'agitait autour d'une fosse, comme s'il combattait quelque chose. Volesprit se risqua à perdre un peu d'altitude pour mieux voir.

Le minotaure, qui mesurait pourtant plus de sept pieds semblait minuscule à côté de son adversaire : un monstre doté d'une épaisse carapace bleu-vert et au dos garni d'une crête. Bien que court sur pattes, il était plus haut que le garde et à peu près deux fois plus long. Il avait renversé le minotaure et, faisant claquer sa redoutable mâchoire au-dessus de lui, l'empêchait de se relever.

Le garde leva son trident et tenta de frapper la créature. Il portait de nombreuses morsures sur le corps. Enfin, il parvint à se redresser et se jeta sur le dos de son adversaire. S'accrochant d'une main, il enfonça les pointes de son arme entre deux plaques de carapace.

Le monstre poussa un cri et fit un bond en l'air. Alors, Volesprit vit que le minotaure avait affaire à une bulette, également appelée requin de terre, un prédateur vorace mais si rare que le kyrie n'en avait jamais rencontré.

Du panier qui pendait à sa ceinture, Volesprit tira un filet de lianes étrangleuses. Il piqua vers la bulette, qui avait réussi à désarçonner le garde et à refermer ses mâchoires autour de son cou.

Le filet enveloppa sa proie et commença à se resserrer. Par chance, la créature, déjà blessée, ne put esquiver cette attaque surprise, ni se dégager à temps. Volesprit se posa à bonne distance et s'approcha avec prudence.

Le monstre ne se débattait pas. Immobile, il regarda le kyrie, ses petits yeux jaunes brillant d'une lueur mauvaise. Au bout de sa tête sans cou, sa mâchoire pointue ressemblait au bec d'une tortue géante.

La bulette avait lâché le minotaure, qui se tordait de douleur sur le sol. Déjà, son sang imbibait le sable grisâtre du désert.

Comme tous les kyries, Volesprit avait une connaissance magique des animaux, ainsi que la faculté de communiquer avec eux. Il savait que les bulettes attaquaient et dévoraient toutes les créatures présentes sur leur territoire, et qu'elles s'enfouissaient sous terre pour dormir, remontant à la surface quand des vibrations leur indiquaient l'arrivée d'une proie.

Malgré la crainte que lui inspirait le monstre, Volesprit décida de lui parler.

— Je ne te veux pas de mal, dit-il dans la langue animale universelle. Je souhaite parler des raisons de ma présence, et des minotaures dont regorge cette île.

— Je me moque de tes discours, répondit la bulette. Me remplir l'estomac est la seule chose qui m'intéresse. Ces stupides hommes-taureaux qui renient leur héritage ne m'intéressent pas.

En plus d'être assoiffée de sang, la créature était stupide, songea Volesprit qui n'en continua pas moins :

— Tu dois aussi t'intéresser à la blessure de ton dos. Elle saigne beaucoup : grâce à mes dons de guérisseur, je pourrai la soigner si tu consens à m'écouter.

— J'ai beau être ta prisonnière, dit la bulette, tu auras du mal à me tuer. Mais parle. Je ne veux pas rester immobilisée plus longtemps que nécessaire.

— Des minotaures de Mithas ont établi un avant-poste sur cette île, expliqua Volesprit. Comme tu dois le savoir, ils exterminent ou réduisent en esclavage tous ceux qui se dressent sur leur chemin. Ce n'est pas dans ton intérêt, ni dans celui des autres créatures de Karthay.

L'éclaireur marqua une pause pour s'assurer qu'il avait toute l'attention de la bulette.

— Mon peuple souhaite évincer les minotaures de l'île, mais nous sommes trop peu nombreux pour y parvenir seuls. Je suis venu avec un groupe de guerriers kyries, une poignée d'humains, un nain et un elfe. Nous serions très honorés qu'un général comme toi, commandant aux animaux de son choix, se joigne à nous pour cette bataille.

Volesprit se disait que flatter l'ego d'un interlocuteur ne faisait jamais de mal.

— Je n'ai besoin de personne pour détruire les minotaures, répliqua la bulette, méprisante. Si je choisissais de le faire, je les exterminerais un à un, très lentement. Pourquoi devrais-je m'allier avec des kyries ?

Volesprit ne doutait pas que le monstre disait vrai. Livré à lui-même, et à condition de prendre son temps, il aurait sans doute pu anéantir les minotaures. Mais le temps était justement ce dont les compagnons manquaient.

— Si tu te joins à nous, nous te concéderons la propriété de cette île comme domaine durant les mille années à venir. Les autres animaux de Karthay reconnaîtront sûrement la suprématie de leur général. Et n'oublie pas ta blessure.

La bulette examina Volesprit des pieds à la tête. Un liquide vert et gluant suintait de sa carapace à l'endroit où le trident du minotaure s'était enfoncé.

— Ma blessure d'abord, dit-elle enfin. Puis nous verrons qui je pourrais enrôler pour lutter contre les minotaures. Les hommes-taureaux n'ont pas beaucoup d'amis sur cette île. (La créature émit ce qui ressemblait à un gloussement.) Moi non plus.

*
* *

Pour soigner la blessure de la bulette, Volesprit dut découper son filet. Plus tard, il utilisa les morceaux pour fabriquer un harnais, afin de soulever et de transporter l'énorme créature.

Toutes ses forces ne furent pas de trop pour ramener la bulette jusqu'au camp. Caramon, Tanis, Sturm, Flint et le reste du groupe regardèrent avec horreur le monstre. Relativement docile, il avait une apparence effrayante et un regard qui leur faisait froid dans le dos.

— Les ruines sont bien défendues, répondit Volesprit à la question muette de ses amis. Nous avons besoin de tous les alliés que nous pourrons trouver.

« Les bulettes sont de redoutables combattantes. Celle-ci a promis d'appeler d'autres créatures terrestres à la rescousse, et elle m'a parlé d'un nid de rocs qui accepteraient peut-être de nous prêter main-forte. »

— Des rocs ! s'étrangla Flint.

Bien qu'ayant grandi dans les collines, il connaissait la réputation de ces oiseaux de proie géants, qui pouvaient faire jusqu'à cent vingt pieds d'envergure et attaquaient souvent les mineurs en montagne.

— Jamais encore un roc n'a aidé un nain, et inversement, déclara Flint avec véhémence.

— Volesprit a raison, fit remarquer Tanis : nous avons besoin d'aide. Kirsig et moi te protégerons de notre mieux...

Croisant les bras sur la poitrine, l'air menaçant, la demi-ogresse approuva avec vigueur.

— Quand nos nouveaux alliés nous rejoindront-ils ? s'enquit Sturm.

Depuis son sauvetage dans la Fosse des Enfers, le Solamnique respectait les kyries, et il ne voyait aucune raison de mettre en doute la sagesse de leurs plans.

— La bulette a déjà envoyé un message ; je vais demander à Fend-Nuage d'envoyer quelqu'un pour négocier avec les rocs. Tout devrait être prêt demain matin. D'ici là, mieux vaut prendre un peu de repos.

Le kyrie s'éloigna pour parler avec son chef. Les autres s'installèrent dans leurs sacs de couchage. Yuril s'adossa au tronc d'un gros arbre pour prendre le premier tour de garde. Plusieurs kyries dormaient déjà.

— Je dois affûter mon épée pour demain, déclara Caramon. Je crois que je vais tenir compagnie à Yuril.

Sturm et Tanis échangèrent un regard amusé.

— Rappelez-vous qu'un de vous deux — au moins — est censé monter la garde, gloussa le demi-elfe.

*

* *

Flint fit des cauchemars toute la nuit. Il s'agitait tellement dans son sommeil que Kirsig dut plusieurs fois remonter la couverture qui avait glissé de ses épaules.

Quand le nain s'éveilla enfin, il lui fallut se frotter les yeux pour se persuader qu'il ne rêvait plus. La bulette se tenait en face de lui, à la lisière sud du camp. Derrière elle, le sol du désert semblait onduler. Flint plissa les paupières.

— Par Réorx ! jura-t-il.

Des dizaines d'insectes géants, au dos couvert d'une carapace chitineuse brillante grouillaient sous la lumière de l'aube. Ils avaient des mandibules noires de petite taille, mais à l'air redoutablement efficace.

— Des horax, expliqua Tanis, qui en avait déjà combattu.

— Des quoi ? sursauta Flint.

— Des horax. Ils vivent sous le sol et peuvent atteindre les sept pieds de long. Ils attaquent généralement en groupe. (Voyant béer la mâchoire du nain, Tanis ajouta :) Ne t'inquiète pas. Ils obéissent à la bulette, et elle est de notre côté, enfin, pour le moment.

Tout le monde était levé dans le camp et regardait la horde avec un mélange d'émerveillement et d'appréhension. A l'arrière-plan d'étranges formations rocheuses s'agitaient.

— K-Kirsig, chuchota Flint en tirant sur la manche de la demi-ogresse.

Les « rochers » bougèrent à nouveau, révélant leur véritable nature. C'étaient les anneaux d'un gigantesque reptile, long de plus de trois cents pieds et au museau garni de crocs effilés. Le monstre était étendu de tout son long, ses « pieds » semblables à des nageoires reposant de chaque côté de son corps. Ce que Flint avait pris pour des cavernes étaient en réalité ses orbites.

— Le grand hatori, approuva Kirsig, dont les connaissances en matière zoologique semblaient inépuisables. Il n'a pas dû manger beaucoup au cours des dernières années. Un hatori affamé est un combattant redoutable, comme disait mon pauvre papa.

Les animaux rassemblés dans le désert étaient des prédateurs qui ne se souciaient guère les uns des autres, mais qui détestaient plus encore les hommes-taureaux.

La bulette leur avait communiqué les termes de l'accord proposé par Fend-Nuage et Volesprit : ils combattraient ensemble pendant une journée. Après, Karthay leur appartiendrait pour les mille ans à venir. Ils avaient reçu l'ordre de ne pas toucher aux humains qu'ils trouveraient dans les ruines : le reste ne regardait qu'eux.

Une rafale faillit renverser Flint. Saisi d'un mauvais pressentiment, le nain leva les yeux. Quatre rocs planaient au-dessus de sa tête : deux adultes et deux plus jeunes, sans doute leurs rejetons.

Quatre paires d'yeux noirs et perçants se posèrent sur les compagnons. Avec leur corps musclé, leur tête en forme de flèche et leurs immenses ailes, les créatures offraient un spectacle impressionnant. Leur plumage brun et jaune et leur bec incurvé brillaient légèrement sous le soleil matinal.

*

* *

Toth-Ur faisait les cent pas devant sa tente, son épaisse fourrure noire gluante de transpiration. Le Maître de la Nuit et ses suivants étaient partis vers le Sommet du Monde. Tout se déroulait comme prévu, mais le commandant minotaure ne pouvait se défaire d'un sentiment de malaise.

La veille Zedhar avait disparu pendant une mission de reconnaissance. Toth-Ur aurait bien envoyé quelqu'un à sa recherche, mais presque toutes ses forces avaient accompagné le Maître de la Nuit jusqu'au lieu du sacrifice, et le prêtre lui avait recommandé la plus grande prudence.

La tente de Toth-Ur se dressait à la lisière ouest des ruines de Karthay, près d'un mur effondré. Les mains sur les hanches, le minotaure balaya le paysage du regard. Quelques soldats se tenaient derrière lui, prêts à exécuter ses ordres.

Soudain, une forme massive jaillit du sol à moins de trois pas de la tente et s'abattit lourdement sur le dos d'un garde. D'un coup de mâchoire, elle lui brisa la nuque.

Les autres soldats eurent à peine le temps de dégainer avant que l'ouverture faite par la bulette commence à cracher des dizaines de horax. Où que regarde Toth-Ur, éberlué, d'étranges animaux sortaient de terre pour attaquer sa petite armée.

Divisées, les forces minotaures n'avaient pas une chance. Les épées des soldats rebondissaient sur la carapace chitineuse de leurs adversaires, les épieux glissaient dessus sans même l'entamer.

La bulette faisait un carnage dans les rangs ennemis.

Les horax étaient assoiffés de sang. Ils devaient s'y mettre à trois pour abattre un garde. Les deux premiers coinçaient ses jarrets dans leurs mandibules pour le faire trébucher. Le troisième lui déchirait la poitrine.

Du sud arrivait un cauchemar pire encore. Le désert semblait monter à l'assaut des ruines. Le hatori serpentait en silence vers un contingent de minotaures qui s'apprêtaient bravement à lui tenir tête. D'un coup de queue, il en renversa une demi-douzaine, leur brisant la colonne vertébrale.

Au nord, les rocs apparurent, leurs ailes gigantesques voilant presque la lumière du soleil. Ils décrivirent des cercles en altitude, tandis que les minotaures projetaient leurs lances vers eux.

Mais les oiseaux géants restaient soigneusement hors de portée.

Avant que les renforts arrivent, ils plongèrent vers les ruines et saisirent au vol de gros rochers couverts de cendres. Reprenant de l'altitude, ils lâchèrent leurs projectiles improvisés sur les soldats, qu'ils écrasèrent par groupes de deux ou trois.

Partout, les minotaures luttaient pour se regrouper. Fuir était impensable, mais l'attaque de ces créatures monstrueuses éveillait en eux une crainte légitime. Leur riposte fut aussi inefficace que désorganisée.

Dans ses pires cauchemars, Toth-Ur n'aurait jamais pensé que les événements puissent tourner ainsi. Il donna l'ordre à ses troupes de battre en retraite.

*
* *

Pendant que les horax, la bulette, le hatori et les rocs faisaient diversion, Caramon, Tanis, Fend-Nuage et les autres kyries devaient pénétrer dans le sanctuaire du Maître de la Nuit pour délivrer Kitiara. Le soleil se couchait déjà, mais personne n'avait encore réussi à localiser Raistlin.

Au centre des ruines, les compagnons eurent la mauvaise surprise de découvrir la cage vide. Malgré le danger, Volesprit se proposa pour survoler les environs. Mais avant qu'il puisse décoller, un épieu à la pointe barbelée utilisé par les minotaures, vint se planter à ses pieds.

Caramon fit volte-face, à temps pour esquiver le coup de hache d'un officier avec lequel il engagea le combat. D'après les bruits et les chocs métalliques qui montaient derrière lui, le jeune homme devina que ses amis avaient fort à faire de leur côté.

Leurs armes en pierre primitives auraient considérablement désavantagé les kyries s'ils n'avaient pas pu s'élever dans les airs pour attaquer les minotaures. Pourtant, un épieu vint se ficher dans l'aile de Fend-Nuage. Le kyrie l'arracha d'une main, puis l'envoya d'un geste vengeur dans l'estomac de son adversaire.

Caramon était en difficulté face à l'officier qui, ambidextre, se battait avec une hache et une massue. Soudain, de la surprise se peignit sur le visage du minotaure. Il bascula en avant et s'immobilisa sur le sol.

Yuril se pencha et posa un pied sur son dos. Tirant à deux mains, elle dégagea son épée, fichée dans les reins de l'officier. L'air nonchalant, elle essuya la lame ensanglantée sur son pantalon, puis s'inclina devant Caramon.

— Toujours ravie de te rendre service, dit-elle avec un sourire éclatant.

*
* *

Sturm, Flint et Kirsig venaient de sauter par-dessus les débris d'une colonne quand un minotaure qui avait échappé aux horax et au hatori bondit sur le nain en brandissant une massue.

Flint esquiva le coup mais trébucha, et se cogna la tête en tombant. Sonné, il regarda le soldat s'approcher, prêt à lui asséner le coup de grâce.

— Noooooon !

Kirsig poussa un hurlement de banshee et se jeta sur le minotaure. Lui entourant les genoux de ses petits bras, elle le plaqua à terre.

Flint s'éloigna en rampant et secoua la tête pour s'éclaircir les idées. Jetant un coup d'œil en arrière, il vit le soldat empoigner Kirsig par le cou et la projeter contre la colonne. Avec un craquement sinistre, la demi-ogresse s'écroula sur le sol, où elle demeura immobile. Sturm planta son épée entre les deux cornes du minotaure, mais il était trop tard. Kirsig était morte.

*

* *

— Mon héros !

Survolant les ruines de Karthay, Volesprit avait enfin repéré la femelle humaine ligotée à une colonne. Il était reparti chercher Tanis : à deux, les compagnons avaient mis quelques instants à se débarrasser du soldat qui gardait Kit.

Epuisée par sa longue captivité, frustrée de ne pouvoir prendre part aux combats qui se déroulaient autour d'elle, la jeune femme avait très fraîchement accueilli ses sauveurs.

— Ça devient une habitude chez toi de voler à mon secours, marmonna-t-elle pendant que Tanis tranchait ses liens.

Elle jeta un regard stupéfait au kyrie, avant d'ajouter à contrecœur :

— Mais cette fois, je suppose que j'en avais besoin.

— *De rien*, grimaça le demi-elfe, conscient qu'il ne tirerait pas plus de remerciements de sa compagne.

Kit était sale et affamée. Tanis fouilla dans son sac et en sortit un morceau de pain, que la jeune femme engloutit voracement. Malgré sa tenue et son attitude, le demi-elfe fut frappé par sa beauté ténébreuse.

Caramon arriva au pas de course et étreignit chaleureusement sa demi-sœur. Sturm et Yuril le suivaient.

— Où est Raist ? demanda le guerrier.

Volesprit secoua la tête.

— Où sont Flint et Kirsig ? demanda Tanis.

— La demi-ogresse est morte, répondit Sturm. Elle a combattu bravement. Flint va bien. Il est quelque part là-bas. Je crois qu'il a un compte à régler avec les minotaures.

Kit se massa les poignets et les chevilles pour rétablir la circulation. Puis, elle tendit un doigt vers le Sommet du Monde.

— Raistlin était ici, mais il s'est porté volontaire pour prendre ma place au cours du sacrifice. Je crois que le Maître de la Nuit l'a emmené là-bas. Nous n'avons pas de temps à perdre…

Fend-Nuage et trois autres kyries venaient d'atterrir près des compagnons.

— En volant, nous pouvons y être dans quelques minutes, proposa le chef des hommes-oiseaux.

Kit eut l'air sceptique. Tanis lui assura que la chose était possible.

— Sturm, ordonna Caramon, va trouver Flint et les autres. Dis-leur de se retirer. Qu'ils laissent les minotaures aux animaux, et qu'ils nous retrouvent au campement.

— Mais..., protesta le Solamnique.

— Il n'y a pas assez de kyries pour nous emporter tous à la fois, coupa Tanis, et il faut que quelqu'un prévienne Flint.

Sturm hocha la tête et s'éloigna en courant.

Fend-Nuage saisit Caramon sous les aisselles et s'envola, pendant que Volesprit en faisait autant avec Tanis, les deux autres kyries se chargeant de Yuril et de Kitiara. Ensemble, les huit compagnons s'élancèrent vers le Sommet du Monde, abandonnant derrière eux le fracas des combats. Ce soir, la bulette, le hatori et les rocs auraient de quoi festoyer.

CHAPITRE XVI

Selon la légende, le Sommet du Monde était entré en éruption pour la dernière fois lors du Cataclysme. Il avait fait pleuvoir la mort sur Karthay, effaçant la cité et ses habitants de la face de Krynn.

Telle une gigantesque dent, le volcan se dressait au nord-ouest des ruines. Ravins profonds et croûtes de lave durcie alternaient sur ses flancs. Les suivants du Maître de la Nuit avaient passé plusieurs mois à tracer un chemin vers son cratère noirci.

Une activité étonnante régnait au sommet du volcan. Des mares de boue fumaient, des jets de vapeur et de gaz toxiques s'échappaient de multiples fissures.

Au centre du cratère s'étendait une dépression ovale plus large que les autres, et au contenu plus volatile. Elle couvrait le bouchon de roche solidifié qui obstruait le cœur du volcan, empêchant la lave de se répandre à nouveau sur l'île.

Au cours des semaines précédentes, le Maître de la Nuit en avait fait enlever une partie d'environ douze pieds de large. C'était ici qu'il incanterait pour ouvrir un portail à Sargonnas. En se penchant sur l'ouverture, on pouvait apercevoir le liquide orange bouillonnant.

Tout était prêt. Les acolytes et une partie des soldats campaient près du cratère depuis plusieurs jours ; ils avaient installé le laboratoire dont leur maître aurait besoin pour lancer son sort, et monté un échafaudage de bois dont la plate-forme surplombait l'ouverture donnant sur le cœur du volcan.

Le jour pâlissait. Les premières étoiles apparaissaient dans le ciel. Le grand soir était venu.

Vêtu de fourrures et de plumes, le Maître de la Nuit avança entre deux rangées d'acolytes et de soldats qui s'inclinèrent devant lui. Les Très-Hauts marchaient quelques pas en arrière, suivis par un humain en robe, que Dogz poussait, et par un kender qui pépiait avec enthousiasme sur la fabuleuse cérémonie à laquelle il allait assister.

*

* *

— Raistlin, comment as-tu deviné que j'allais lancer ce sort ? La plupart des mages ont oublié jusqu'à son existence. Puisque tu vas mourir, tu peux bien satisfaire ma curiosité, dit le Maître de la Nuit en se penchant vers le jeune homme.

Assis sur un rocher, les pieds et les mains liés, Raistlin refusa de céder à la terreur. Il ne voulait pas manifester d'émotion devant le prêtre minotaure. Un sourire énigmatique se dessina sur ses lèvres.

— C'est par le plus pur hasard. Il y a quelques années, j'ai lu ce sort dans un grimoire jauni. Il était accompagné d'une citation de Sargonnas, et semblait décrire une cérémonie minotaure. Mais je n'en possédais pas les composants, et de toute façon, il ne m'intéressait pas…

« Puis un ami de Tasslehoff m'apprit qu'un herboriste minotaure installé en Ergoth Méridional vendait de la jalopine, un des ingrédients nécessaires au lancement du sort. Intrigué, j'envoyai mon frère en acheter. Dans ma profession, on s'intéresse beaucoup aux plantes exotiques. Je ne pensais pas que ça irait plus loin.

« Mais mon frère disparut en mer avec les deux amis qui l'accompagnaient, Tass et Sturm. Quelque temps après, je reçus du kender un message magique me racontant l'étrange exécution de l'herboriste minotaure.

« La personne qui m'apporta ce message ajouta de curieux détails sur le vaisseau englouti et son équipage. Après avoir trahi ses passagers, il semble que le capitaine du navire ait été assassiné par magie. »

Les yeux de Raistlin brillaient d'intelligence.

— Ensuite, il m'a suffi d'additionner deux et deux et de formuler quelques hypothèses. J'ai de nouveau consulté le grimoire, et discuté de la situation avec son propriétaire.

« Nous avons convenu que l'endroit le plus logique pour la cérémonie serait les ruines de Karthay, là où le Seigneur de la Vengeance s'était manifesté dans notre monde pour la dernière fois, voilà plusieurs siècles. »

— Je suis bien content que tu aies reçu ma bouteille ! s'écria Tass en bondissant de joie. Je craignais qu'elle se soit...

Le Maître de la Nuit s'empara du kender, dont le babillage incessant lui portait sur les nerfs, et le fourra sans cérémonie sous son bras gauche avant de le bâillonner de la main droite.

— Si je comprends bien, ronronna le prêtre tandis que Tass, rouge de colère, se débattait dans son étreinte, le kender et toi êtes de vieux amis ? Comment le trouves-tu depuis que ma potion l'a rendu maléfique ?

— C'est ainsi que vous avez procédé, murmura Raistlin. Avec une potion. C'est étrange : je croyais qu'elles n'avaient pas d'effet à long terme.

Le Maître de la Nuit eut un sourire indulgent.

— Exact, mon jeune ami. (Il se tourna vers Dogz et lui tendit le kender.) Veux-tu bien administrer une double dose à Tasslehoff ?

Le minotaure ne put pas soutenir le regard de son maître. Il déglutit et hocha la tête.

— Merci de m'y avoir fait penser, lança le prêtre à l'attention de Raistlin.

Malgré les protestations de Tass, Dogz l'assit de force dans une chaise et le força à boire le contenu d'une petite fiole. Le kender se débattit encore quelques minutes, puis sa tête tomba sur sa poitrine et il parut s'assoupir.

Dans le cratère, les préparatifs touchaient à leur fin. Fesz et les deux autres Très-Hauts jetaient dans l'ouverture des poignées de composants. Après des siècles d'inactivité, le Sommet du Monde recommençait à gronder et à cracher. Un halo orange entourait déjà la dépression ovale au bord de laquelle se tenaient les chamanes.

Dogz revint vers Raistlin et le Maître de la Nuit.

— J'aurais pu sacrifier le kender, mais il est trop insignifiant. Sargonnas préférera un humain, surtout s'il possède des pouvoirs magiques. Ça devrait augmenter l'efficacité du sort...

Il plissa les yeux en détaillant Raistlin.

— Je ne connais guère les coutumes de ton peuple. Pourquoi tu ne portes pas la robe d'un des trois Ordres traditionnels.

— Parce que je n'ai pas encore passé l'Epreuve, répondit le jeune mage, ni choisi ma future allégeance.

— Si tu appartenais aux Robes Noires, dit rêveusement le Maître de la Nuit, nous serions du même côté. Tu vénérerais Sargonnas comme moi.

— Je ne sais rien du Seigneur de la Vengeance. C'est pourquoi je suis venu.

— Non ! Tu es venu pour sauver ton frère ! ricana le prêtre.

— En partie, concéda Raistlin, mais aussi parce que je m'intéresse aux trois Ordres de magie.

— Vraiment ?

Les Très-Hauts avaient terminé leurs travaux préliminaires. Les bras croisés sur sa poitrine, Dogz attendait, un peu en retrait. Fesz s'approcha de son maître et l'interrompit :

— Je vous demande pardon, Excellence, mais nous sommes prêts.

Le Maître de la Nuit hocha la tête. Il se pencha vers Raistlin, lui soufflant son haleine fétide au visage, et l'examina avec un regain d'intérêt.

— Ainsi, voilà pourquoi tu t'es porté volontaire pour prendre la place de ta sœur, dit-il lentement. Tu voulais assister à la cérémonie et rencontrer Sargonnas... Rassure-toi : ton vœu sera exaucé, puisque c'est toi qui lui permettra d'entrer dans ce monde !

Raistlin attendit un long moment avant de répondre.

— Ou d'en sortir à tout jamais, lâcha-t-il enfin, impassible.

Le Maître de la Nuit le gifla à la volée. Déséquilibré, le jeune mage tomba du rocher où il était assis. Le prêtre lui flanqua un coup de pied vicieux dans les côtes sans lui arracher le moindre cri.

— Gardes ! appela-t-il.

Deux minotaures rompirent les rangs et se précipitèrent.

— Amenez ce pathétique humain près du cratère et tenez-le jusqu'à ce que je sois prêt !

Obéissants, les soldats traînèrent Raistlin au-dessus de l'ouverture. Une bouffée de chaleur monta au visage du jeune homme.

Les Très-Hauts se placèrent face à la victime. Le Maître de la Nuit enfila sa cape écarlate et monta la douzaine de marches conduisant à la plate-forme, où un énorme grimoire reposait sur un pupitre.

Raistlin secoua la tête. Il était encore un peu étourdi. Se tordant le cou, il repéra Tasslehoff, toujours affalé sur sa chaise, derrière les Très-Hauts.

Le Maître de la Nuit leva sa tête cornue, prit une profonde inspiration et fixa les étoiles qui brillaient comme autant de phares dans le ciel sans nuages.

La nuit était glaciale, bien qu'il n'y eût pas le moindre souffle de vent. Mais Raistlin ne sentait que la chaleur dégagée par le volcan, et il n'entendait que le bouillonnement de la lave qui montait lentement vers la surface.

Le Maître de la Nuit lut le sort dans un ancien dialecte minotaure, sa voix gutturale montant peu à peu. En fond sonore, le murmure des Très-Hauts était à peine audible. Raistlin ne distinguait aucun mot, à part le nom de Sargonnas.

En incantant, le prêtre dessinait dans les airs de gracieux symboles qui contrastaient avec le son de sa voix. Ses mains puissantes bougeaient sans relâche, accompagnées par le tintement de ses grelots. Sa cape écarlate voletait derrière lui.

Clonk ! Jailli de nulle part, un objet atteignit un des gardes avec une telle force que le minotaure lâcha Raistlin, porta les mains à sa gorge et s'écroula raide mort. Avant que quiconque puisse réagir, un objet encore plus gros pénétra dans le champ de vision du jeune mage.

C'était Tasslehoff Racle-Pieds. Le kender se jeta sur le dos du second garde et fit de son mieux pour l'étrangler, bien qu'il fût trois fois plus haut et six fois plus lourd que lui. Mais il ne s'en sortait pas trop mal, car sa victime n'était pas assez souple pour le déloger.

Il fallut à Fesz quelque secondes pour se précipiter vers Tass, l'empoigner et le jeter à terre. Le kender se releva aussitôt, mais il titubait. Fesz le saisit par le col de sa tunique et le souleva jusqu'à son visage bovin.

— Tu me fais honte ! gronda-t-il en secouant Tass si fort que celui-ci eut le hoquet. Toi, en qui j'avais confiance, toi, que j'ai rendu maléfique, toi, qui a le grand privilège d'assister à l'arrivée de Sargonnas, toi, toi...

Livide de rage et de déception, le chamane n'arrivait plus à trouver ses mots.

Le deuxième garde, qui n'avait pas lâché Raistlin, se remettait peu à peu de l'attaque surprise. Le jeune mage chercha désespérément un sort sans composants gestuels. En vain.

— Tu parles d'un *hic !* privilège ! cracha Tass à la figure de Fesz. Vous, les grosses vaches, vous *hic !* confondez l'honneur et la *hic !* bouse. J'en ai ras-le-bol de vos *hic !* gueules qui puent, des *hic !* tournebroches qui vous tiennent lieu de cornes, de vos *hic !* fringues immondes et de vos manières de *hic !* péquenots...

Un rugissement interrompit le kender. Tous levèrent les yeux vers la plate-forme où se tenait le Maître de la Nuit. Les poings serrés, un rictus sur les lèvres, le prêtre était l'image vivante de la rage.

— Silence ! tonna-t-il. Vous interrompez le lancement du sort !

— Mais, geignit Fesz, le kender...

— Débarrasse-toi de lui ! ordonna son maître. Jette-le dans le cratère !

— Oui, dit Fesz.

— Non ! s'exclama une autre voix.

Raistlin tourna la tête à temps pour voir Fesz porter les mains à sa gorge, d'où émergeait le manche en forme de H du katar de Dogz. Le chamane lâcha Tass, qui atterrit sur les fesses, et bascula en arrière.

— Gardes ! Emparez-vous de lui ! hurla le Maître de la Nuit, tendant un index vers Dogz.

Le minotaure ne tenta ni de s'enfuir ni de résister. Il n'aurait pu expliquer les raisons de son geste… Tout ce qu'il savait, c'était qu'il aimait bien Tasslehoff Racle-Pieds, surtout depuis que le kender était redevenu lui-même. Il avait obéi à un instinct qu'il ignorait posséder, celui de l'amitié. Entouré de lances et d'épées menaçantes, il tomba à genoux.

Tass se releva en hoquetant. Alors Raistlin songea au sort d'invisibilité qu'il avait utilisé un peu plus tôt. Il ne lui servirait à rien maintenant, mais s'il pouvait en faire bénéficier quelqu'un d'autre... Ses effets seraient assez longs pour permettre à Tass de s'échapper.

Le jeune mage se concentra, remuant les doigts derrière son dos. Il incanta en remplaçant son nom par celui du kender. Avec un léger « plop ! », Tasslehoff disparut.

Le Maître de la Nuit, qui s'apprêtait à lui lancer un éclair magique, jura entre ses dents.

— Imbécile ! Je suis un imbécile ! J'aurais dû y penser ! enragea-t-il.

Il se pencha par-dessus la balustrade pour crier au garde qui tenait Raistlin :

— Bâillonne-le, et assure-toi qu'il ne puisse pas parler. Puis amène-le-moi.

Le minotaure jeta Raistlin à terre et lui noua un morceau de tissu sale sur la bouche. Puis il l'empoigna par le dos de sa robe et commença à le traîner vers les marches de bois.

— Le kender est invisible, cria le Maître de la Nuit au reste des gardes. Retrouvez-le et tuez-le !

Les minotaures se déployèrent, fouillant l'air du bout de leur arme. Chaque fois qu'ils entendaient un hoquet, ils se précipitaient vers sa source, mais ils ne réussissaient qu'à se bousculer.

Le Maître de la Nuit se pencha vers les deux Très-Hauts survivants et cria :

— Continuez ! L'incantation est presque finie !

Surpris par la mort de Fesz, les chamanes s'étaient tus. Ils semblaient désorientés, mais le regard meurtrier du Maître de la Nuit suffit à les galvaniser. A nouveau, ils entonnèrent leur chant.

Le grand prêtre se concentra sur Raistlin, que le garde venait de lui amener. Saisissant le bras du jeune mage, il le poussa vers le bord de la plate-forme, au-dessus de l'ouverture béante.

— Grave bien cet instant dans ta mémoire, siffla le Maître de la Nuit, car c'est le dernier que tu vivras en ce monde.

Il lâcha Raistlin et vint se placer derrière son pupitre. S'efforçant d'oublier le vacarme qui régnait autour de lui, il reprit sa lecture.

*
* *

— Psst, Dogz ! C'est moi, Tass !

Les yeux du minotaure s'agrandirent de stupeur. Autour de lui, les trois gardes assignés à sa surveillance avaient reculé. Le museau en l'air, ils observaient avec fascination les gestes gracieux du Maître de la Nuit.

Dogz cligna des paupières pour montrer qu'il avait entendu.

— Merci d'avoir tué Fesz ! chuchota Tass. Tu es un véritable ami ! Je l'aurais fait moi-même depuis longtemps si je...

Du regard, Dogz indiqua au kender qu'il devrait s'enfuir le plus loin possible.

— Dis, tu n'aurais pas une dague ou quelque chose de ce genre ?

— Fesz, souffla le minotaure le plus doucement qu'il put.

Un des gardes l'entendit et le dévisagea d'un air soupçonneux. Dogz haussa les épaules. Le soldat lui flanqua un coup dans l'estomac avec la hampe de sa lance. Dogz gémit et se plia en deux.

Sur la plate-forme, le Maître de la Nuit arrivait à la dernière page de son grimoire. Il sortit des feuilles séchées d'une petite bourse et les jeta dans le cratère. Un nuage rouge orangé, chaud et sec, s'échappa de l'ouverture.

— La jalopine, grommela le prêtre, satisfait. Le dernier composant du sort.

Plus bas, une main invisible tentait d'arracher le katar du cou de Fesz. Personne ne faisant attention au cadavre du chamane, Tass put dégager l'arme sans être inquiété. Il la glissa dans sa tunique, où elle disparut.

Son hoquet avait cessé depuis quelques minutes : du coup, les gardes, plus intéressés par ce qui se passait sur la plate-forme, avaient arrêté de le chercher. Hélas, le sort d'invisibilité touchait à sa fin.

Tass monta l'escalier le plus discrètement qu'il put et se dirigea vers Raistlin. Le mage entendit un léger craquement derrière lui et se figea. Le métal froid d'une lame se glissa entre ses poignets et commença à trancher ses liens.

Jetant un coup d'œil par-dessus son épaule, Raistlin vit Tass réapparaître graduellement sur la dernière marche de l'échafaudage. Il grimaça pour avertir le kender. Absorbé par sa tâche, celui-ci ne se rendit compte de rien.

Quand il releva la tête, le Maître de la Nuit le toisait de toute sa hauteur, les yeux exorbités par la colère.

— Oh oh, murmura Tass avant de prendre ses jambes à son cou.

Trop tard. Le minotaure le saisit à la gorge et, poussant un hurlement furieux, le projeta vers la gueule du cratère.

Tass se sentit dégringoler vers la fournaise...

... Une silhouette plongea vers lui et l'attrapa dans ses serres. Eberlué, le Maître de la Nuit regarda un kyrie arracher le kender à une mort certaine, et le déposer sur le sol vingt pas plus loin.

Un petit groupe de kyries venaient de bondir sur les soldats minotaures. Plusieurs gisaient déjà à terre, morts ou agonisants ; d'autres avaient battu en retraite derrière les monticules de lave solidifiée, d'où ils tiraient des flèches sur les intrus.

Le Maître de la Nuit repéra Kitiara parmi les assaillants. En revanche, il ne vit nulle trace de ses deux Très-Hauts, qui avaient lâchement abandonné leur poste.

Au pied de l'échafaudage, un humain musclé aux longs cheveux bruns engagea le combat avec le seul garde qui protégeait encore le Maître de la Nuit. Le prêtre n'en croyait pas ses yeux. Tous ses efforts étaient réduits à néant par un kender, quelques kyries et une poignée d'humains minables !

Cette pensée raviva la colère du prêtre. Il avança d'un pas et, levant les bras vers le ciel, cria une injonction magique. De l'index droit, il visa les importuns.

Une douzaine de boules de feu explosèrent au milieu des humains et des kyries. Des langues de flammes rouges éclairèrent brièvement la scène. Deux soldats minotaures furent incinérés en un clin d'œil. Les ailes d'un homme-oiseau prirent feu ; il se jeta sur le sol en hurlant.

Le Maître de la Nuit éclata de rire et se prépara à lancer un autre sort. Alors un bruit, sur sa droite, lui rappela la présence de Raistlin Majere.

*
* *

Tasslehoff bondissait et zigzaguait pour éviter les boules de flammes qui fusaient autour de lui. Les étranges créatures alliées de Caramon, de Tanis et Kitiara volaient au-dessus de lui.

La fumée lui piquait les yeux. A quatre pattes, il tâtonna jusqu'à ce que ses mains se referment sur ce qu'il cherchait. Alors qu'il se relevait, un pied se posa rudement sur son avant-bras. Il leva les yeux et grimaça.

— Bonjour, Tanis ! Ça fait plaisir de te revoir ! Où est Flint ?

Le demi-elfe lui jeta un regard sévère.

— De quel côté es-tu, Tasslehoff ?

— Comment ça ? demanda le kender, peiné. Du tien, bien sûr. N'es-tu pas du mien ? Pour l'instant, Raistlin et moi sommes seuls contre les minotaures, et nous avons sacrément besoin d'aide !

Tanis dévisagea le kender, puis ôta son pied. Tass saisit son bâton et se releva en se massant le bras.

— Tu n'aurais pas une épée, par hasard ? demanda-t-il, plein d'espoir.

Tanis secoua la tête, puis sortit une dague de son fourreau et la tendit au kender.

— Tiens. Bien sûr que je suis de ton côté... Si tu es du mien. Ces derniers temps, d'étranges rumeurs ont couru à ton sujet.

— Vraiment ? fit Tass, souriant d'une oreille à l'autre. Il faut dire que les dernières semaines ont été plutôt mouvementées. D'abord, le capitaine du *Vénora* nous a trahis. J'avais bien dit à Caramon que sa tête ne me revenait pas, mais...

Trois minotaures se précipitèrent vers les deux amis. Tanis pivota, évita leur charge, puis s'enfuit dans une direction. Tass prit ses jambes à son cou et partit dans une autre.

*
* *

Le soldat était aussi obstiné que bon combattant. Il maniait une lance aux deux extrémités garnies d'une lame en forme de croissant. Caramon n'arrivait pas à le contourner pour monter sur l'échafaudage.

Aucune de ses attaques ne parvenait à percer la garde du minotaure.

Le duel aurait pu se prolonger indéfiniment si Tanis n'avait volé à la rescousse de son ami. Tous deux se placèrent sur les flancs du garde et le harcelèrent sans relâche.

Pour la première fois, Caramon aperçut une lueur de panique dans les yeux du minotaure. Le soldat était à bout de souffle et ne tiendrait sans doute plus très longtemps.

*
* *

Tasslehoff courait en tous sens à la recherche de Dogz. Les gardes l'avaient traîné au bord du cratère, l'un d'eux se chargeant sa surveillance. Dogz était assis en tailleur sur le sol, qu'il contemplait d'un air désolé.

Un « clonk ! » sonore retentit. Il leva la tête juste à temps pour voir le garde tomber à genoux, puis s'effondrer dans les cendres pour révéler la silhouette triomphante du kender.

— Tout est dans le poignet, se vanta Tass. Je ne connais pas beaucoup de gens qui manient le bâton à fronde aussi bien que moi. J'irai même jusqu'à dire que *personne* ne le manie aussi bien que moi, à part peut-être mon oncle Chausse-Trappes, mais c'est lui qui m'a appris !

Le kender profita de la confusion qui régnait autour d'eux pour détacher Dogz. Celui-ci ne bougea pas.

— Tu es revenu, ami Tass, constata-t-il bas.

— Je te devais bien ça, non ?

— Il est bon de te voir redevenu toi-même, sourit le minotaure. Ainsi, l'antidote de la femelle humaine a fonctionné.

*

* *

Sur l'échafaudage, le Maître de la Nuit pivota pour affronter Raistlin. Débarrassé de ses liens, le jeune homme était prêt à bondir, tel un animal pâle et trempé de sueur.

— Les choses ne se passent pas aussi bien que vous l'aviez espéré, n'est-ce pas ? dit-il.

A dire vrai, le Maître de la Nuit se sentait un peu dépassé par les événements. Mais à la vue du misérable humain qui avait deviné ses plans et conspiré pour les faire échouer, il sentit sa combativité revenir. Toisant Raistlin, il remarqua avec satisfaction que celui-ci ne portait pas d'arme.

— Le sort est terminé, gronda le Maître de la Nuit. Il ne me reste plus qu'à procéder au sacrifice, et je vois que tu es toujours là. Sargonnas a assez attendu. Il est temps pour toi de mourir !

Avant que le minotaure puisse réagir, Raistlin bondit vers le pupitre et s'empara du grimoire. Il brandit l'épais volume devant lui.

— Que fais-tu, humain ? ricana le Maître de la Nuit. Crois-tu avoir le temps d'apprendre un sort pour te défendre ? A moins que tu comptes t'en servir comme d'un bouclier...

Sans répondre, Raistlin fit volte-face et jeta le grimoire dans le cratère.

— Nooooon ! hurla le minotaure, tendant les mains vers son précieux livre de sorts. Non !

Tandis qu'il tournait le dos à Raistlin, Caramon et Tanis débouchèrent sur la plate-forme. Avec un bel ensemble, ils plongèrent leurs épées dans les flancs du prêtre. Celui-ci tituba, puis perdit l'équilibre et alla rejoindre son grimoire au fond du cratère.

Caramon et Tanis étreignirent Raistlin.

— Kit va bien, dit Caramon. Tasslehoff aussi. Nous faisons de notre mieux pour contenir les minotaures.

— Nous n'avons plus le temps ! lança Raistlin. Il faut déguerpir !

Déjà, un nuage rouge se formait au-dessus du volcan. Les trois compagnons durent détourner la tête pour se protéger de la chaleur insoutenable qu'il dégageait.

Un grondement pareil au galop d'un millier d'étalons monta du cratère. Raistlin saisit ses amis par le bras et les entraîna au pied de l'échafaudage.

*
* *

— L'antidote de Kitiara ? répéta Tass, ébahi.

— Je l'ai échangé contre la potion qui te rendait maléfique, expliqua Dogz.

— Justement, je voulais t'en parler. Ce truc n'a jamais eu bon goût, mais la dernière fois, il était vraiment dégueulasse...

Le kender s'interrompit. Il entendait un bruit étrange, comme si une tempête se préparait. Levant les yeux vers l'échafaudage, il vit qu'il était vide. En revanche, la gueule du volcan crachait un ouragan de feu.

— Oh oh, souffla Tass. Nous en reparlerons plus tard. Pour l'instant, nous ferions mieux de filer !

Il prit la main de Dogz et voulut l'aider à se lever. Le minotaure ne bougea pas d'un pouce.

— Je ne viens pas, dit-il en secouant la tête.

— Hein ? Mais pourquoi ?

— J'ai trahi les miens. J'ai désobéi aux ordres. Je suis déshonoré.

— Que racontes-tu ? demanda Tass, désespéré.

Partout, les minotaures lâchaient leurs armes et s'enfuyaient. La fumée et les flammes empêchaient le kender de voir ce que faisaient ses amis.

— Dogz, tu m'as sauvé la vie ! Tu es un héros ! insista Tass.

Le minotaure prit le kender par les épaules.

— Va-t'en, ami Tass, dit-il à regret. Sauve-toi. Je ne mérite pas de vivre. Je suis déshonoré.

Ses épaules s'affaissèrent.

Tass allait répliquer vertement quand une créature ailée plongea vers lui et le souleva dans les airs. L'homme-oiseau rejoignit un vol de ses semblables, qui portaient chacun un passager.

Les kyries s'élancèrent vers les cieux. Derrière eux, une explosion assourdissante retentissait. Se tordant le cou, Tass aperçut une gigantesque langue de flammes rouges qui jaillissait de la gueule du volcan.

Un moment, elle dessina la silhouette d'un condor géant, qui fit pleuvoir la mort sur tous ceux qui demeuraient encore sur le Sommet du Monde. Puis elle s'évanouit, la fumée se dissipa et le volcan sombra à nouveau dans un profond sommeil.

Sargonnas était venu et reparti.

ÉPILOGUE

Les compagnons se regroupèrent à l'endroit où ils avaient campé la veille.

Les minotaures s'étaient éparpillés. Ceux qui étaient restés au sommet du volcan avaient été calcinés par la langue de flammes rouges. Après la fin du combat, les créatures des sables enrôlées par la bulette s'étaient retirées dans leurs terriers.

Flint creusa lui-même la tombe de Kirsig et prononça l'éloge funèbre de la demi-ogresse.

— Kirsig se prétendait femme de ménage et guérisseuse, dit-il, essuyant les larmes dont il se montrait si avare d'ordinaire. Mais ceux qui ont eu l'honneur de la côtoyer savent que dans sa poitrine battait le cœur d'une vraie guerrière. Elle nous manquera.

Deux des anciennes du *Castor* et trois kyries, dont Volesprit, avaient été tués au cours de la bataille. Sturm fut très touché par la perte de l'ami qui l'avait tiré de la Fosse des Enfers.

Yuril avait reçu au flanc une blessure très grave. Elle survécut, mais devrait en garder une certaine raideur jusqu'à la fin de ses jours. Caramon veilla tendrement sur elle durant sa convalescence.

— Il me rappelle Kirsig, dit Flint à Tanis. Regarde-le : il se conduit comme une femmelette !

Le demi-elfe eut un sourire amusé et ne répondit pas.

Un jour, un des éclaireurs kyries rapporta que le *Castor* cabotait le long de la côte méridionale de l'île. A la nouvelle, Yuril et ses deux compagnes survivantes tinrent un conciliabule, puis annoncèrent leur départ. Caramon tenta de les dissuader.

— Tu ne comprends pas ! protesta Yuril. Le capitaine Nugetre n'est pas facile à vivre, mais j'appartiens à l'océan, et il le sait. Tu as retrouvé ton frère : je dois rejoindre mon navire.

Caramon bouda un peu. Puis, en guise d'au revoir, il planta sur les lèvres de Yuril un baiser si profond que la jeune femme en eut le souffle coupé.

Tasslehoff dut lui taper sur l'épaule pour qu'il la laisse partir.

Trois kyries ramenèrent les femmes à bord et revinrent avec un messager venant de Mithas. Les nouvelles n'étaient pas gaies. Matinciel venait de mourir dans la prison d'Atossa. Jusqu'au dernier instant, il avait gardé les lèvres closes.

Fend-Nuage pleura longuement son aîné.

— Tu dois rentrer, dit le messager. Plumesoleil t'attend. Tu es son héritier légitime...

Le kyrie rassembla ses guerriers et annonça qu'ils partaient. Les compagnons se rassemblèrent pour faire leurs adieux aux hommes-oiseaux qui les avaient tant aidés à lutter contre Sargonnas.

— Nous nous reverrons, déclara Raistlin, solennel.

— J'en suis certain, répondit Fend-Nuage.

Sturm étreignit maladroitement ses nouveaux amis. Caramon s'avança vers leur chef, dont il était devenu très proche en peu de temps. Il savait qu'il ne l'oublierait jamais.

Fend-Nuage leva les yeux vers le jeune homme, puis remonta une manche de sa tunique, révélant la cicatrice que Caramon s'était faite au cours de la Nuit du Dragon Aquatique. Touchant celle-ci avec le majeur et l'index, il porta ses doigts à ses lèvres.

— Guerrier, dit-il. Mon frère.

— Guerrier, répéta Caramon. Mon frère.

Les kyries s'envolèrent.

*
* *

Une semaine était passée depuis la défaite du Maître de la Nuit, deux jours depuis le départ des hommes-oiseaux. Pourtant, les compagnons ne se résolvaient pas à s'en aller.

Tasslehoff tenta de convaincre ses amis qu'il n'avait jamais été maléfique, car il avait joué la comédie tout du long. Personne ne voulut le croire. Sturm resta convaincu qu'il avait failli périr dans la Fosse des Enfers par la faute du kender.

— Et toi, Raistlin, qu'en penses-tu ? s'enquit Tass en se tournant vers le jeune mage.

— Moi, je suis sûr que tu dis vrai.

— Oui ! triompha Tass. Raistlin me croit !

— Mon frère est très sage, fit sèchement Kitiara, mais il a une faiblesse pour les kenders.

— Alors, tu partages mon avis ? demanda Sturm, plein d'espoir.

— Je te l'ai déjà dit. D'après moi, Tass est resté maléfique jusqu'à ce que Dogz substitue ma fiole de salive de leucrotta à la potion du chamane. Sans le minotaure, nous serions probablement morts.

Tasslehoff ne protesta pas. Il aimait cette version de l'histoire parce qu'elle faisait de son ami un héros.

— De la salive de leucrotta ? répéta Sturm, perplexe.

— Normalement, c'est un antidote contre les philtres d'amour, intervint Tanis. Kit s'est dit que ça neutraliserait peut-être les effets de la potion. Je suppose que c'est le cas, puisque Tass est redevenu lui-même.

Le demi-elfe se tourna vers Kit :

— Au fait, tu ne m'as jamais expliqué comment tu avais pu arriver si vite à Karthay.

La jeune femme se leva et saisit un seau.

— Il faut que j'aille chercher de l'eau pour le souper, dit-elle.

Quand elle revint, ses amis avaient trouvé un autre sujet de conversation, le même depuis une semaine : que devaient-ils faire et où iraient-ils ?

— Moi, déclara Caramon, j'aimerais retourner à Mithas et aider Fend-Nuage à combattre les minotaures. Je voudrais venger la mort de Matinciel.

— Et moi, je flanquerais bien une raclée à ce gros balourd de Tossak, maintenant que je suis remis, déclara Sturm avec un rictus féroce.

— Y a-t-il des trésors à conquérir dans les cités des minotaures ? s'enquit Kitiara, curieuse.

— Pour sûr ! s'écria Tass.

— Je ne sais que dire, soupira Tanis. Solace me manque, mais puisque nous avons fait ce chemin, nous devrions en profiter pour explorer cette partie du monde. Qu'en penses-tu, Raistlin ?

Le vent s'était levé. Dans le ciel, Lunitari s'élançait à la rencontre de Solinari.

— Nous ne pouvons pas rester ici éternellement, répondit le jeune mage. Et la maison est loin. Nous mettrons toutes les propositions au vote demain matin.

— C'est ça, grommela Flint en soulevant le couvercle de la marmite qui bouillait sur le feu. Et maintenant, assez bavardé. A table !

Achevé d'imprimer en avril 1998
sur les presses de Cox & Wyman Ltd
(Angleterre)

FLEUVE NOIR – 12, avenue d'Italie
75627 PARIS – CEDEX 13.
Tel: 01.44.16.05.00

Dépôt légal : mai 1998
Imprimé en Angleterre